CRITICISM OF CRUSADING
1095-1274

CRITICISM OF CRUSADING

1095-1274

ELIZABETH SIBERRY

CLARENDON PRESS · OXFORD

1985

Oxford University Press, Walton Street, Oxford OX2 6DP
Oxford New York Toronto
Delhi Bombay Calcutta Madras Karachi
Kuala Lumpur Singapore Hong Kong Tokyo
Nairobi Dar es Salaam Cape Town
Melbourne Auckland
and associated companies in
Beirut Berlin Ibadan Nicosia

Oxford is a trade mark of Oxford University Press

Published in the United States
by Oxford University Press, New York

British Library Cataloguing in Publication Data
Siberry, Elizabeth
Criticism of crusading, 1095–1274.
1. Crusades—History
I. Title
909.07   D156.58
ISBN 0-19-821953-9

Library of Congress Cataloging in Publication Data
Siberry, Elizabeth.
Criticism of crusading.
Bibliography: p.
Includes index.
1. Crusades.   I. Title.
D160.S49   1985   909.07   85-13579
ISBN 0-19-821953-9

Set by Joshua Associates Limited, Oxford
Printed in Great Britain by
Billing & Sons Ltd., Worcester

To my parents

Preface

ALTHOUGH contemporaries seem to have had a clear idea of what a crusade was, there was no specific terminology to describe such expeditions. Medieval writers used a variety of vernacular and Latin terms such as *croiserie, iter*, and *peregrinatio*.[1] This ambiguity has created a certain amount of disagreement amongst modern historians about the correct definition of a crusade. I have decided to adopt that given by Jonathan Riley-Smith, namely that a crusade was

> a holy war authorized by the pope, who proclaimed it in the name of God or Christ . . . Proposed, like all justifiable Christian violence, as a defensive reaction to injury or aggression or as an attempt to recover Christian territories lost to the infidels, it answered to the needs of the whole church or of all Christendom . . . rather than to those of a particular nation or region.[2]

This covers the expeditions launched by the papacy against heretics, schismatics, and Christian lay powers in the West as well as the campaigns against the Muslims in the Near East. But it does not include outbursts of popular fervour such as the so-called Children's Crusade of 1212 and the Shepherds' Crusade of 1251.

All proper names are translated into their English equivalents unless it seems to me that there is an established usage to the contrary (thus Raymond of Aguilers and Peter of Vaux de Cernay, but Raimon de Miraval and Peire Cardenal). I have used the Rheims–Douai–Challoner translation for all Biblical references and quotations because it is closest to the Latin Vulgate, but I have substituted more familiar proper names from the Authorized Version, for example Ezra for Esdras.

This book is a revised version of a dissertation which was accepted for the degree of Ph.D. in Cambridge in 1982;

[1] J. S. C. Riley-Smith, *What Were the Crusades?* (London, 1977), 12.
[2] J. S. C. and L. Riley-Smith, *The Crusades: Idea and Reality, 1095–1274* (London, 1981), 1.

I should like to thank all those who have given me advice and encouragement during its preparation. The staff of the Reading Room of the British Museum and Cambridge University Library have shown great patience in finding books for me and answering my queries. I also owe debts of gratitude to many individuals: in particular I should like to thank the late Dr L. T. Topsfield, Dr P. Johnson, Dr G. Evans, Professor C. N. L. Brooke, Dr R. C. Smail, and Dr B. Hamilton for their criticisms and suggestions. My two greatest debts are to my research supervisor in Cambridge and my parents. Those who have had the privilege of being taught by Professor Jonathan Riley-Smith know the value of his wide-ranging knowledge, enthusiasm, kindness, and patience. To my parents I owe more than I can say. They have been a constant source of support and encouragement and to them this book is dedicated.

London   ELIZABETH SIBERRY
February 1984

Contents

List of Abbreviations

The full title is not given here if the work is listed in the Bibliography

COD		*Conciliorum oecumenicorum decreta*, ed. G. Alberigo *et al.*	
EHR		*English Historical Review*. London 1886–	
Gratian,			
Decretum,	C	Gratian, *Decretum*,	Causa
	q		quaestio
	c		canon
	d.a.c.		Dictum Gratiani
			ante canonem
	d.p.c.		Dictum Gratiani
			post canonem
HD		*Historia Diplomatica Friderici Secundi*	
HGL		*Histoire générale de Languedoc*	
HMC		Historical Manuscripts Commission	
HMSO		Her Majesty's Stationery Office	
Liber extra,	Lib.	*Liber extra*,	Liber
	tit.		titulus
	c.		canon
Matthew Paris,			
CM		Matthew Paris, *Chronica maiora*	
MF		*Minnesangs Frühling*	
MGH		Monumenta Germaniae Historica, ed. G. H. Pertz *et al.* Hanover, Weimar, Stuttgart and Cologne. 1826 ff	
MGH SS		MGH Scriptores (folio and quarto). 32 vols. 1826–1934	
MGH Scr. rer. Germ.		MGH Scriptores rerum Germanicarum in usum scolarum. Hanover, 1839–	
n.s.		new series	
PL		Patrologiae cursus completus. Series Latina, publ. J. P. Migne. 217 vols. and 4 vols. of indexes. Paris, 1844–64	
Ralph Niger, *DRM*		Ralph Niger, *De re militari*	

RHC	Recueil des historiens des croisades
RHC Doc. arm.	RHC Documents arméniens. 2 vols. Paris, 1869–1906
RHC Occ.	RHC Historiens occidentaux. 5 vols. Paris, 1844–95
RHGF	Recueil des historiens des Gaules et de la France, ed. M. Bouquet *et al.* 24 vols. Paris, 1737–1904
RIS	Rerum Italicarum scriptores, ed. L. A. Muratori. 25 vols. Milan, 1723–51
RS	Rolls Series. Rerum Britannicarum Medii Aevi Scriptores. 99 vols. London, 1858–1911
TRHS	*Transactions of the Royal Historical Society.* London, 1871–

Introduction

THE subject of this study is criticism of crusading in the Near East and Europe between 1095 and 1274. During this period, eight major expeditions and many minor ones were sent to the East, and a series of campaigns was launched against pagans, heretics, schismatics, and Christian lay powers in the West. Some themes of criticism can be traced from the time of the First Crusade to at least the end of the thirteenth century, but the year 1274 provides a convenient *terminus ad quem*. In modern thought 1274 is a watershed, more important than the fall of Acre in 1291, because from the Second Council of Lyons onwards new policies began to emerge which were maintained well into the fourteenth century.[1]

The critics of the crusading movement in the Central Middle Ages have already received some treatment from historians. But there are serious gaps in our knowledge. The first penetrating work on twelfth-century criticism was done by the Canadian historian, G. B. Flahiff. In an article issued in 1940, he drew attention to an unpublished treatise by the twelfth-century English scholar Ralph Niger, entitled *De re militari et triplici via peregrinationis Ierosolimitane*, which questioned the advisability of crusading; and he promised that an edition of this work would appear in the near future.[2] In the event all Flahiff did was to publish some extracts as an appendix to an article. In this he contrasted Ralph's criticism of the crusade with the opinions advanced by his contemporaries. Flahiff admitted that from the beginning certain individuals had been reluctant to go to the Holy Land and described the sense of despair after the failure of the Second Crusade. But he stressed that only Ralph

[1] See S. Schein, 'The West and the Crusades: Attitudes and Attempts, 1291–1312' (unpubl. thesis, Cambridge, 1980), 1-2, 7, 23, 262-3; Riley-Smith, *The Crusades*, 35.

[2] G. B. Flahiff, 'Ralph Niger: An Introduction to his Life and Works', *Mediaeval Studies*, ii (1940), 119-20.

questioned whether another expedition should be launched at all.[3] The task of preparing an edition of *De re militari* was eventually taken up by the German scholar Ludwig Schmugge, who built upon the foundations established by Flahiff but challenged some of his conclusions. He maintained that Flahiff's argument was misleading because it ignored the parts of *De re militari* which did not deal with the crusade; and, whilst he agreed that the range of Ralph's criticism of the crusading movement was unique, and that he alone questioned the advisability of sending another expedition to the East, he showed that most of the elements of his argument could be found in the works of other contemporaries, drawing parallels with satirical works such as Walter Map's *De nugis curialium*.[4] Apart from the detailed studies of Flahiff and Schmugge, however, twelfth-century criticism has been virtually ignored, although objections to crusading were raised almost from the beginning.

Most attention has been focused on the thirteenth century. Even here the picture is not clear. In 1940 the American historian Palmer A. Throop published a work entitled *Criticism of the Crusade*, in which he sought to answer the question why the crusade had declined in the thirteenth century. He argued that the heart of the matter was to be found, not in military or political causes, but rather in public antagonism towards the crusading movement; and he maintained that the crucial point was reached between 1270 and 1291.[5] Throop intended to discuss this period as a whole, but he published only his research upon Gregory X's pontificate, the years 1271 to 1276. His main sources for this study were the memoirs submitted to the Second Council of Lyons by Gilbert of Tournai, Bruno of Olmütz, William of Tripoli, and Humbert of Romans, but he also drew on material provided by contemporary Old French, Provençal, and Middle High German literature and, to provide some background, devoted one chapter to vernacular and Latin criticism of papal crusading policy in Europe in the first half of the

[3] Flahiff, 'Deus non vult: A Critic of the Third Crusade', ibid. ix (1947) 162-88.

[4] Ralph Niger, *DRM* 40-1, 68-73.

[5] P. A. Throop, *Criticism of the Crusade: A Study of Public Opinion ana Crusade Propaganda* (Amsterdam, 1940), pp. vii-viii.

thirteenth century.[6] Throop uncovered a wealth of valuable material, but he presented his evidence in a confused and often repetitive way; and, although he traced some themes of criticism back to the twelfth century, he made no real attempt to analyse their development or assess their importance. Moreover, he tended to exaggerate the extent of the opposition to crusading. For example, he quoted four trouvères who denounced Cardinal Pelagius' interference during the Fifth Crusade and concluded that the legate's behaviour was 'widely discussed' and aroused a 'great deal of indignation'.[7] In fact there is no evidence that these writers represented public opinion; on the contrary they were all members of a small circle of determined critics of the papacy.[8]

Sir Steven Runciman's paper on the decline of the crusading idea[9] was really a summary of previous research and relied heavily upon Throop; the same is true of Joshua Prawer's discussion of opposition to crusading in his history of the Latin Kingdom of Jerusalem.[10] More recently Maureen Purcell has published a study of papal crusading policy between 1244 and 1291, but the analysis of criticism is incidental to her main theme: the tension between the spiritual notion of the crusade and its practical application; its diversion from the Holy Land and its use against enemies of the faith in Europe.[11] And, although Erwin Stickel, in his examination of the Western reaction to the fall of Acre, traced some themes of criticism back to the twelfth century, like Throop he made no real attempt to assess their significance.[12]

Criticism of crusading is, however, to be found in a wide

[6] This was first published as an article, 'Criticism of Papal Crusading Policy in Old French and Provençal', *Speculum*, xiii (1938), 379-413. All references below are to the later book.

[7] Throop, 32-3.

[8] See below, p. 10.

[9] S. Runciman, 'The Decline of the Crusading Idea', *Storia del medioevo, Relazioni del X Congresso internazionale di scienze storiche*, iii. Biblioteca storica Sansoni, n.s. XXIV (Florence, 1955), 637-52.

[10] J. Prawer, *Histoire du royaume latin de Jérusalem* (Paris, 1969-70), ii. 379-96.

[11] M. Purcell, *Papal Crusading Policy, 1244-91* (Leiden, 1975). Purcell also published an article entitled 'Changing Views of the Crusade in the Thirteenth Century', *Journal of Religious History*, ii (1972), 3-20. All references below are to the later book.

[12] E. Stickel, *Der Fall von Akkon* (Frankfurt, 1975), 158-252.

variety of sources before 1274; and the subject merits more detailed attention, for it gives an indication of the popularity or unpopularity of the crusading movement in this period. For the purposes of analysis it is necessary to divide the sources into certain categories. At one level there are the works of the crusading apologists and preachers such as Peter of Blois and Henry of Albano. As clerks they put forward the standard ecclesiastical defence of Christian warfare, but they also had direct experience of the views and prejudices of the laity and some of their arguments can be regarded as attempts to assuage their doubts and answer their criticisms of the crusading movement.[13]

This was also the great age of the clerical and monastic chronicler in England, France, and Germany and the lay municipal annalist in Italy. Naturally these chroniclers drew upon the more detailed accounts of earlier crusading historians such as Fulcher of Chartres and Odo of Deuil, but they also had access to important local information and their location and circumstances often determined their attitude towards the crusades. For example, in the thirteenth century certain writers in Italy and Germany adopted a Guelf or Ghibelline stance with regard to the crusades against the Staufen.[14] In England there seems to have been a tradition of opposition to papal crusading policy centering upon the monastery of St Albans.[15]

The major lay sources for criticism of crusading are the poems of the Provençal troubadours, Northern French trouvères, and German minnesingers. As literary sources they present certain unique problems, and it is necessary to analyse the nature of the evidence which they provide. The earliest troubadours were to be found in the Languedoc at the turn of the eleventh and twelfth centuries; but later poets travelled widely and their songs exerted a profound influence upon the poetry of Western Europe. At the height

[13] For this two-way traffic in ideas, see Riley-Smith, 'An approach to Crusading Ethics', *Reading Medieval Studies*, vi (1980), 3–20.

[14] See C. Merkel, 'L'opinione dei contemporanei sull'impresa italiana di Carlo I d'Angiò', *Atti della R. Accademia dei Lincei*, 4th ser., Classe di Scienze morali, storiche e filologiche, iv. 1 (1888), 275–435; T. C. Van Cleve, *The Emperor Frederick II of Hohenstaufen* (Oxford, 1972), 543–52.

[15] See below, pp. 13–14.

of the movement, from *c.*1150 to *c.*1250, troubadours flourished at the courts of France, Italy, Spain, Germany, Hungary, Cyprus, Malta, and the Latin East, and poets of many nationalities composed in Provençal.[16] The supreme genre of troubadour poetry was the *canso*, or love-song, and these make up the majority of the poems which have survived. But a few poets also composed moral or political songs known as *sirventes*[17] and the crusade songs are classified amongst these. According to their biographies or *vidas*,[18] a number of troubadours took part in the crusades to the Holy Land. They lamented that they must leave their lady or *domna*, but they denounced those who remained at home or postponed their departure. Like the crusading apologists, the troubadours declared that it was the duty of the faithful to repay God for his sacrifice and they emphasized that the crusade provided an opportunity for penance and offered a reward of eternal felicity.[19] The same themes are to be found in the works of the Northern French trouvères and German minnesingers and close parallels have been drawn between some poems and the sermons of preachers of the cross.[20] In this limited respect the vernacular poets can be used as an index of public opinion: an indication that, to a certain extent at least, the crusading ideas put forward by the clergy were adopted by the laity. The poets' condemnation of recalcitrant crusaders can also be regarded as a reflection of more widespread criticism and their works provide valuable evidence of disillusionment after a defeat or the failure of an expedition.

[16] L. T. Topsfield, *Troubadours and Love* (Cambridge, 1975), 5.

[17] For a definition of this term, see *Doctrina de compendre dictats*, ed. P. Meyer, 'Traités catalans de grammaire et de poétique', *Romania*, vi (1877), 356; *Guilhem Figueira, ein provenzalischer Troubadour*, ed. E. Levy (Berlin, 1880), 16; A. Jeanroy, *La Poésie lyrique des troubadours* (Paris, 1934), ii. 177-8.

[18] The *vidas* include much legendary material, but scholars now accept that the main biographical details are reasonably accurate. See Jeanroy, 'Les "biographies" des troubadours et les "razos"; leur valeur historique', *Archivum Romanicum* i (1917), 289-306.

[19] See Jeanroy, *La Poésie lyrique*, ii. 206-7.

[20] M. Colleville, *Les Chansons allemandes de croisade* (Paris, 1936), 134, 148-9, 155-6; G. Wolfram, 'Kreuzpredigt und Kreuzlied', *Zeitschrift für deutsches Alterthum und deutsche Litteratur*, xxx (1886), 97-132; C. Morris, 'Propaganda for War: the Dissemination of the Crusading ideal in the Twelfth Century', in *Studies in Church History*, xx (1983), 94.

At the same time, certain troubadours, trouvères, and min-nesingers condemned the use of the crusade in Europe; they are a major source for criticism of the Albigensian Crusade and the papal campaigns against the Staufen. Various explanations have been put forward for the poets' opposition to papal crusading policy in the West. It is important to establish whether they represented a large body of public opinion or merely expressed their personal views. The deriva-tion of the word *sirventes* is obscure, but it has been suggested that it meant 'a poem composed by a *sirven* for his master', reflecting the master's views and prejudices in an attempt to influence public opinion.[21] This has prompted some literary scholars to argue that the Provençal troubadours were employed as propagandists by Counts Raymond VI and VII of Toulouse and the Emperor Frederick II.[22]

According to this thesis, so long as Count Raymond VI had hopes of reaching an honourable agreement with the French and Innocent III, he kept the troubadours in check, but after the humiliating settlement imposed by the Fourth Lateran Council both he and his son encouraged them to denounce the Albigensian Crusade. Admittedly Guilhem Rainol d'Apt wrote after the Southern victory at Beaucaire:

I must turn back to my former employment because there appears to be a great need . . . Shall I sing then? Yes since it will please my count. From my themes of consolation I will draw a song of anger and send it to Simon of Montfort.[23]

But this is the only indication that either count actually urged poets to compose *sirventes* against the French. Indeed only a very small proportion of the poets writing in the Languedoc even mentioned the crusade in passing.[24] And, if the few critics became more outspoken after 1215, this should be attributed to a change in their own

[21] Jeanroy, *La Poésie lyrique*, ii. 175-6, 181; *Guilhem Figueira*, 20-1.

[22] Jeanroy, *La Poésie lyrique*, ii. 215-17; J. Anglade, *Histoire sommaire de la littérature méridionale au moyen âge* (Paris, 1921), 91.

[23] 'A tornar m'er enquer al premier us', *Anthologie des troubadours, XIIme-XIIIme siècles*, ed Jeanroy, rev. J. Boelcke (Paris, 1974), 244-8.

[24] R. H. Gere, 'The Troubadours, Heresy and the Albigensian Crusade' (un-publ. thesis, Columbia, 1955), 59, 61.

attitude rather than to an attempt to use them as propagandists.[25]

From the last quarter of the twelfth century onwards, a number of troubadours also found patronage in the North Italian courts of the Montferrat, Malaspina, and D'Este families.[26] But, although poets were anxious to win his favour, there is no evidence that Frederick II encouraged them to join the imperial entourage and compose *sirventes* against the pope:[27] Guilhem Figueira's famous denunciation of Rome, 'D'un sirventes far', was written in Toulouse.[28] After Frederick's death other troubadours denounced the papal campaigns against his heirs, Conrad, Manfred, and Conradin. But again they did so for their own reasons, not at another's prompting. Whilst some may have expressed sentiments calculated to win their lord's favour, it is significant that several of the Italian poets who criticized the Angevin crusades against the Staufen were merchants who had no need of princely patrons.[29]

Another explanation which has been advanced for the troubadours' opposition to papal crusading policy is that they were Cathars.[30] Admittedly Guilhem Figueira and Peire Cardenal were bitter opponents of the papacy, and some of the accusations levelled against Rome in their poetry resembled statements made by the heretics.[31] But this anticlericalism stemmed from the poets' resentment of abuses in the church; at the same time they stressed their orthodox beliefs. For example, in one *sirventes* Peire Cardenal wrote:

[25] See below, pp. 161–5.

[26] J. Longnon, 'Les troubadours à la cour de Boniface de Montferrat en Italie et en Orient', *Revue de synthèse*, n.s. xxiii (1948), 45–51; Jeanroy, 'Les Troubadours dans les cours de l'Italie du Nord aux XIIe et XIIIe siècles', *Revue historique*, clxiv (1930), 2–20.

[27] See V. De Bartholomaeis, 'Osservazioni sulle poesie provenzali relative a Federico II', *Memorie della R. Accademia delle scienze dell'Istituto di Bologna*, Classe di scienze morali, 1st ser. vi (1911-12), 97–125; Jeanroy, 'Les troubadours', 20–3.

[28] *Poesie provenzali storiche relative all'Italia*, ed. De Bartholomaeis, (Rome, 1931), ii. 98 n.

[29] Ibid. i, pp. lxi–lxii.

[30] D. de Rougemont, *Passion and Society* (London, 1940), 97–9.

[31] See Jeanroy, *La Poésie lyrique*, ii. 119–20; L. Varga, 'Peire Cardenal était-il hérétique?', *Revue de l'histoire des religions*, cxvii (1938), 205–31.

I believe in a God who was born of a Holy Virgin mother and through whom the world is saved. He is father, son, and Holy Trinity and these are three persons and one unity.[32]

There is certainly no indication that the church sought to prevent the circulation of troubadour poems for fear that they might corrupt the faithful. The literary scholar Jeanroy cited as an example of this ecclesiastical persecution the case of Bernart Raimon Baranhon, a burgher of Toulouse, who, when he was questioned by the Inquisition in 1274, confessed to knowing Guilhem Figueira's savage denunciation of Rome, 'D'un sirventes far'.[33] The deposition makes it clear, however, that the Inquisitors were seeking a vernacular work entitled *La Bible*, which began with the same phrase, 'Roma tricharitz', as the third stanza of Guilhem's poem; there is no indication that Bernart's acquaintance with the latter was regarded as incriminating.[34] Only a tiny proportion of the troubadours writing in the Languedoc are known to have been practising Cathars, and their heretical beliefs do not seem to have influenced their poetry.[35]

The real explanation for the troubadours' opposition to papal crusading policy in Europe seems to have been their location and circumstances; they all came from areas already hostile to the papacy such as the Languedoc and Ghibelline Italy. For this reason, although they had a wide variety of backgrounds and experience, including a merchant, a knight, a tailor, and a judge, they cannot be used, as Throop suggests, as an index of public opinion.[36] All that one can say is that, whilst their *sirventes* may have been performed initially before sympathetic audiences, they may later have spread and influenced a wider circle of people.[37]

Most manuscripts of Provençal poetry date from the late thirteenth or fourteenth centuries[38] and the *sirventes* seem to

---

[32] Peire Cardenal, 'D'un estribot farai', *Poésies complètes du troubadour Peire Cardenal*, ed. R. Lavaud (Toulouse, 1957), 206. See also ibid. 660-1; Guilhem Figueira, 'Totz hom qui ben comensa' ed. cit., 49-52.

[33] Jeanroy, *La Poésie lyrique*, ii. 225 n. 1.

[34] Gere, 'The Troubadours', 113-21.

[35] See R. Nelli, *Le Phénomène cathare* (Paris, 1964), 150-61; Gere, 96-150.

[36] Throop, 27-36.

[37] See Morris, *Medieval Media: Mass Communication in the Making of Europe* (inaugural lecture, Southampton, 1972), 7, 10.

[38] Jeanroy (ed.), *Bibliographie sommaire des chansonniers provençaux* (Paris,

have been preserved by oral tradition before they were written down.[39] The use of a recurring phrase or refrain at the end of each stanza by such poets as the Tarascon knights Tomier and Palazi suggests that their works were sung in various public places as well as at court.[40] Whereas each *canso* had to have a new rhyme-scheme or melody, a *sirventes* could imitate others; and, according to a late thirteenth-century literary treatise, the term meant 'a poem which was an inferior servant to the *canso*, from which it could borrow its music and rhyme-scheme'.[41] An obvious way of ensuring that the message of a *sirventes* would spread was to use the melody and rhyme of a popular song; a good example of this is Guilhem Figueira's poem 'D'un sirventes far', which imitated the verse-structure of a hymn to the Virgin.[42] It is interesting to note that when Bernart Raimon Baranhon was questioned by the Inquisitors, he stated that he had often heard Figueira's poem sung and had frequently recited it himself in public.[43] We have no real means of judging what proportion of the audience agreed with Figueira's views, but 'D'un sirventes far' has survived in five different manuscripts and the virulence of this attack prompted another troubadour Gormonda de Montpellier to compose a lengthy defence of papal policy, using the same metre and rhyme-scheme.[44]

There is also evidence of criticism of papal crusading policy in certain Middle High German political poems or *sprüche*. Little is known about the minnesingers except what can be gleaned from their poetry and in a few cases from documentary sources. But linguistic evidence sometimes provides an indication of their provenance and it is occasionally possible to identify their patrons.[45] Once again the poets' attitude towards

1916), 1–34; T. Karp, 'Troubadours and trouvères', in *The New Grove Dictionary of Music and Musicians* (London, 1980), xix. 196–7.

[39] H. van der Werf, *The Chansons of the Troubadours and Trouvères* (Utrecht, 1972), 26–30.

[40] 'De chantar farai', *Poesie provenzali*, i. 55–6.

[41] *Doctrina de compendre dictats*, 358.

[42] *Guilhem Figueira*, 23. See also ibid. 19–20, 22–9.

[43] See Y. Dossat, 'Les Vaudois méridionaux d'après les documents de l'Inquisition', *Cahiers de Fanjeaux*, ii (1967) 221–2.

[44] 'Greu m'es a durar', in *Guilhem Figueira*, 8, 74–8.

[45] J. Bumke, *Mäzene im Mittelalter* (Munich, 1979).

the crusades in Europe seems to have been dictated by their location and circumstances. For example, Freidank, the author of the satirical poem *Bescheidenheit*, came from the Staufen heartland of Germany and Walther von der Vogelweide held an imperial fief. It is possible to suggest that the message of certain Provençal *sirventes* may have spread because their authors used popular melodies; but unfortunately no music for the *sprüche* has survived,[46] although Gerhoh of Reichersberg declared that German was a particularly good language for singing in.[47] Our only real clue about the influence of the political poems comes from the Italian moralist Thomasin von Zirclaira. In his treatise *Der wälsche Gast*, he complained of a certain poet who had led thousands astray because of his virulent criticism of the papacy,[48] and it has been suggested that this was a reference to Walther von der Vogelweide,[49] who composed several *sprüche* denouncing papal levies for the Fifth Crusade.[50] One should be wary, however, of placing too much reliance upon the testimony of Thomasin, for he may have sought to blacken Walther's reputation because he regarded him as a rival for the patronage of the Patriarch of Aquileia.

We have very few details about the lives of the Northern French trouvères such as Guillaume le Clerc, Guiot de Provins, and Gautier de Coincy; but they seem to have belonged to a small literary circle which, in the late twelfth and thirteenth centuries, composed moral treatises attacking what it regarded as abuses in lay and ecclesiastical society.[51] It is against this background that one should interpret their criticism of papal crusading policy; there is no evidence that they represented a large body of opinion.

[46] B. Kippenberg, 'Minnesang', in *The New Grove Dictionary of Music and Musicians*, xii. 340-1.

[47] Gerhoh of Reichersberg, *Commentarius in Psalmos*, MGH Libelli de lite, iii (Hanover, 1897), 437.

[48] Thomasin von Zirclaira, *Der wälsche Gast*, ed. H. Rückert (Quedlinburg, 1852), ll. 11191-5, 11223.

[49] See D. Rocher, *Thomasin von Zerklaere—Der wälsche Gast 1215-16* (Paris, 1972), 144-6, 300-1, 702-3.   [50] See below, pp. 128-9.

[51] See M. M. Wood, *The Spirit of Protest in Old French Literature* (New York, 1917), 3-5; E. Lommatzsch, *Gautier de Coincy als Satiriker* (Halle, 1913), 16-47; Guiot de provins, *Les Œuvres*, ed. J. Orr (Manchester, 1915), pp. xxi, xxviii; C. V. Langlois, *La Vie en France au moyen âge d'après quelques moralistes du temps* (Paris, 1908), 30-68, 89-112.

To sum up, it seems likely that, when the vernacular poets denounced recalcitrant crusaders or expressed disillusionment after the failure of a campaign, they were reflecting a wider body of public opinion. But the same cannot be said of their attacks upon papal crusading policy in Europe. Although they were neither heretics nor propagandists, the attitude of the Provençal troubadours, Northern French trouvères, and German minnesingers was dictated by their location and circumstances and coloured by a deep-seated prejudice against the papacy. To a certain extent the Provençal *sirventes* may have circulated orally and their ideas influenced a wider circle of people, but we have no real means of assessing their effect upon public opinion. The same applies to the Middle High German *sprüche* and the works of the Northern French trouvères.

Most critics will be discussed in more detail as they occur in the text. But it is necessary at this stage to say more about the work of a few individuals—Ralph Niger, the chroniclers of St Albans, and the authors of the memoirs submitted to the Second Council of Lyons—for their criticisms covered many aspects of crusading and will be quoted throughout this study.

Relatively little is known about the life of Ralph Niger, but he seems to have been born about 1140 and to have been a student at the schools in Paris in the 1160s: he was referred to as *magister* in *c*.1166. As a young man, Ralph was acquainted with prominent ecclesiastics such as John of Salisbury, later Bishop of Chartres, and the Archbishops of Mainz and Rheims, and he appears to have been one of the supporters of the Archbishop of Canterbury, Thomas Becket. Perhaps for this reason he incurred Henry II's displeasure and was exiled to France some time before Becket's murder in 1170. We have few details about this stage in Ralph's career, but he seems to have become a member of the Young King's court and the latter probably acted as his literary patron. During his stay on the continent Ralph composed a number of theological treatises and biblical commentaries; after his return to England in *c*.1194, he also wrote two chronicles.[52]

[52] For further details see Flahiff, 'Ralph Niger: An Introduction'; Ralph Niger, *DRM* 3-11.

His most important work for our purposes, however, is the treatise *De re militari*, which was addressed to King Philip II of France. Schmugge dated this to the turn of 1187-8, in other words to the months after the fall of Jerusalem to Saladin and Pope Gregory VIII's decision to launch a new crusade, probably before Philip took the cross at Gisors on 21 January 1188. Flahiff treated Ralph's criticism of the crusading movement in isolation, but Schmugge showed that it formed part of a general attack upon abuses in lay and ecclesiastical society and was founded upon traditional biblical exegesis.[53] In the first three books of *De re militari* Ralph was concerned to remind those who took the cross that their undertaking would be in vain if they did not undergo a spiritual as well as a physical pilgrimage, and discussed the significance of the three pilgrimages to Jerusalem described in the Bible: the exodus of the Israelites from Egypt, their return from the Babylonish captivity, and Peter's escape from Herod's prison. Towards the end of Book III and throughout Book IV, Ralph turned his attention to the crusade itself. He argued that the loss of Palestine was a divine punishment for the sins of the Christians in the Latin East and advanced three main reasons why men should not hasten to the Holy Land. He questioned whether it was justifiable for Christians to expose themselves to the physical and spiritual dangers posed by the journey to the East and declared that they would do better to devote their energies to combating the rise of heresies in the West, rather than to involve themselves in the affairs of other regions. Indeed, Ralph urged the French king to postpone his departure for the Holy Land.[54] The most interesting and controversial part of Ralph's thesis, however, was the suggestion that God might not wish the faithful to end the Muslim domination of Palestine, for this called into question the whole basis of the crusade.[55] Ralph seems to have been aware that such extreme views would find little support in the general atmosphere of crusad-

[53] Ralph Niger, *DRM* 15-16, 23-40.

[54] This proposal was calculated to appeal to Ralph's patron, Archbishop William of Rheims, who had made repeated attempts to stamp out heresy in his own diocese. See Flahiff, 'Ralph Niger', 120. n. 88.

[55] See below, p. 84.

ing enthusiasm. He therefore concluded his treatise with some words of advice about the proposed expedition, in particular who should and who should not take the cross, drawing upon the lessons of previous campaigns.[56]

It has been suggested that the twelfth-century abbot, John de Cella, was the founder of the St Albans historical school,[57] but in fact this title should probably be given to Roger Wendover.[58] He began writing his *Flores historiarum* in *c.*1219; although for the most part it draws heavily upon the work of other historians, it seems to provide an original account of events from *c.*1201 to 1236. After Roger's death this task was taken up by his associate and pupil Matthew Paris. His main work was the *Chronica maiora*, but he also produced a series of abridgements with various alterations and additions, including his most popular chronicle, the *Flores historiarum*, and continued writing until his death in *c.*1259.[59] Both Roger and Matthew benefited from St Albans' position on one of the main routes from London to the North; they derived much of their information from important visitors, such as King Henry III and Earl Richard of Cornwall, who stayed at the abbey.[60] Nevertheless theirs was a personal record rather than an official history of the period. Matthew has been singled out for his prejudices against foreigners, friars, the king, and the papacy, but in fact he inherited these from Roger and they stemmed from the same root. Both monks were very aware of the tradition of autonomy in Benedictine houses and they were anxious to defend St Albans' established wealth and privileges from all forms of outside interference, whether the encroachments of new orders or royal or papal aggrandizement.[61] These

---

[56] See below, pp. 27, 29-30, 41-2, 45-6.

[57] C. Jenkins, *The Monastic Chronicler and the Early School of St. Albans* (London, 1922), 38-41; R. Vaughan, *Matthew Paris* (Cambridge, 1958), 22-3.

[58] V. H. Galbraith, *Roger Wendover and Matthew Paris* (David Murray Lecture, University of Glasgow, 1944), 15-16; F. M. Powicke, 'The Compilation of the *Chronica maiora* of Matthew Paris', *Proceedings of the British Academy*, xxx (1944), 147-51.

[59] Vaughan, 21-35, 49-77.   [60] Ibid. 11-17, 135.

[61] Galbraith, 6; H. Plehn, 'Der politische Charakter von Matheus Parisiensis', *Staats- und sozialwissenschaftliche Forschungen*, iii. 14 (1897), 42-5; A. Gransden, *Historical Writing in England c.550 to c.1307* (London, 1974), 367-8; Vaughan, 263-5.

grievances also seem to be the most satisfactory explanation
for the chroniclers' opposition to certain aspects of papal
crusading policy. It is hardly surprising that Roger and
Matthew resented the burden imposed upon St Albans and
the English church as a whole by papal taxation, to finance
expeditions against the Muslims in the East and Christian
lay powers in the West; and they seem to have regarded the
inhabitants of the Languedoc and the Staufen emperors
as fellow victims of papal avarice.[62] It is significant that
Matthew's enthusiasm for Frederick II waned after 1245,
when he learned of the emperor's plans to confiscate
ecclesiastical property.[63] In spite of these similarities,
however, there are important differences between Roger's
and Matthew's accounts of events, even in the years before
1236: Matthew's style was more vigorous and direct than his
predecessor's, and he added details and phrases to increase
the dramatic effect and underline the political moral. Indeed,
one has to be careful when using his evidence, for he often
put his own views into the mouths of his characters and
tended to invent stories or embellish the facts in order to
emphasize his point.[64]

The memoirs submitted to the Second Council of Lyons
in 1274 were composed at the request of Pope Gregory X.
As a former crusader, he was aware of the desperate situation
of the Christians in the Latin East; in his summons to the
clergy to attend the council, he asked for advice about possible
means of recovering the Holy Land. He also seems to
have requested information about the attitude of the faithful
towards the crusading movement as a whole.[65] Four of these
replies have survived; they express a variety of views. Bishop
Bruno of Olmütz advocated the diversion of the crusade
against the pagans of north-eastern Europe, who he maintained
were the greatest threat to Christendom,[66] whereas

[62] Vaughan, 147-8; Plehn, 99-100.

[63] Matthew Paris, *CM* iv. 476-8; A. L. Smith, *Church and State in the Middle Ages* (Oxford, 1913), 176-7.

[64] Vaughan, 32-4, 126-8, 135, 143, 149.   [65] See Throop, 11-24, 215-20.

[66] Bruno of Olmütz, 'Bericht des Bischof Bruno von Olmütz an Papst Gregor X. über die kirchlichen und politischen Zustände Deutschlands bei der Thronbesteigung Rudolphs von Hapsburg', ed. C. Höfler, in 'Analecten zur Geschichte Deutschlands und Italiens', *Abhandlungen der historischen Classe der Königlich Bayerischen Akademie der Wissenschaften*, 3rd ser. iv (1846), 20-2.

the Dominican William of Tripoli listed the similarities between Islam and Christianity and discussed the likelihood of the peaceful conversion of the Muslims.[67] Two ecclesiastics, however, sought to give a more specific answer to the pope's appeal. The main theme of Gilbert of Tournai's treatise was corruption in the church; in this context he highlighted certain abuses which affected the crusades and pointed out to Gregory X that the misuse of vow-redemptions and excessive taxation had deterred men from taking the cross.[68] The fullest treatment was, however, to be found in the memoir composed by Humbert of Romans, who had been Minister-General of the Dominican Order from 1254 to 1263. Whereas Gilbert tended to repeat criticisms put forward by earlier writers such as James of Vitry and Peter of Blois,[69] Humbert actually attempted to report and analyse public opinion. Some years previously he had written a treatise on crusade-preaching in which he listed the various factors which deterred men from taking the cross, including domestic cares and physical fear.[70] Now he addressed himself to the more fundamental problem of public hostility towards the crusading movement. He distinguished seven main classes of critics, ranging from those disillusioned by the failure of previous expeditions to pacifists, and he quoted their arguments in full before proceeding to put forward his own defence of the crusading movement.[71]

In addition to these four treatises, we also have an interesting memoir composed by Fidenzio of Padua, the Provincial-General of the Franciscans in the Holy Land, who was a member

[67] William of Tripoli, *De statu Saracenorum*, in H. Prutz, *Kulturgeschichte der Kreuzzüge* (Berlin, 1883), 573-98. William stated that he was writing in 1273, but he may have begun his task in 1270 or 1271, with a personal commission from the crusading Archdeacon Teobaldus, later Pope Gregory X. See Throop, 115-19.

[68] Gilbert of Tournai, *Collectio de scandalis ecclesiae*, ed. P. A. Stroick, *Archivum Franciscanum Historicum*, xxiv (1931), 39-40. For the authorship of this work, see Stroick, 'Verfasser und Quellen der *Collectio de scandalis ecclesiae*, ibid. xxiii (1930), 15-41, 273-92.

[69] Stroick, 292-9, 433-66.

[70] Humbert of Romans, *De praedicatione sancte crucis* (Nuremberg, 1490). A. Lecoy de la Marche, 'La prédication de la croisade au treizième siècle', *Revue des questions historiques*, xlviii (1890), 11-13, dates this treatise c.1266.

[71] Humbert of Romans, *Opus tripartitum*, ed. E. Brown, in *Fasciculus rerum expetendarum et fugiendarum*, ii (London, 1690), 185-206.

of the convent at Tripoli until 1268 and witnessed the Mamelukes' gradual reconquest of the Latin East. Because of his
experience, Fidenzio was one of those summoned to the
Second Council of Lyons to give Gregory X advice about his
proposed crusade; but he then seems to have returned to
the East, and his ideas were not set out in the form of
a treatise until c.1291.[72] In his memoir Fidenzio drew upon
his local knowledge and put forward various suggestions for
the reacquisition and maintenance of the Holy Land, including improvements in tactics and in the general conduct of
the army.[73]

Certain themes of criticism can be traced from the early
twelfth century to 1274; it is the aim of this book to chart
their development and assess their significance. The nature of
the material demands that the work should be divided into
two parts. In the first three chapters I shall discuss criticism
of the crusaders: their qualifications to take the cross, their
commitment to crusading, and their behaviour during expeditions. Then in Part II, I shall turn to criticism of the crusades
themselves: of the movement as opposed to the participants.
In this period a large body of opinion expressed complaints
about abuses such as frequent royal and papal demands for
taxation and the use of vow-redemptions as a source of
revenue, and certain groups protested about the use of the
crusade against heretics, schismatics, and Christian lay
powers in the West. As early as the mid twelfth century there
were also a few critics who attacked the very idea of the
crusade, including a small group of pacifists, and it is important to establish whether or not these reflected more widespread opposition to the crusading movement. This in turn
will shed some light upon the question whether support for
the crusade was declining in the second half of the thirteenth
century.

Before I go any further, however, it is necessary to refute
certain theories which have been put forward about criticism
of the crusading movement in this period. The first of these

[72] A. S. Atiya, *The Crusade in the Later Middle Ages* (London, 1938), 36-48.
[73] Fidenzio of Padua, *Liber recuperationis Terre Sancte*, ed. P. G. Golubovich,
Biblioteca Bio-Bibliografica della Terra santa e dell'Oriente francescano (Florence,
1906-27), ii.

is the suggestion that almost from the beginning there was a significant body of individuals who condemned the military conquest of the Holy Land and advocated peaceful conversion of the Muslims by means of a programme of missionary work.[74] The proponents of this thesis cite the example of Peter the Venerable, Abbot of Cluny, who, as early as the 1140s, commissioned a series of translations of the Koran and several other Islamic treatises and declared that the Muslims should not be approached, 'as our people often do with arms, but with words; not with force but with reason; not in hatred but in love'.[75] But there is no evidence that Peter was opposed to the idea of the crusade.[76] His main aim in commissioning the translations was to strengthen the faithful against Muslim propaganda and to provide Christians with a weapon for future ideological conflicts. He did not reject the use of force as a means of maintaining and defending the Holy Land. On the contrary, he played an important part in the preparations for the Second Crusade and was closely involved in Abbot Suger's attempts to send another expedition to the East in the early 1150s.[77]

Far from their being an obstacle to conversion, contemporaries, with a few important exceptions, seem to have regarded the crusades as a means to that end. For example, in the early thirteenth century, James of Vitry, Bishop of Acre, and Oliver, later Bishop of Paderborn, exhorted the Muslims to abjure their faith, pointing out the similarities between Islam and Christianity. But they also preached the cross and took part in the Fifth Crusade;[78] and it seems that one of the main purposes of Louis IX's North African expedition was to persuade the Sultan of Tunis to accept

[74] See J. E. Siberry, 'Missionaries and Crusaders, 1095-1274: Opponents or Allies?', *Studies in Church History*, xx (1983) 103-10.

[75] Peter the Venerable, *Liber contra sectam sive haeresim Saracenorum*, ed. J. Kritzeck, *Peter the Venerable and Islam* (Princeton, 1964), 231.

[76] See Kritzeck, 20-3; J. Leclercq, *Pierre le Vénérable* (Abbaye S. Wandrille, 1946), 245-9.

[77] See V. G. Berry, 'Peter the Venerable and the Crusades', *Studia Anselmiana*, xl (1956), 141-62.

[78] James of Vitry, *Lettres* ed. R. B. C. Huygens (Leiden, 1960), 89, 108; Oliver of Paderborn, *Epistolae, Die Schriften*, ed. H. Hoogeweg, (Tübingen, 1894), 299; J. Richard, *La Papauté et les missions d'Orient au moyen âge, XIIIe-XVe siècles* (Rome, 1977), 34-7; R. C. Schwinges, *Kreuzzugsideologie und Toleranz* (Stuttgart, 1977), 273-4.

Christianity.[79] It was agreed that it was wrong to force Muslims to renounce their beliefs, but it was thought that conquest would create the right political conditions for them to enter the Christian fold of their own volition.[80]

It is also wrong to suggest that in the thirteenth century the crusading movement aroused opposition from the new orders of friars, the Franciscans and Dominicans, who advocated the peaceful conversion of the Muslims.[81] Admittedly, during his stay at Damietta on the Fifth Crusade, St Francis sought to convert the Sultan al Kāmil by preaching.[82] Moreover, he denounced the behaviour of the Christian army[83] and predicted that it would be defeated.[84] But there is no indication that he objected to the actual use of force against the Muslims.[85] In the following decades, the Franciscans and Dominicans launched a series of missions to the East,[86] but at the same time they became the papacy's principal agents for preaching the cross.[87] One who combined these two functions to great effect was the former Dominican Master-General, Raymond of Peñafort. Between 1240 and 1275 he organized missions among the Muslims of North Africa and Spain and founded colleges to teach Arabic; but he also accepted Gregory IX's commission to preach the *Reconquista*.[88] When Henry III took the cross in 1250, the English Franciscan Adam Marsh praised his devotion to the

[79] Longnon, 'Les vues de Charles d'Anjou pour la deuxième croisade de Saint Louis: Tunis ou Constantinople', *Septième centenaire de la mort de Saint Louis: Actes des colloques de Royaumont et de Paris, Mai 1970*, ed. M. Roche and L. Carolus-Barré (Paris, 1976), 191-2, 195.

[80] For the peaceful conversion of the Muslims on the First Crusade, see *Gesta Francorum*, ed. R. M. T. Hill (London, 1962), 66-7, 71, 83; Raymond of Aguilers, *Historia Francorum qui ceperunt Iherusalem*, ed. J. H. and L. L. Hill (Paris, 1969), 112.   [81] Prawer, ii. 396.

[82] Bonaventure, *Vita S. Francisci*, ed. Golubovich, *Biblioteca*, i. 33-5; Thomas of Celano, *Vita S. Francisci*, ibid. 17.

[83] *L'estoire d'Eracles empereur et la conqueste de la terre d'Outremer*, RHC Occ. ii. 348-9.   [84] Bonaventure, 35; Thomas of Celano, 17.

[85] See K. Haines, 'Attitudes and Impediments to Pacifism in Medieval Europe', *Journal of Medieval History*, vii (1981), 374; P. Rousset, *Histoire d'une idéologie: La Croisade* (Lausanne, 1983), 111, 115.

[86] Richard, *La Papauté et Les Missions*, 384-7.

[87] J. R. H. Moorman, *A History of the Franciscan Order* (Oxford, 1968), 300-1.

[88] Vita S. Raymundi, in 'Raymundiana seu Documenta quae pertinent ad S. Raymundi de Pennaforti vitam et scripta', ed. F. Balme and C. Paban, in *Monumenta Ordinis Fratrum Praedicatorum Historica*, vi (Rome and Stuttgart, 1900), 7, 31-2.

Holy Land and, far from denouncing the king's proposed expedition, prayed for its success and exhorted clerks to take the opportunity to emulate the apostles and spread the Christian faith.[89]

Apart from a few Joachites, who will be discussed later, it was only in the 1260s that critics such as Roger Bacon began to argue that the crusades hindered the conversion of the Muslims and advocated preaching and teaching alone. The extent of their opposition has not been sufficiently studied hitherto.[90]

In this period missionaries and crusaders could work in partnership because, although in certain circumstances the crusade might act as a stimulus to conversion, there was never any suggestion that actual force should be used to compel the Muslims to abjure their faith. In fact the condemnation of conversion by force was laid down in canon law; this ruling was quoted in Gratian's *Decretum*[91] and the works of other twelfth-century canonists and theologians.[92] Ralph Niger and Walter Map reemphasized that God was not pleased with forced service;[93] and the church's position was stated clearly by Thomas Aquinas. In his *Summa Theologica* he declared that, although Christians were justified in waging war against the Muslims, the latter could not be compelled to abandon their faith, for belief depended upon free will.[94]

Attitudes towards the crusades in north-eastern Europe were more complex, for they formed part of the great German expansion eastwards in which conversion and conquest went hand in hand.[95] This fusion of interests led

---

[89] Adam Marsh, *Epistolae*, ed. J. S. Brewer, *Monumenta Franciscana*, i (London, 1858), 416, 431, 434-7. See also M. W. Bloomfield and M. Reeves, 'The Penetration of Joachism into Northern Europe', *Speculum*, xxix (1954), 785-6; Throop, 132.   [90] See below, pp. 207-8.

[91] Gratian, *Decretum*, ed. A. Friedberg, *Corpus iuris canonici* (Leipzig, 1879-81), i, C. 23, q. 6 c. 4, 1.

[92] See *Summa 'Elegantius in iure divino' seu Coloniensis*, ed. G. Fransen and S. Kuttner (New York, 1969), 74; Peter Lombard, *Summa Theologica*, PL cxcii. col. 711.

[93] Ralph Niger, *DRM*, 149, 168, 196, 207; Walter Map, *De nugis curialium*, ed. M. R. James, rev. R. A. B. Mynors and C. N. L. Brooke (Oxford, 1983), 60.

[94] Thomas Aquinas, *Summa Theologica*, ed. P. Caramello (Turin, 1962), iii (2), q. 10 art. 8.

[95] E. Christiansen, *The Northern Crusades* (London, 1980); E. Johnson, 'The German Crusades in the Baltic', in *History of the Crusades*, (Madison, Wis. 1969-), iii. 57.

two prominent crusading apologists to make outspoken statements which have puzzled generations of historians. At the time of the Wendish Crusade, St Bernard offered pagans a clear choice between conversion and destruction[96] and in 1209 Innocent III exhorted the King of Denmark to take the cross, 'to stamp out the error of paganism and extend the frontiers of the Christian faith'.[97] The German scholar Lotter has recently put forward a possible explanation for St Bernard's apparent rejection of the church's ruling about forcible conversion, namely that he meant the destruction of the heathen nations rather than the slaughter of individual pagans;[98] but this interpretation has been questioned by other historians.[99] Even if the Abbot of Clairvaux intended to make this distinction, we do not know how his audience interpreted the phrase; the same applies to Innocent III's extraordinary remark.

Another aim of this study is to challenge the thesis that the only true crusades were those directed to conquer Jerusalem and defend the Latin East and that the papacy's use of the crusade against heretics, schismatics, and Christian lay powers in the West was a late and unpopular development.[100] In Chapter Six I intend to analyse the extent and significance of opposition to the crusades in Europe. But it should be noted at this stage that as far as popes, preachers, and canonists were concerned, these expeditions formed part of a general campaign against the enemies of the faith and participants were usually awarded the same indulgence as those who fought against the Muslims. Far from its being a late development, the 'political' crusade was first preached in the 1130s; and it could be argued that this crusade against Roger II of Sicily and the antipope Anacletus II had its precursor in Bohemond of Antioch's expedition against the schismatic Greeks in 1107-8.[101]

---

[96] Bernard of Clairvaux, *Opera*, ed. Leclercq, C. H. Talbot, and H. M. Rochais (Rome, 1957-77), viii. 433.

[97] Innocent III, *Opera*, PL ccxvi. cols. 116-17.

[98] F. Lotter, *Die Konzeption des Wendenkreuzzugs*, (Sigmaringen, 1977), 12.

[99] J. A. Brundage, review of F. Lotter, *Speculum*, liv (1979), 172-3; H. E. J. Cowdrey, review of Lotter, *EHR*, xciv (1979), 166-7.

[100] See H. E. Mayer, review of Riley-Smith, *What were the Crusades?*, *Speculum*, liii (1979), 841-2; id. *The Crusades* (London, 1972), 202-3.

[101] E. D. Hehl, *Kirche und Krieg im 12. Jahrhundert* (Stuttgart, 1980), 14-16, 38-45.

Throop described Christendom in 1274 as 'profoundly discouraged, sceptical and disgusted'[102] and several other historians have highlighted the 'diversion' of the crusade to Europe as one of the factors which led to increasing disillusionment and ultimately to the decline of the crusading movement as a whole.[103] Gregory X's failure to send an expedition to the East has been regarded as proof of this decline in enthusiasm; but in fact the whole subject needs to be more carefully analysed. In recent years there have been a number of detailed studies of various aspects of the crusading movement in the Later Middle Ages, which emphasize the continued popular support for the crusading ideal.[104] And the arguments advanced by the various critics should be placed in the context of repeated attempts to launch crusades to the Holy Land in the thirteenth and fourteenth centuries.

---

[102] Throop, 25, 68, 163, 214, 284.

[103] Purcell, 3, 184-5; Runciman, 'Decline', 644-6; Prawer, ii. 380-4; Stickel, 176-90; P. Toubert, 'Les Déviations de la Croisade au milieu du XIIIe siècle: Alexandre IV contre Manfred', *Le Moyen Âge*, lxix (1963), 391-2.

[104] See N. J. Housley, *The Italian Crusades: The Papal-Angevin Alliance and the Crusades against Christian Lay Powers, 1254-1343* (Oxford, 1982); C. J. Tyerman, 'Marino Sanudo Torsello and the Lost Crusade: Lobbying in the Fourteenth Century', *TRHS*, xxxii (1982), 57-75; F. Cardini, 'The Crusade and the "Presence of Jerusalem" in Medieval Florence', in *Outremer: Studies in the History of the Crusading Kingdom of Jerusalem presented to J. Prawer*, ed. B. Z. Kedar, R. C. Smail, and H. E. Mayer (Jerusalem 1982), 332-46; M. Keen, 'Chaucer's Knight, the English Aristocracy and the Crusade', in V. J. Scattergood and J. W. Sherborne (eds.), *English Court Culture in the Later Middle Ages* (London, 1983), 45-63; Siberry, 'Criticism of Crusading in Fourteenth-century England', in *'Crusade and Settlement' Papers: Proceedings of the First Society for the Study of the Crusades and Latin East Conference, Cardiff 1983*, ed. P. W. Edbury (forthcoming).

PART I

CRITICISM OF THE CRUSADERS

CHAPTER I

The qualifications of a crusader

IT was agreed that crusaders should generally be laymen and that the laymen best fitted to crusade were those who were physically fit and active and could afford to equip and support themselves for the duration of the expedition. And, from the beginning of the crusading movement, attempts were made to restrict participation to those who possessed these qualifications.

According to Robert of Rheims's account of Urban II's sermon at Clermont, the pope tried to persuade the old and weak not to join the First Crusade,[1] but many disregarded his advice. During the march through Asia Minor, these non-combatants proved a severe burden upon the army's resources;[2] it is significant that, when Bruno of Lucca returned to his native city after the siege of Antioch with a request for reinforcements, he carried the warning that the poor should be left at home.[3] The problems of provisioning a large army and protecting the weak from enemy attacks became acute during the Second Crusade.[4] After the disastrous journey through Asia Minor, Louis VII apparently suggested that 'the defenceless mob which has always harmed us and because of which food is more expensive and progress slower' should be separated from the main body of the army and entrusted to the fleet; and, in his account of the expedition, the king's chaplain, Odo of Deuil, expressed the hope that future pilgrims would be 'the more cautious because of our experiences'. He lamented:

[1] Robert of Rheims, *Historia Iherosolimitana*, RHC Occ. iii. 729. See also R. Somerville, 'The Council of Clermont and the First Crusade', *Studia Gratiana*, xx (1976), 330-3.

[2] See W. Porges, 'The Clergy, the Poor, and the Non-combatants on the First Crusade', *Speculum*, xxi (1946), 1-4, 9-12.

[3] *Die Kreuzzugsbriefe aus den Jahren 1088-1100*, ed. H. Hagenmeyer (Innsbruck, 1901), 167.

[4] *Annales Herbipolenses*, MGH SS xvi. 5; Gerhoh of Reichersberg, *De investigatione Antichristi*, MGH Libelli de lite, iii. 374-6.

would that he (Pope Eugenius III) had instructed the infantry . . . to keep the weak at home . . . for the weak and unarmed are always a burden to their comrades and a source of prey to their enemies.[5]

A similar explanation for the failure of the Second Crusade was advanced by Abbot Suger's secretary, William of St Denis. In a dialogue said to have taken place between himself and another monk Geoffrey, William posed the question why 'scarcely anyone survived from such a great multitude of men and the army of two very powerful kings and (why) the few who escaped the sword and famine returned without any result'. In his reply his companion drew parallels between the crusade and Xerxes' Greek campaign described in Seneca's treatise De Beneficiis. He recalled the advice of Demaratus, who alone had told Xerxes that the disorganized and unwieldy multitude in which he had trusted had weight rather than strength and would be a burden to its commander.[6]

The disastrous experience of the Second Crusade led to official measures in England, France, and Germany to prevent those unable to bear arms or to support themselves from going to the East. At the Councils of Geddington and Le Mans, Henry II and Philip Augustus penalized runaway serfs who attempted to join the Third Crusade,[7] and the Emperor Frederick I decreed that those who could not finance themselves for two years should remain at home.[8]

---

[5] Odo of Deuil, De profectione Ludovici VII in Orientem, ed. Berry (New York, 1948), 28–30, 94, 130.

[6] William of St Denis, 'Dialogus', ed. A. Wilmart, Revue Mabillon, xxxii (1942), 107–8; Seneca, De Beneficiis, vi. 31. 1–4, 7–12. For this use of Seneca, see H. Glaser, 'Wilhelm von Saint Denis: Ein Humanist aus der Umgebung des Abtes Suger und die Krise seiner Abtei von 1151 bis 1152', Historisches Jahrbuch, lxxxv (1965), 296; K. D. Nothdurft, 'Studien zum Einfluß Senecas auf die Philosophie und Theologie des zwölften Jahrhunderts', Studien und Texte zur Geistesgeschichte des Mittelalters, vii (Leiden and Cologne, 1963), 106–7.

[7] Roger of Howden, Gesta regis Henrici secundi, ed. W. Stubbs (London, 1867), ii. 32–3. For similar measures enacted at the Council of Messina, see ibid. 131. For Roger's authorship of the Gesta, see now D. Corner, 'The Gesta Henrici secundi and Chronica of Roger, Parson of Howden', Bulletin of the Institute of Historical Research, lvi (1983), 126–45 and J. B. Gillingham, 'Roger of Howden on Crusade', in D. O. Morgan (ed.), Medieval Historical Writing in the Christian and Islamic Worlds (London, 1982), 60–76.

[8] Historia peregrinorum, ed. A. Chroust, MGH Scr. rer. Germ. n.s. v (Berlin, 1928), 126; Annales Marbacenses, MGH SS xvii. 60. See also Continuatio Sanblasiana, MGH SS xx. 319; Itinerarium peregrinorum, ed. Mayer (Stuttgart, 1962), 290.

The most detailed discussion of the qualifications for crusading is to be found in Ralph Niger's treatise *De re militari*. Ralph accepted that Pope Gregory VIII had exhorted all men to take the cross, promising them an indulgence, but he emphasized that the pope's appeal should be correctly interpreted so that it was in conformity with justice and equity. Ralph was anxious to prevent a repetition of the events of the Second Crusade and maintained that only certain classes, such as knights, were justified in going to the Holy Land. He admitted that some poor youths might be subsidized by wealthy crusaders and act as messengers, guards, and menials in the camp. But otherwise he believed that the poor served no good purpose, since they could not afford to bring supplies and fell prey to enemy ambushes. As for old men, they might give valuable advice and guard equipment, but this did not justify the burden which they imposed upon the army.[9] A similar criterion of utility was advocated by Innocent III. In 1200 the Archbishop of Canterbury, Hubert Walter, who himself had been on the Third Crusade, requested the pope's advice 'about those who took the cross for the relief of the Holy Land and who, because of infirmity or poverty or some other just reason, could not usefully fulfil their undertaking'. Innocent replied:

the weak and the poor go thither more to the disadvantage than to the advantage of the enterprise, since the former cannot fight and the latter are obliged to beg, unless they (the weak) happen to be nobles or great men who are taking soldiers with them at their own expense, or are craftsmen or farmers who can gain the necessities of life by their own labours and contribute to the support of the land;

and he instructed the archbishop to encourage those who could not usefully fulfil their vows to redeem them according to their means or pay for soldiers in their place. Innocent subsequently made a further exception for men who, although unable to fight themselves, could give mature counsel; but otherwise his emphasis upon the military nature of the crusade remained unchanged.[10] These directives were amongst the instructions sent to the papal legate Peter Capuano on

[9] Ralph Niger, *DRM* 224, 227.
[10] *Liber extra*, ed. Friedberg, *Corpus iuris canonici*, ii, Lib. 3, tit. 34 c. 8-9.

the Fourth Crusade[11] and they were incorporated in later collections of canon law under the title *De voto*.[12] In the course of the thirteenth century, a series of papal letters exhorted preachers to examine the physical fitness of prospective crusaders[13] and the annalist of Waverley recorded that some who had undertaken to go on the Fifth Crusade were absolved from their vows because of 'want of means or weakness of body'.[14] There was a protest by the French barons in 1213 when Innocent authorized his legates in France, Robert Courson and Archbishop Simon of Tyre, to distribute the cross freely in order to save time and then to consider whether the votaries were capable of fulfilling their vows, using the money obtained from redemptions as a source of finance for the crusade.[15] According to the chronicler known as William le Breton, the barons laid aside their crosses because they feared that the army would be hampered by the presence of the poor, the old, and the weak.[16]

In his sermon at Clermont and his letter to the Bolognese, Urban II had decreed that no layman should go to the Holy Land without the licence of his parish priest and that married men should seek the consent of their wives.[17] Nevertheless, laymen were considered more free than other classes to make a crusading vow.

It was accepted that some clerks were needed to accompany the crusading army in the Near East and Europe: to preach, to give communion, to lead penitential processions,

[11] 'Die Dekretalensammlungen des Gilbertus und Alanus nach den Weingartener Handschriften', ed. R. von Heckel, *Zeitschrift der Savigny-Stiftung für Rechtsgeschichte*, Kanonistische Abteilung lxxiii (1940), 328-9. See also *Devastatio Constantinopolitana*, MGH SS xvi. 10.

[12] *Compilatio III, Quinque compilationes antiquae*, ed. Friedberg (Leipzig, 1882), Lib. 3. tit. 26 c. 4-5.

[13] Innocent III, *Opera*, PL ccxv, cols. 1500-3; Gregory IX, *Registres*, ed. L. d'Auvray, (Paris, 1896-1955), nos. 4222, 4635; Innocent IV, *Registres*, ed. E. Berger, (Paris, 1884-1921), nos. 3523, 3727.

[14] *Annales de Waverleia*, ed. H. R. Luard, *Annales monastici* (London, 1864-9), ii. 289.

[15] G. Tangl, *Studien zum Register Innocenz' III.* (Weimar, 1929), 93-4. See also Innocent III, *Opera*, PL ccxvi, cols. 904-5.

[16] William le Breton, *Gesta Philippi Augusti*, ed. H. F. Delaborde (Paris, 1882), 303.

[17] Robert of Rheims, 729; *Die Kreuzzugsbriefe*, 138. For a discussion about the vows of married men, see Brundage, 'The Crusader's Wife: A Canonistic quandary', *Studia Gratiana*, xii (1967), 425-41.

to care for the poor, and to help maintain morale;[18] and priests who took the cross were granted special financial privileges.[19] But at the same time they were reminded that they had obligations to their parishioners. Writing in France in *c.* 1093-4,[20] on the eve of the First Crusade, the canonist Ivo of Chartres had recognized that a few clerks might accompany a military force in order to minister to the soldiers' religious needs, but he emphasized that they must have their bishop's permission to travel and denounced priests who abandoned their parishes to go on pilgrimage.[21] This anxiety about pastoral duties was shared by Urban II. According to one account of his sermon at Clermont, the pope exhorted clerks to seek their bishop's consent before they took the cross; and, in his letter to the Bolognese, Urban warned priests that they would derive no benefit from the expedition if they left without their superior's authorization.[22] The same qualification was incorporated in later collections of canon law.[23]

This concern about parochial duties led to criticism of certain clerical crusaders by fellow ecclesiastics. For example, Ralph Niger accepted that a few clerks were needed to hear confessions and celebrate mass, but he argued that, apart from these, priests were of no practical value to the army and consumed valuable supplies. Ralph declared that those who had a charge in the community should fulfil it and he deemed the provision of a substitute unsatisfactory. He recognized that clerks took the cross in order to acquire remission of sins, but questioned whether it would not be

[18] Ralph Niger, *DRM* 227; *COD* 267; *Liber extra*, Lib. 3 tit. 34 c. 9. See also Porges, 9-11, 15-17; M. H. Vicaire, 'Les clercs de la croisade', *Cahiers de Fanjeaux*, iv. (1969), 268-73.

[19] See Purcell, 139-40; Brundage, *Medieval Canon Law and the Crusader* (Madison, Wis., 1969), 177-9.

[20] For the dating of Ivo of Chartres's *Decretum* and *Panormia*, see P. Fournier and G. Le Bras, *Histoire des collections canoniques en Occident depuis les fausses décrétales jusqu'au Décret de Gratien* (Paris, 1931-2), ii. 82-3, 96-7.

[21] Ivo of Chartres, *Decretum*, PL clxi. cols. 424, 484-5.

[22] Robert of Rheims, 729; *Die Kreuzzugsbriefe*, 138. See also Urban's letter to the monks of Vallombrosa, 'Papsturkunden in Florenz', ed. W. Wiederhold, *Nachrichten von der Königlichen Gesellschaft der Wissenschaften zu Göttingen, Philologisch-historische Klasse*, (1901), 313.

[23] *Liber extra*, Lib. 3 tit. 34 c. 7; Hostiensis, *Summa aurea* (Basle, 1573), col. 896.

better for them to do penance in their own churches. They
should discharge the duties of their office, not desert their
flock and expose themselves to the dangers of a pilgrimage.[24]
In a similar way, at the beginning of the thirteenth century,
Adam, Abbot of Perseigne, a participant in the Fourth
Crusade,[25] wrote to Bishop Hamelin of Le Mans criticizing
clerks who abandoned their parishes to go to the Holy Land,
'hastening on their own initiative to a task which God does
not impose upon them'. Adam recalled the virtues of Christian
charity and the perils to which these priests exposed their
congregations, and he begged the bishop to dissuade them
from their undertaking:

Christ did not shed his blood for the acquisition of Jerusalem, but
rather to win and save souls. And it seems to me that those who seek
to acquire this land and in so doing neglect the salvation of souls cloak
with an appearance of piety the business of their own perdition.

Adam was particularly critical of priests who used their
churches merely as a source of income and had no concept
of parochial duties, and maintained that they would derive
no spiritual benefit from the expedition.[26]
   In 1260 Odo Rigaud, Archbishop of Rouen, granted
Sylvester, a priest at Varangeville, permission to go to
the Holy Land, on condition that if he had not returned
within two years he should be considered to have resigned
his benefice. But during a tour of his province several
years later, the archbishop witnessed the disruption caused
by the absence of a parish priest on crusade. This experience seems to have had a profound effect upon him and in
1265 Odo's deputies ordered Sylvester to postpone his
departure until he had discussed the matter with his
superior.[27]
   In a similar way certain bishops were urged to pay attention

[24] Ralph Niger, *DRM* 195, 224-5.
[25] See J. Bouvet, 'Biographie d'Adam de Perseigne', *Collectanea Ordinis
Cisterciensium Reformatorum*, xx (1958), 147.
[26] Adam of Perseigne, 'Lettres d'Adam de Perseigne à ses correspondants du
Maine, XIIᵉ-XIIIᵉ siècles', ed. Bouvet, *La Province du Maine*, 2nd ser. xxxii
(1952), 12-13.
[27] Odo Rigaud, *Regestrum visitationum archiepiscopi Rothomagensis*, ed. T.
Bonnin (Rouen, 1852), 495, 520, 664.

to the needs of their diocese.[28] Ralph Niger conceded that some prelates might go on crusade if this served the common good of their subjects, but he warned them to be careful lest they imperilled themselves and ninety-nine of their flock for the sake of the one sheep that had strayed (Luke 15: 14). And he was highly critical of bishops who went on pilgrimages in order to escape their burdens and thus set a bad example for their subordinates.[29] Unlike Ralph, Peter of Blois was one of the great advocates of the Third Crusade.[30] But as Archdeacon of Bath he was concerned about what might become of the diocese if Bishop Savaric went to the Holy Land. He begged the bishop not to place himself in danger, and not to abandon the churches committed to his care, and he asked what good this journey would do. Peter pointed out that Christ had told his apostles to flee in times of persecution (Matt. 10: 23), not in times of peace; he reminded Bishop Savaric that clerks, monks, and laity lamented his departure. He stressed that it would not be considered a fault if he gave up his plans; on the contrary he would be welcomed back with honour and glory.[31] Peter's appeal may have had an effect upon Bishop Savaric, for in June 1205 he paused in Rome on his way to Palestine and was released from his crusading vow by Innocent III because of his own inability to fight and the poverty of his diocese.[32] He died soon afterwards.

In his *Decretum*, dated c. 1140,[33] the canonist Gratian had ruled that a bishop must seek papal permission before he accompanied a military expedition.[34] And the anxiety about pastoral duties seems to have led in the early thirteenth century to the extension of this provision to the

[28] See Roderick of Toledo, *De rebus Hispaniae*, ed. A. Schott, *Hispaniae illustratae seu rerum urbiumque Hispaniae, Lusitaniae, Aethiopiae et Indiae scriptores varii* (Frankfurt am Main, 1603-8), ii. 107; Bernard, *Opera*, vii. 144.

[29] Ralph Niger, *DRM* 211, 225.   [30] See below, pp. 54-5.

[31] Peter of Blois, *Opera*, ed. J. A. Giles (Oxford 1846-7), ii. 79. See also Gerald of Wales, *Itinerarium Kambriae, Opera*, ed. Brewer *et al.* (London, 1861-91), vi. 125-6.

[32] Innocent III, PL ccxv, col. 668.

[33] See Fransen, 'La date du Décret de Gratien', *Revue d'histoire ecclésiastique*, li (1956), 530.

[34] Gratian, *Decretum*, C. 23 q. 8 d.p.c. 25. See also F. H. Russell, *The Just War in the Middle Ages* (Cambridge, 1975), 109-11, 186-7.

crusades.[35] When, moreover, in 1205 Innocent III authorized the Bishop of Soissons to remain in Constantinople for three years, he wrote to the bishop's chapter exhorting them to bear his absence humbly and devoutly and explaining that in this instance public utility should have precedence over a more local need.[36] And an anonymous thirteenth-century collection of *notabilia* included the observation that a bishop should receive the permission of both his chapter and the pope before he undertook a lengthy pilgrimage.[37] The decretal *Magne* went even further and suggested that a bishop should seek the consent of his flock before he made a vow which would separate him from it.[38] This notion was not taken up by later canonists, although Hostiensis limited a bishop's power to make a pilgrimage vow because of the marriage-bond relationship which he had established with his church.[39] But a few crusading prelates seem to have taken the idea to heart: we know, for example, that, before Archbishop Odo of Rouen went on Louis IX's second crusade, he toured his province and sought the blessing of his clergy and people.[40]

Ivo of Chartres had recognized that some clerks were needed to perform spiritual functions during a campaign,[41] but in his *Decretum* he repeated the canonical ruling that they could not bear arms;[42] a similar provision was enacted by the Council of Clermont in 1095.[43] The role of clerks in warfare in general and in the crusades in particular was discussed at length by other canonists and theologians in the twelfth and thirteenth centuries.[44] They accepted that priests could

---

[35] See *Liber extra*, Lib. 3 tit. 34 c. 7; Raymond of Peñafort, *Summa de casibus penitentiae* (Verona, 1744), 61; Hostiensis, col. 896.

[36] Innocent III, PL ccxv, col. 638.

[37] Brundage, *Medieval Canon Law*, 85, n. 70.

[38] *Liber extra*, Lib. 3 tit. 34 c. 7.

[39] Hostiensis, col. 896.

[40] Odo Rigaud, 638.

[41] Ivo of Chartres *Decretum*, cols. 424, 524.

[42] Ibid. cols. 505, 508.

[43] *Decreta Claromontensia*, in Somerville, *The Councils of Urban II*, i, Annuarium Historiae Conciliorum, Supp. i (Amsterdam, 1972), appendix iii, 143.

[44] See Russell, 72-83, 105-12, 186-8, 251-2; Brundage, 'Holy War and the Medieval Lawyers', in T. P. Murphy (ed.), *The Holy War* (Columbus, Ohio, 1974), 110-12.

exhort others to defend the oppressed and attack the enemies of God,[45] but they emphasized that their weapons were to be prayers and tears.[46] Admittedly a number of clerks ignored this prohibition and fought against the Muslims,[47] and some were even praised for their military skills.[48] But the church never conceded that this was compatible with their profession[49] and such behaviour also aroused criticism. In his commentary on the Book of Kings dated c. 1180,[50] Ralph Niger condemned Bishop Otto of Freising for his part in promoting the Second Crusade: 'usurping arms, he promised aid . . . against (the rules of) his order';[51] and in his treatise *De re militari* he observed that it was not lawful for priests to shed blood; when they were attacked they should obey Christ's injunction and turn the other cheek (Matt. 5: 39).[52] The chronicler Richard of Devizes charged the Archbishop of Rouen, Walter of Coutances, with cowardice, because he abandoned the army of the Third Crusade at Sicily, but the latter apparently excused his action on the grounds that 'the shepherds of the church should preach not fight; and it is not fitting for a bishop to bear any arms other than those of the virtues'.[53]

A few clerks seem to have been valued for their wise counsel in military affairs,[54] but others were criticized for

[45] Gratian, *Decretum*, C. 23 q. 8 d.p.c. 6. For a portrait of such a clerical crusader, see Peter of Vaux de Cernay, *Hystoria Albigensis*, ed. P. Guébin and E. Lyon (Paris, 1926–30), i. 178–80.

[46] Gratian, *Decretum*, C. 23 q. 8 d.p.c. 6 c. 3. Russell (78, n. 83) questions the authenticity of this canon: he points out that it is not found in any manuscript before the 13th c. and suggests that it was added at this stage to reinforce the prohibition on direct clerical participation in warfare, which hitherto had not been properly observed.

[47] Raymond of Aguilers, 104, 111; *Itinerarium regis Ricardi*, ed. W. Stubbs (London, 1864), 372.

[48] *Itinerarium regis Ricardi*, 96, 116; Robert of Clari, *La Conquête de Constantinople*, ed. P. Lauer (Paris, 1974), 75–6, 96.

[49] Anna Comnena, *Alexiad*, ed. B. Leib (Paris, 1937–45), ii. 218–19, gave a description of a bellicose clerk who took up arms against the Greeks. She was, however, mistaken in believing that the Western church differed from her own and permitted priests to bear arms.

[50] Flahiff, 'Ralph Niger: An Introduction', 118–19.

[51] Ralph Niger, *Liber regum*, quoted in *DRM* 79–80.

[52] Ralph Niger, *DRM* 196, 224; Flahiff, 'Deus non vult', 174 n. 59.

[53] Richard of Devizes, *Cronicon de tempore regis Ricardi Primi*, ed. J. T. Appleby (London, 1963), 27–8.

[54] For the controversy about the role of the papal legate Bishop Adhémar

intervening in matters which did not concern them;[55] and some contemporaries even went so far as to draw a connection between clerical interference and a defeat. John of Salisbury believed that the main cause of the failure of the Second Crusade was the dissension among the participants about its objective, and in this context he singled out for particular criticism the Bishops of Langres and Lisieux, who 'were in such constant disagreement that rarely, if ever, could they agree on any plan'.[56] In a similar way the papal legate Cardinal Pelagius was held responsible for the disastrous outcome of the Fifth Crusade. According to the terms of his appointment, his role was to maintain peace and unity in the army.[57] But a small group of Northern French poets accused the legate of avarice and complained that he disregarded the advice of John of Brienne, the principal lay commander of the expedition, and led the army to a humiliating surrender at Mansurah.[58] The most explicit of these critics was the Norman cleric known as Guillaume le Clerc. In his didactic religious poem *Le Besant de Dieu*, composed in 1226 or 1227, he commented:

of Le Puy on the First Crusade, see Hill, 'Contemporary Accounts and the Later Reputation of Adhémar, Bishop of Puy', *Medievalia et Humanistica*, ix (1955), 31-6; Brundage, 'Adhémar of Puy: The Bishop and his Critics', *Speculum*, xxxiv (1959), 202-8; Richard, 'La papauté et la direction de la première croisade', *Journal des savants* (1960), 52-4, 57-8; Mayer, 'Zur Beurteilung Adhémars von le Puy', *Deutsches Archiv für Erforschung des Mittelalters*, xvi (1960), 547-53.

[55] Ambroise, *L'estoire de la guerre sainte*, ed. G. Paris (Paris, 1897), ll. 1612-17; *Itinerarium regis Ricardi*, 192-3; Gerald of Wales, *De principis instructione, Opera*, viii. 207.

[56] John of Salisbury, *Historia Pontificalis*, ed. M. Chibnall (London, 1956), 54-6. See also Odo of Deuil, 68-80. For John's attitude towards Arnulf of Lisieux, see *Historia Pontificalis*, pp. xxxv-vii.

[57] Honorius III, *Regesta*, ed. P. A. Pressutti (Rome, 1888-95), nos. 1350. 1433; Richard of San Germano, *Chronica*, MGH SS xix. 339. For the controversy about Pelagius' role, see J. P. Donovan, *Pelagius and the Fifth Crusade* (Philadelphia, 1950), 44-9; Van Cleve, 'The Fifth Crusade', in *History of the Crusades*, ii. 402-3.

[58] Gautier de Coincy, *De sainte Léocade* ed. E. Vilamo-Pentti, *Annales Academiae Scientiarum Fennicae*, lxvii. 2 (1950), ll. 908-20; Huon de St Quentin, 'Rome, Jherusalem se plaint', in *La Langue et la littérature française*, ed. K. Bartsch and A. Horning (Paris, 1887), cols. 373-80; Anon. 'Bien mostre Dieus apertement', *Chansons satiriques et bacchiques du XIIe siècle*, ed. Jeanroy and A. Langfors (Paris, 1921), 10. In the manuscript this poem is attributed to the trouvère Moniot, but this seems doubtful.

because of a legate who governed and led the Christian host, everyone says in truth, we lost that city [Damietta] through folly and sin . . . For when the clergy have the task of leading knights certainly that is contrary to the law. The clerk should recite aloud from his scripture and his psalms and let the knight go to his great battlefields. He [the clerk] should remain before his altars and pray for the warriors and absolve the sinners. Greatly should Rome be humiliated for the loss of Damietta.[59]

Guillaume's remark, 'everyone says in truth', prompted Throop to argue that this criticism represented a large body of opinion in the French-speaking provinces.[60] But there is no real evidence to support this conclusion. As we have seen, the trouvères belonged to a small literary circle which denounced various abuses in the church, and it was against this background that they condemned Pelagius' conduct.[61]

The critics cited above seem to have been concerned about too large a contribution from the clergy, rather than with the concept of clerical participation itself. But the same cannot be said about the critics of monastic crusaders. Monastic apologists were aware of the attractions of the Holy Land for those in the cloister, and, although they accepted that a few monks were needed on crusade as spiritual counsellors and chaplains to the army,[62] they were anxious to point out the overriding superiority of the monastic vocation.

A chronicler of the First Crusade, Abbot Guibert of Nogent, had declared that a knight was no longer forced to abandon the secular world and assume a religious way of life in order to attain salvation, for the crusade enabled him to practise his profession and win God's grace.[63] But other monastic writers stressed that a monastic vow should have

[59] Guillaume le Clerc, *Le Besant de Dieu*, ed. P. Ruelle (Brussels, 1973), ll. 2547-63.

[60] Throop, 32-3.

[61] See Guillaume le Clerc, ed. cit. 33-4; Lommatzsch, 16-26; Langlois, 89-112. See also above, p. 10.

[62] Anselm, *Opera*, ed. F. S. Schmitt, (Edinburgh, 1946-61), v. 355. See also *Gesta abbatum S. Bertini Sithiensium: continuatio*, MGH SS xiii. 664; Anonymous of Halberstadt, 'De peregrinatione in Greciam et adventu reliquiarum de Grecia libellus', ed. P. Riant, *Exuviae sacrae Constantinopolitanae* (Paris, 1877-1904), i. 12.

[63] Guibert of Nogent, *Gesta Dei per Francos*, RHC Occ. iv. 244. See also Morris, 'Equestris Ordo: Chivalry as a Vocation in the Twelfth Century', *Studies in Church History*, xv (1978) 87-97.

precedence over a crusade vow even when a crusader had undertaken to go to the Holy Land before he became a monk. Writing on the eve of the First Crusade, St Anselm had maintained that a pilgrimage vow was superseded by entry to a monastery: 'for those who through a vow surrender themselves to God partially may later submit themselves to God totally (and) do not subsequently have to render the part in the whole.'[64] And this theme was taken up by Peter the Venerable, Abbot of Cluny, with reference to crusading. He reminded Hugh of Châlons, a knight who had vowed to become a Cluniac but was reported to be planning to join the Second Crusade: 'lesser goods can be put aside for greater, but greater ought never to be exchanged for lesser . . . to serve God perpetually in humility and poverty is truly greater than making the journey to Jerusalem in pride and luxury'.[65] In his collection of spiritual anecdotes for the edification of novices, which was composed in c.1213 and took the form of a dialogue between a novice and his master, the Cistercian Caesar of Heisterbach related an incident said to have taken place when St Bernard was preaching the crusade at Liège. A canon of the cathedral, who can probably be identified as Archdeacon Philip of Liège,[66] apparently asked to join the Cistercian Order rather than take the cross because he had observed that those who had been to the Holy Land soon reverted to their evil ways and that few had benefited spiritually from the expedition. This story prompted the novice to ask whether the Order was considered superior to the crusades. His master replied:

The Cistercian Order has this indult from the apostolic see that a crusader or a man bound by any other vow of pilgrimage is absolved before God and the church if he wishes to enter the Order.[67]

[64] Anselm, *Opera*, iii. 222. See also ibid. iv. 73-4. Elsewhere Anselm and his pupil Gilbert Crispin attributed this phrase to the Abbot of Cluny. See Anselm, *Opera*, v. 417; Gilbert Crispin, 'La lettre de Gilbert Crispin sur la vie monastique', ed. Leclercq, *Studia Anselmiana*, xxxi (1953) 119 n. 3, 123.

[65] Peter the Venerable, *Letters*, ed. G. Constable (Cambridge, Mass., 1962), i. 152. Hugh apparently accepted the abbot's reasoning and became a monk. See *Vita altera*, PL clxxxix, col. 34.

[66] See Peter the Venerable, *Letters*, ii. 220.

[67] Caesar of Heisterbach, *Dialogus miraculorum*, ed. J. Strange (Cologne, 1951), i. 12-13.

In fact there is no evidence that this indult ever existed. But a decretal of Alexander III, which stated that any vow could be commuted to a vow to enter a religious house, with the implication that this was the highest form of votive obligation, was incorporated in two major thirteenth-century collections of canon law[68] and certain crusaders are known to have commuted their vows and entered the cloister. For example, William, Count of Nevers, a survivor of the 1101 Crusade, decided to join the Carthusian Order rather than take part in the Second Crusade;[69] and in 1216 or 1217 Morgan, provost of Beverley, an illegitimate son of Henry II, resigned his benefices, commuted his crusading vow, and became an oblate at the Cistercian abbey of Fountains.[70]

St Paul had described two Jerusalems (Gal. 4: 25-6); this imagery was taken up by later monastic apologists, who claimed that the monk was superior to the crusader because he aspired to the heavenly rather than the earthly city.[71] In a letter written at the time of the First Crusade, Abbot Geoffrey of Vendôme urged Abbot Odo of Marmoutier not to stray from the journey of his profession to travel to the Holy Land;[72] and Peter the Venerable reminded Hugh of

---

[68] *Compilatio II, Quinque compilationes*, Lib. 3 tit. 21 c. 2; *Liber extra*, Lib. 3 tit. 34 c. 4.

[69] *Magna vita Sancti Hugonis*, ed. D. L. Douie and H. Farmer (London, 1961-2), ii. 57. The reference in the text is actually to a Count Gerard of Nevers, who, according to the editors, has never been satisfactorily identified by any modern scholar, but this seems to have been a mistake on the part of the author of the *Vita*, the Benedictine Adam of Eynsham. Several contemporaries observed that Count William of Nevers refused to go on crusade and entered a monastery. See *Origo et historia brevis Nivernensium comitum*, extr. RHGF xii. 316; *Historia Vizeliacensis monasterii*, extr. RHGF xii. 318-19; Odo of Deuil, 14.

[70] Walter Gray, Archbishop of York, *Register*, ed. J. Raine (Surtees Society, Durham, 1872), 130. Fears about the effect of this ruling may have prompted William of Rennes, in his gloss to Raymond of Peñafort's *Summa de casibus*, to suggest an exception. He declared that great noblemen could not be freed of the obligation incurred by making a crusade vow if they entered a monastery, although lesser persons might be. Brundage, *Medieval Canon Law*, 94.

[71] Y. M. J. Congar, 'Eglise et cité de Dieu chez quelques auteurs cisterciens à l'époque des croisades', *Mélanges offerts à Étienne Gilson* (Paris, 1959), 193-201; Leclercq, *The Love of Learning and the Desire for God* (2nd rev. edn., New York, 1974), 66-71. See also A. H. Bredero, 'Jérusalem dans l'Occident médiéval' in P. Gallais and Y. J. Riou (eds.), *Mélanges René Crozet* (Poitiers, 1966), i. 259-72.

[72] Geoffrey of Vendôme, *Opera*, PL clvii, col. 162. See also ibid. col. 127;

Châlons that 'if it is good to visit Jerusalem where the feet of the Lord stood, it is far better to long for heaven where he can be seen face to face'.[73] According to these commentators, a monk had no need to visit the Holy Places; he could pray more effectively in his cell.[74]

Apologists of the crusades argued that the true crusader, the *miles Christi*, had a cross inscribed upon his heart, mind, or body as well as one sewn upon his clothing.[75] But monastic writers countered that the laity possessed only the inferior outward symbol.[76] Thus St Bernard appealed to the brethren who had joined the Second Crusade: 'why do you sew the sign of the cross upon your clothes when you always bear it upon your hearts so long as you observe the religious way of life?'[77] And according to Caesar of Heisterbach the canon of Liège deemed it

more wholesome to impress a long cross upon his mind than to sew a short cross for a brief period to his garment. For he had read the words of the Saviour's, 'He that taketh not his cross daily and followeth after me is not worthy of me' (Luke 9: 23). He said not 'for one or two years' but 'daily so'.[78]

All these arguments were intended to convince monks of the superiority of their vocation. But apologists also pointed out that crusading, although a worthy activity for the laity, was incompatible with the monastic way of life. In his Rule, St Benedict had laid great emphasis upon the vow of stability[79] and a series of early church councils had condemned

'Le récit de la fondation de Mortemer', ed. Bouvet, *Collectanea Ordinis Cisterciensium Reformatorum*, xxii (1960), 152.

[73] Peter the Venerable, *Letters*, i. 152. See also Bernard, *Opera*, viii. 437.

[74] *Liber de poenitentia et tentationibus religiosorum*, PL ccxiii. cols. 891-4; *Annales Corbeienses*, MGH SS iii. 13-14; Peter the Venerable, *Letters*, i. 215-17. This argument is reminiscent of a sentence of Jerome (*Epistolae*, ed. I. Hilberg, Corpus Scriptorum Ecclesiasticorum Latinorum, LIV, Leipzig, 1909, no. 58, p. 529) often quoted by critics of monastic pilgrimages: 'Non Hierosolymis fuisse sed Hierosolymis bene vixisse laudandum est'. See also Ivo of Chartres, *Decretum*, col. 877; Geoffrey of Vendôme, cols. 127-8.

[75] See below, pp. 97-8.   [76] 'Récit', loc. cit.

[77] Bernard, *Opera*, viii. 511-12. See also Ralph Niger, *DRM*, 196.

[78] Caesar of Heisterbach, *Dialogus miraculorum*, i. 12. See also *Magna vita Sancti Hugonis*, ii. 57.

[79] Benedict of Nursia, *Regula monachorum*, ed. E. C. Butler (Freiburg, 1912). ch. 1, 29, 58, 67.

the *gyrovagi*, monks who wandered from place to place.[80] In later centuries this notion of *stabilitas* formed one of the bases of opposition to monastic pilgrimages,[81] and the arguments developed in this context were repeated by critics of monastic participation in the crusades. According to canon law some monks were permitted to break their vow of stability and go to the Holy Land if they had their abbot's permission,[82] but on the whole this practice seems to have been discouraged. In his letters to the Bolognese and the monks of Vallombrosa, Urban II, a former prior of Cluny, reminded monks who were anxious to join the First Crusade of their vow of stability,[83] and this theme was taken up by other monastic writers. When he heard that Abbot Odo of Marmoutier was planning to join the expedition, Geoffrey of Vendôme recalled St Benedict's views on pilgrim monks and to underline his point, he quoted the pope's sermon at Clermont:[84]

going to Jerusalem is enjoined upon laymen but forbidden for monks by the apostolic see. I know this myself because I heard it from the mouth of Pope Urban when he instructed laymen to make the pilgrimage and forbade the same pilgrimage to monks.[85]

St Anselm also recognized the importance of the Benedictine concept of stability[86] and, whilst he encouraged laymen to take the cross,[87] he warned a monk of St Martin of

---

[80] For a list of these conciliar decrees, see H. Waddell, *The Wandering Scholars* (London, 1927), Appendix E. See also Benedict of Aniane, *Opera*, PL ciii, cols. 736-40.

[81] See Constable, 'Opposition to Pilgrimage in the Middle Ages', *Religious Life and Thought (Eleventh and Twelfth Centuries)* (London, 1979), 130-2.

[82] See Brundage, 'A Transformed Angel (X 3.31.18): The Problem of the Crusading Monk' in *Studies in Medieval Cistercian History Presented to J. F. O'Sullivan*, Cistercian Studies Series, XIII. (Shannon, 1971) 57-61.

[83] *Die Kreuzzugsbriefe*, 137-8; 'Papsturkunden in Florenz', 313.

[84] Geoffrey of Chalard's biographer, writing after 1127, is the only source to suggest that Urban encouraged monks to go on crusade. See *Vita beati Gaufredi*, ed. J. Bosvieux, *Mémoires de la Société des sciences naturelles et archéologiques de la Creuze*, iii (1862), 93.

[85] Geoffrey of Vendôme, col. 162; L. Compain, *Étude sur Geoffroi de Vendôme* (Paris, 1891), 67-8, 269.

[86] See H. de Sainte-Marie, 'Les lettres de saint Anselme de Cantorbéry et la Règle Bénédictine', *Mélanges bénédictins* (Abbaye S. Wandrille, 1947), 259-321.

[87] For Anselm's attitude towards the crusade, see Cowdrey, 'Pope Urban II's Preaching of the First Crusade', *History*, lv (1970), 183-5.

Sées that his desire to go to the Holy Land had no good origin:

For it is contrary to your profession, in which you have promised before God to remain fixed in the monastery in which you took the monastic habit; and it is contrary to the obedience owed to the pope [Urban II], who with his great authority ordered monks not to make this journey, except for some religious person who might be useful in governing the church of God and instructing the people; and even the latter should not go without the advice of and in obedience to a prelate. I was present when the pope declared this judgement. It is also contrary to the obedience (owed) to your abbot, who . . . condemns this (plan) as perilous to your soul.

Later as Archbishop of Canterbury, Anselm wrote to his suffragan bishop, Osmund of Salisbury, seeking to secure the correction of the Abbot of Cerne, who had encouraged his monks to go on the First Crusade. He ordered the bishop not to allow any monks from his diocese to join the expedition under pain of anathema and asked that this instruction should be passed on to the Bishops of Bath, Exeter, and Worcester.[88]

St Bernard, Abbot of Clairvaux, was the great advocate of the Second Crusade and a supporter of the Templars, who combined the monastic and military ways of life.[89] But he was careful to make a clear distinction between the latter and ordinary monks who took the cross. In 1147 Bernard wrote to all Cistercian abbots, prohibiting, in the pope's name, under pain of excommunication, any monk or lay brother from joining the expedition; and, after the retreat from Damascus, he declined to lead a new crusade, protesting 'what is more remote from my profession, even if my strength were sufficient, even if the skill were not lacking?'[90] The Cistercian Chapter-General may also have forbidden monks to go on the expedition, for in 1157 it decreed that those who had gone to Jerusalem should be banished to another house.[91] In a similar way, Peter the Venerable prayed for the success of the crusade and exhorted knights to take the cross, but declared that the monastic order forbade him

[88] Anselm, *Opera*, iv. 85–6; v. 355.

[89] See Bernard, *De laude novae militae, Opera*, iii. 213–39.

[90] Bernard, *Opera*, viii. 163–5, 511–12. See also ibid. 379–80.

[91] *Statuta Capitulorum Generalium Ordinis Cisterciensis, 1116–1786*, ed. J. Canivez (Louvain, 1933–5); i. 66, no. 53.

to go and worship in the Holy Places.[92] And a vision attributed to him by close associates, although dated 1161, five years after his death, emphasized the importance of the vow of stability. The vision concerned a Cistercian novice who in secular life had been famed for his strength and who longed to go to Jerusalem. The novice apparently consulted his abbot, who advised him to remain in his monastery and fulfil his vows, but he paid little heed to this counsel, and when he was asleep one night he was visited by a demon. After struggling with this enemy of virtue, he lapsed into unconsciousness for three days. During this period the novice had a vision in which St Benedict appeared and exhorted him to obey monastic discipline and the Virgin begged him to persevere in her house, and as a final admonition he was taken on a journey to the other worlds by St Raphael and shown the glories of the blessed and the torments of the damned.[93] This emphasis upon *stabilitas* can also be found in an anonymous dialogue composed by a monk in Southern Germany at the time of Frederick I's crusade. In this dialogue, which was said to have taken place between himself and another brother, the monk lamented the decline of training in the cloister and the wickedness of the world, and it was in this context that he discussed monastic participation in the crusades. The other brother apparently wanted to take the cross as a sign of penance but he countered that he would do better to remain in his cell and fulfil his vows. He accepted that some monks had already joined the expedition, but argued that they were wrong and had been led astray 'by the spirit of the Deceiver [Satan]'.[94]

It is significant that all these proponents of the concept of *stabilitas* lived according to the Benedictine Rule. The only exception was Ralph Niger. Ralph was probably a clerk rather than a monk,[95] but like the monastic apologists he believed that the religious were not justified in taking the cross. He argued that there was nothing worse than a broken

[92] Peter the Venerable, *Letters*, i. 220; Berry, 'Peter the Venerable and the Crusades', 147–55.

[93] The Vision of Gunthelm and Other Visions Attributed to Peter the Venerable', ed. Constable, *Revue Bénédictine*, lxvi (1956), 102–13.

[94] *Liber de poenitentia*, cols. 890–4.

[95] Flahiff, 'Ralph Niger: An Introduction', 114–15.

vow and that those who had undertaken to live in hardship
and stay in a fixed place should not take another cross so
that they might wander.[96]   Ralph admitted that a monk
might sometimes be called upon to do something beyond the
requirements of his vow, but declared that this was like being
indebted to the extent of five talents and then having one's
debt raised to ten: the new debt incorporated the old one, it
did not absolve the debtor from his earlier obligation.
According to canon law a monk could make a pilgrimage or
crusade vow if he had his abbot's consent, but Ralph questioned whether this was wise.[97] He pointed out that an abbot
could not grant a monk permission to marry after he had
entered a religious house, yet to go on crusade was just as
contrary to his vocation as marriage. Ralph concluded that
if an abbot gave his authorization he could be held to be
as much at fault as the monk. He added that since a monk
renounced his property when he entered the cloister he could
go to the Holy Land only at the expense of another and this
would seem to rob the undertaking of much of its merit.[98]

Another fear expressed by monastic writers was that the
crusade might make a monk forget his vocation and return
to the secular world and its values.[99] At the time of the First
Crusade, Urban II reminded the monks of Vallombrosa that
they had left the world and enrolled in the spiritual army;[100]
and St Bernard wrote of the Cistercians who had joined the
Second Crusade:

They have scorned the holy way of life and are trying to involve themselves in the tumults of the world . . . Why do you seek the glory of
the world when you have elected 'to lie forgotten in the house of
God?' (Ps. 83: 11). What have you to do with wandering around the
countryside when you are professed to lead a life in solitude?[101]

This type of criticism may have prompted Abbot Theobald
of St Columba in Sens, who had taken the cross at Vézelay,

---

[96] For similar criticism of monastic pilgrimages, see Gratian, *Decretum*,
C. 20 q. 4 d.p.c. 3; Hostiensis, col. 897.
[97] See also Stephen of Grandmont, *Opera*, PL cciv. col. 1114; Caesar of
Heisterbach, *Dialogus miraculorum*, i. 13.
[98] Ralph Niger, *DRM* 203–4, 225–6.
[99] See Geoffrey of Vendôme, col. 162; Ralph Niger, *DRM* 226.
[100] 'Papsturkunden in Florenz', 313.
[101] Bernard, *Opera*, viii. 511.

to ask Peter the Venerable for guidance about his behaviour on the expedition. In his reply Peter praised the abbot's piety and devotion, but advised him to shun levity, instability, and curiosity, and to be careful lest he were corrupted by avarice and the love of vain praise, for he would only derive spiritual benefit from the crusade if his intentions were sincere and his conduct befitted a monk rather than a knight.[102] Master Isenbold of St Paul at Halberstadt gave a similar warning to the monk Elvingus of Corbie. He praised the latter's desire to visit Jerusalem, but at the same time he urged caution: he reminded Elvingus that when he entered a religious house he had renounced the world and its vices, and suggested that a change of places might make his conduct worse not better.[103] Isenbold chose a phrase from Horace which was popular among critics of monastic pilgrimages and crusades to emphasize this point:

Caelum non animum mutant qui trans mare currunt.[104]

All these criticisms were directed at monks who went as spiritual counsellors to the army. But a few threw aside their monastic habits and put on fighting garb.[105] This was clearly contrary to their profession, for, although the religious might exhort others to battle, they could not themselves bear arms;[106] the behaviour of these bellicose monks, like that of their clerical counterparts, was condemned.[107] In fact it has been suggested that Ralph Niger was thinking of the number of monks who had taken up arms at Gisors in 1188 when he launched his fierce attack upon monastic crusaders.[108]

A few abbots who wished to go on crusade were reminded of their vow of stability.[109] But on the whole their participation

---

[102] Peter the Venerable, *Letters*, i. 358-60.

[103] *Annales Corbeienses*, 13-14.

[104] Horace, *Epist.* i. 11.27. See also *Liber de poenitentia*, col. 891; Peter the Venerable, *Letters*, i. 216; *Annales Stadenses*, MGH SS xvi. 344.

[105] Bernold of St Blasien, *Chronicon*, MGH SS v. 464; *Itinerarium peregrinorum*, 277.

[106] 'Papsturkunden in Florenz', 313; Odo of Deuil, 116; Peter of Vaux de Cernay, 158; Ralph Niger, *DRM* 196.

[107] *Liber de poenitentia*, col. 893.

[108] See Flahiff, 'Deus non vult', 177 n. 65.

[109] Geoffrey of Vendôme, cols. 162-3; Matthew Paris, *CM* v. 101.

does not seem to have aroused as much opposition as that of ordinary monks. There may have been a ruling that abbots should seek the consent of the pope or, in the case of the heads of Cistercian houses, the Abbot of Cîteaux and the Chapter-General,[110] before they went on crusade. But, as with bishops, the critics' main concern was that they should not neglect their official duties.[111] According to his biographer, the followers of Geoffrey, founder and prior of Chalard, were alarmed by his desire to join the First Crusade and he decided not to go to the Holy Land after receiving a vision from Christ in which a fellow abbot foretold the evils which would befall the young community if it was abandoned.[112] In a similar way Wibald of Corvey denounced a German abbot who deserted his house to join the Second Crusade.[113] And, in his idealized portrait of the crusading Abbot Martin of Pairis, the monk Gunther was anxious to stress his superior's concern for the welfare of the brethren and his desire to return to the cloister. Conscious of his duties to his house, Martin apparently refused offers of high ecclesiastical preferment in the Latin Empire of Constantinople.[114]

Women were regarded as a third class who were particularly unsuited to crusading. According to Robert of Rheims, in his sermon at Clermont Urban II urged women not to join the First Crusade unless they were accompanied by their husband, brother, or guardian.[115] And after the suffering caused by the protracted siege of Antioch the leaders of the army reiterated that all non-combatants should remain at home.[116] Canonists also listed women as one of the classes who were not free to take the cross because of the binding nature of

[110] *Statua Ordinis Cisterciensis*, i. no. 16, 200; no. 37, 270; no. 38, 282; Gunther of Pairis, *Historia Constantinopolitana*, ed. Riant, *Exuviae*, i. 66. See also E. Willems, 'Cîteaux et la seconde croisade' *Revue d'histoire ecclésiastique*, xlix (1954), 150; E. A. R. Brown, 'The Cistercians in the Latin Empire of Constantinople and Greece, 1204-76', *Traditio*, xiv (1958), 65-9.

[111] See Bernard, *Opera*, vii. 24-7, 214-16.

[112] *Vita beati Gaufredi*, 93-5.

[113] Wibald of Corvey, *Epistolae*, ed. P. Jaffé, *Monumenta Corbeiensia, Bibliotheca rerum Germanicarum* (Berlin, 1864-73), i. 244.

[114] Gunther of Pairis, 72-3, 79, 109, 114-15; F. R. Swietek, 'Gunther of Pairis and the *Historia Constantinopolitana*', *Speculum*, liii (1978), 72-6.

[115] Robert of Rheims, 729.

[116] *Die Kreuzzugsbriefe*, 148, 167; Porges, 13-14.

the marriage vow.[117] Nevertheless the main fear seems to have been that their presence would compromise the moral standing of the army.[118] During the First Crusade the clergy continually reminded the host of the connection between human sinfulness and a defeat; setbacks were attributed to God's anger at men's fornication and adultery and at times of crisis women were expelled from the camp.[119] A divine judgement upon men's sins was also found to be the most satisfactory explanation for the reversal of Christian fortunes at Damascus on the Second Crusade and, reflecting upon this disaster, some chroniclers questioned whether it had been wise to allow women to accompany the host. The annalist of Würzburg commented that it had been at least indiscreet to give women the cross. But Vincent of Prague went further and blamed the failure of the expedition upon their presence and the resultant immorality in the camp.[120] Rumours circulated particularly about the misconduct of Queen Eleanor,[121] and the experiences of the Second Crusade probably led to official measures in 1188 to restrict the number of female camp-followers. In fact the Councils of Geddington and Le Mans forbade any women except laundresses to go on the Third Crusade, and it was emphasized that they were to be above suspicion.[122] Some seem to have ignored this prohibition and set out with the crusading army, but there were further attempts to enforce it in the Latin East and a number of female camp-followers were sent home to Europe.[123] Not surprisingly Ralph Niger expressed unreserved disapproval of women crusaders. He argued that their presence on the expedition might prove to be the snare of the Devil and cited the example of the Midianite woman

[117] Brundage, *Medieval Canon Law*, 44–77.
[118] See Bernold of St Blasien, 464–5.
[119] See below, pp. 102–3.
[120] *Annales Herbipolenses*, 3; Vincent of Prague, *Annales*, MGH SS xvii. 663. See also Gislebert of Mons, *Chronicon Hanoniense*, MGH SS xxi. 516; William of Newburgh, *Historia rerum Anglicarum*, ed. R. Howlett (London, 1884–5), i. 92–3.
[121] John of Salisbury, *Historia Pontificalis*, 52–3; Gerhoh of Reichersberg, *De investigatione Antichristi*, 376. These rumours were still circulating at the time of the Third Crusade. See Richard of Devizes, 25–6.
[122] Roger of Howden, *Gesta*, ii. 32–3.
[123] Ambroise, ll. 5681–700; *Itinerarium regis Ricardi*, 248.

who had caused God's people to sin (Num. 25: 6–11). Ralph recognized that some women would be needed to help colonize the Holy Land but deemed it more prudent to leave them at home to await the outcome of the crusade. He believed that the success of the expedition was dependent upon God's favour and women might prove to be an impediment or danger to the whole campaign.[124] It is significant that one of the first actions of the papal legate on the Fourth Crusade was to order female camp-followers to leave the host at Venice;[125] and in 1260 the legate at Acre, Thomas Agni, appealed to the prelates of Frisia to prevent women journeying to the Holy Land, on the grounds that their presence in the army led to fornication and adultery. Thomas argued that female crusaders would be of more use if they contributed financially towards the expedition,[126] and in the thirteenth century preachers were instructed to compel women to redeem their vows unless they were accompanied by a contingent of soldiers.[127] As an incentive, after 1252, Innocent IV granted women who remained at home the same indulgences as their husbands who fought in the East.[128]

---

[124] Ralph Niger, *DRM* 227. See also ibid. 154, 223.

[125] *Devastatio Constantinopolitana*, 10.

[126] Menko, *Chronicon*, MGH SS xxiii. 549. Kedar, 'A Passenger List of a Crusader Ship: Towards the History of the Popular Element on the Seventh Crusade', *Studi medievali*, ser. 3, xiii (1972), 273 n. 31 argues that this formed part of a general appeal throughout the West.

[127] William of Andres, *Chronica Andrensis*, MGH SS xxiv. 758. See also *Liber extra*, Lib. 3 tit. 34 c. 8; Hostiensis, col. 898.

[128] Innocent IV, no. 5980.

CHAPTER II

Commitment to crusading

SOME crusaders were allowed to redeem their vows if it was deemed more important for them to remain in the West.[1] But generally those who were functionally qualified to take the cross were expected to go on crusade, and there was criticism of crusaders who failed to fulfil their vows or postponed their departure.

Guibert of Nogent and Orderic Vitalis maintained that Urban II pronounced excommunication upon members of the First Crusade who left the ranks of the army before it reached Jerusalem;[2] and, although their chronicles date from the early twelfth century and were compiled from second-hand information, other more reliable evidence confirms that, from the beginning, the crusade vow was regarded as a binding obligation.[3] Fulcher of Chartres remarked that those who abandoned the army at Calabria in the winter of 1096-7 'became vile before God and men',[4] and the leaders of the expedition appear to have assumed that those who returned to the West would be treated as excommunicates. The papal legate Bishop Adhémar of Le Puy, writing from Antioch in October 1097, called upon bishops to ensure that all renegade crusaders were compelled to fulfil their vows under pain of anathema, and similar messages were sent to the West in January and July 1098 by the Greek Patriarch of Jerusalem and Anselm of Ribemont.[5] Stephen of Blois and the other crusaders who had fled from the siege

---

[1] See Richard of Devizes, 6.

[2] Guibert of Nogent, 140; Orderic Vitalis, *Ecclesiastical History*, ed. Chibnall (Oxford, 1969-81), v. 268. Chibnall (v. 269 n. 4, 322) suggests that Orderic wrote Urban II in mistake for Paschal II, since the latter issued a similar ruling in 1099.

[3] See Brundage, 'The Army of the First Crusade and the Crusade Vow: Some Reflections on a Recent Book', *Mediaeval Studies*, xxxiii (1971), 334-44.

[4] Fulcher of Chartres, *Historia Hierosolymitana*, ed. Hagenmeyer (Heidelberg, 1913), 168.

[5] *Die Kreuzzugsbriefe*, 142, 148, 160.

of Antioch attracted particular opprobrium.[6] In a letter addressed to French ecclesiastics dated December 1099, Pope Paschal II decreed that they should remain excommunicate until they had discharged their obligations.[7] This ruling was reiterated by the Synod of Anse in 1100, and according to Orderic Vitalis many chose to redeem their reputation by joining the crusade of 1101.[8] The most famous of these was Stephen of Blois, who was captured and slain by the Muslims after the battle of Ramla.[9]

The problem posed by crusaders who had taken the cross in a burst of enthusiasm and then regretted their decision continued to preoccupy the church in the twelfth century. In 1123 the First Lateran Council formally enacted penalties against those who had not fulfilled their vows. According to canon 10, *Eis qui Hierosolymam*, crusaders who had failed to discharge their obligations by the following Easter were to be forbidden to enter churches and an interdict was to be placed upon their lands.[10] This canon was not included in Gratian's *Decretum*, but a decretal on this subject issued by Alexander III was incorporated in John of Wales's collection *Compilatio II*, compiled between 1210 and 1212.[11]

This strain of criticism was taken up by vernacular poets. The minnesinger Frederick von Hausen warned those who took the cross at the time of the Third Crusade, and then sought to avoid the journey to the Holy Land, of the perils they would face at the Last Judgement.[12] And this was also the theme of a vision recorded by Adam, subprior of Eynsham, and subsequently attributed to Peter the Venerable

---

[6] See Fulcher of Chartres, 222-4, 228; Orderic Vitalis, v. 268, 324.

[7] *Die Kreuzzugsbriefe*, 175.

[8] Hugh of Flavigny, *Chronicon*, MGH SS viii. 487; Orderic Vitalis, v. 322-4.

[9] For Stephen of Blois's career, see Brundage, 'An Errant Crusader: Stephen of Blois', *Traditio*, xvi (1960), 380-95; Rousset, 'Étienne de Blois, croisé, fuyard et martyr', *Genava*, n.s. xi (1963), 183-95.

[10] *COD* 191-2.

[11] *Regesta Pontificum Romanorum*, comp. P. Jaffé *et al.*, (Leipzig, 1885-8), no. 14077; *Compilatio II, Quinque compilationes*, Lib. 3 tit. 21 c. 3. See also Brundage, *Medieval Canon Law*, 74-5.

[12] 'Si waenent dem tôde entrunnen sîn', *MF* 93. See also Reinmar der Fiedler, 'Ez ist in . . . vil swaere', *Minnesinger: deutsche Liederdichter des zwölften, dreizehnten und vierzehnten Jahrhunderts*, ed. F. von der Hagen (Leipzig, 1838), ii. 172.

by Stephen of Bourbon and Vincent of Beauvais.[13] According to Adam, a poor, sickly monk of Eynsham named Edmund fell into a trance on Good Friday, 1196, and remained unconscious for two days. When he awoke he claimed that he had been led to other worlds by St Nicholas and described the sufferings of many whom he had known on earth. Amongst those whom he saw in Purgatory was an insincere crusader, who had taken the cross out of vainglory rather than devotion and then cast it aside. As a punishment for this he was forced to repeat his pilgrimage every night, undergoing all the hardships along the way, and in the daytime the demons returned to torment him in the fire. This example was obviously intended to serve as a warning to other recalcitrant crusaders, and having related his misfortunes the knight exhorted them to repent of their sins before it was too late:

All those who put aside their cross having vowed to go to Jerusalem will be compelled to make their pilgrimage in a similar way. But if . . . at the end they truly repent, then through the wholesome remedy of confession this deadly sin will be changed to a venial one. Otherwise . . . they will endure eternal damnation.[14]

In the late twelfth century the church was still trying to ensure that those capable of going to the Holy Land fulfilled their vows. In 1196 the Archbishop of Canterbury, Hubert Walter, instructed clerks in the diocese of York to compel deserters to resume the cross.[15] Before such a policy could be implemented it was necessary to know who was bound by a crusading vow and officials drew up lists of those who had undertaken to go to the East. Only those from the

[13] For this attribution, see 'Vision of Gunthelm', 95-6; *Catalogue of Romances in the Department of Manuscripts, British Museum*, ed. J. A. Herbert, iii (London, 1910), 83; Vincent of Beauvais, *Speculum morale* in *Biblioteca mundi* (Douai, 1624), ii. 739. In his article on the vision of Gunthelm, Constable failed to note the similarity between the vision attributed to Peter the Venerable and that recorded by Adam of Eynsham. He argues that 'in Emesamensi monasterio' referred to the house of Augustinian canons at Embsay in Yorkshire, but it could also have meant Eynsham.

[14] *Vision of the Monk of Eynsham*, ed. H. E. Salter, *Cartulary of the Abbey of Eynsham*, Oxford Historical Society Publications (Oxford, 1908), 338-9. See also ibid. 257-76.

[15] Roger of Howden, *Chronica*, iii. 317-19. See also C. R. Cheney, *Hubert Walter* (London, 1967), 124-32.

archdeaconry of Cornwall and the deanery of Holland in Lincolnshire have survived. For the most part they consist of names alone, but some entries specify whether or not the votary has fulfilled his obligations and give reasons for his failure to do so.[16] Although Innocent III exhorted preachers of the crusade to redeem the vows of those unqualified to take the cross,[17] he was determined that those who could usefully fulfil this undertaking should go to the Holy Land. In 1201 he sent a mandate to Hubert Walter which required English prelates to denounce and excommunicate crusaders who would not abide by their commitment and at the Council of Westminster the archbishop enjoined his suffragans to make sure that those who had undertaken to go on the Fourth Crusade had left by February 1202.[18] Innocent also threatened reluctant French crusaders such as the Counts of Beaumont and Boulogne with anathema; in 1203 he actually excommunicated the Count of Eu because he had torn off his cross and refused to leave for the Holy Land.[19]

In 1215 the Fourth Lateran Council reaffirmed the ecclesiastical censures to be inflicted upon laggard crusaders.[20] Even so there were complaints that many votaries refused to join the Fifth Crusade. Abbot Gervais of Prémontré lamented that the poor were unable to fulfil their vows because there was no one to lead the French contingent, and in 1220 Honorius III sent Conrad of Mainz to Germany to compel apathetic crusaders to leave for the East.[21] This pattern of events was repeated at the time of Louis IX's first crusade. The First Council of Lyons had reiterated the provisions of 1215,[22] but again Innocent IV protested that many had laid aside their crosses and ordered bishops to

[16] *HMC Report on Manuscripts in Various Collections*, i (London, 1901), 235-6 and *Fifth Report* (London, 1876), 462. See also Brundage, *Medieval Canon Law*, 130-1.

[17] *Liber extra*, Lib. 3 tit. 34 c. 8-9; Cheney, *Innocent III and England* (Stuttgart, 1976), 248-56.

[18] Roger of Howden, *Chronica*, iv. 166, 173.

[19] *Gesta Innocentii*, PL ccxiv, cols. cxxxvi–cxxxvii; Innocent III, PL ccxv, cols. 184-5. See also id. PL ccxvi, col. 729.

[20] *COD* 268.

[21] Gervais of Prémontré, *Epistolae*, ed. C. L. Hugo, *Sacrae antiquitatis monumenta historica, dogmatica, diplomatica*, i (Estival, 1725), 3-4, 7; *HD* i. 783-4. See also Gregory IX, nos. 1, 1957.

[22] *COD* 298.

force them to depart for the East under pain of anathema.[23] Innocent's successors, Clement IV and Gregory X, issued further warnings to recalcitrant crusaders,[24] and form-letters for this purpose were included in several contemporary formularies. Nevertheless non-fulfilment of vows remained a problem and was a source of criticism throughout the thirteenth century.[25]

There was also criticism of certain prominent crusaders who postponed their departure for the East. After the failure of the Second Crusade and subsequent disasters in the Holy Land, a series of appeals for aid were sent to the West; as a result the papacy made attempts to launch a new expedition. Henry II and Louis VII professed themselves eager to take the cross; as part of the preparations in the late 1160s negotiations began in earnest to settle the dispute with Becket and restore peace to the English church.[26] These initiatives came to nothing and it began to be realized in the 1170s that an essential preliminary to a new crusade was a settlement between England and France and between Henry II and his sons. In the following years a series of papal representatives and ambassadors from the Latin Kingdom of Jerusalem urged the kings to abandon their private wars and to devote their energies to a campaign against the Muslims. An agreement was reached in 1172, but, although both rulers promised to take the cross, it was not long before the wars in France had recommenced.[27] A more permanent treaty was signed at Ivry in 1177 and in the opening words of their statement Louis VII and Henry II announced their intention of going to Jerusalem.[28] When Louis died in 1180, however, plans for the expedition were no further advanced.

[23] Innocent IV, nos. 2054, 3970, 4926, 5979.

[24] Clement IV, *Registres*, ed. E. Jordan (Paris, 1893-1945), no. 1675; Gregory X, *Registres*, ed. J. Guiraud (Paris, 1892-1906), no. 539.

[25] See Brundage, *Medieval Canon Law*, 129, 131.

[26] See Gilbert Foliot, *Letters and Charters*, ed. A. Morey and C. N. L. Brooke (Cambridge, 1967), 541; Morey and Brooke, *Gilbert Foliot and his Letters* (Cambridge, 1965), 173; John of Salisbury, *Letters*, ed. W. J. Millor and Brooke (Oxford, 1955-79), ii. 568, 630-4, 692-6.

[27] *Materials for the History of Thomas Becket*, ed. J. B. Sheppard and J. C. Robertson (London, 1875-85), vii. 516, 520.

[28] Roger of Howden, *Gesta*, i. 191; R. C. Smail, 'Latin Syria and the West 1149-87', *TRHS* xix (1969), 16-17.

In 1184 Patriarch Heraclius of Jerusalem headed a major embassy to the West to seek aid against Saladin. But, although Henry II and Philip Augustus offered financial assistance,[29] neither was prepared to lead a new crusade, for fear that his absence might jeopardize the safety of the kingdom.[30]

This situation changed dramatically in July 1187, when the army of the Latin Kingdom was decisively defeated by Saladin at the Horns of Hattin. During the battle King Guy was captured and many nobles were either taken prisoner or slain; and a few months later, after the submission of most other towns and castles in the realm, the Holy City, Jerusalem, surrendered. The survival of the Latin Kingdom itself now depended upon the defence of Tyre, which had been saved from falling into Muslim hands by the chance arrival of Conrad of Montferrat. News of the disaster and appeals for aid soon reached the West and in October Gregory VIII issued his great crusading bull *Audita tremendi*.[31] Richard I, then Count of Poitou, took the cross in November 1187 and Henry II and Philip Augustus followed his example at Gisors in January 1188.[32] At the same time the papal legate, Archbishop Joscius of Tyre, persuaded the kings to declare a truce[33] and later that month they held assemblies at Paris and Le Mans, at which they promulgated various crusading decrees including the Saladin tithe.[34] Henry II professed himself eager to aid the Holy Land, but in June Richard invaded Toulouse and Philip retaliated by attacking Berry. By the end of the summer the wars in France had resumed.[35] A series of abortive peace negotiations was held during the autumn and winter of 1188 and a settlement was finally

---

[29] See Mayer, 'Henry II of England and the Holy Land', *EHR* xcvii (1982), 721–40.

[30] Roger of Howden, *Gesta*, i. 338; Gerald of Wales, *De principis instructione, Opera*, viii. 208; Rigord, *Gesta Philippi Augusti*, ed. Delaborde (Paris, 1882), 47–8; Smail, 17–19.

[31] *Historia de expeditione Friderici imperatoris*, ed. A. Chroust, MGH Scr. rer. Germ., n.s.v. (Berlin, 1928), 6–10. See also Roger of Howden, *Gesta*, ii. 15.

[32] Ralph of Diceto, *Opera historica*, ed. W. Stubbs (London, 1876), ii. 50–1; Rigord, 83.

[33] Gregory VIII had himself declared a seven-year truce. See Roger of Howden, *Gesta*, ii. 15.

[34] Roger of Howden, *Gesta*, ii. 30–2; Rigord, 84–90.

[35] Roger of Howden, *Gesta*, ii. 34–6, 38–40; Rigord, 90–1.

reached in July 1189.[36] A few days afterwards Henry II died. That autumn Richard and Philip reaffirmed their intention of going to the Holy Land and in December they met at Nonancourt to complete the arrangements.[37] According to the chronicler Richard of Devizes, Richard was anxious not to be the last to set out.[38] But the English and French contingents did not assemble at Vézelay to begin their journey to the East until July 1190 and the kings did not arrive at Acre until the following summer.[39]

The defeat at Hattin and the desperate situation in the Latin Kingdom seem to have produced a highly charged crusading atmosphere in Western Europe and the vacillations of Henry, Richard, and Philip sparked off a storm of criticism from many quarters: their dilatory behaviour was contrasted with the crusading zeal of Emperor Frederick I, who had taken the cross in March 1188 and had left for the Holy Land in May 1189.[40]

At an ecclesiastical level the delays of the kings aroused complaints from preachers and apologists of the crusade. In the late 1170s Cardinal Henry of Albano had been closely involved in the attempts to send a new expedition to the East.[41] It was probably because of this experience that in 1187 he was commissioned by Gregory VIII to preach the Third Crusade in France and Germany.[42] In the course of these duties Henry presided over the assembly at Mainz at which Frederick I and several German princes took the cross; and in the thirteenth tract of his treatise *De peregrinante civitate Dei*, he praised their crusading zeal and condemned the renewed rivalry between the Kings of England and France which prevented them from fulfilling their crusading vows. This passage was probably written in the summer or autumn of 1188, shortly after Philip's invasion

---

[36] Ralph of Diceto, ii. 55, 57-8, 62-4; Roger of Howden, *Gesta*, ii. 47, 49, 51, 61, 66, 70.

[37] Roger of Howden, *Gesta*, ii. 92-3, 104-5; Ralph of Diceto, ii. 71, 73-4.

[38] Richard of Devizes, 5.

[39] Roger of Howden, *Gesta*, ii. 111.

[40] *Historia de expeditione Friderici*, 14, 17.

[41] Henry of Albano, *Opera*, PL cciv, cols. 215-16; Alberic of Troisfontaines, *Chronica*, MGH SS xxiii, 855; Congar, 'Henri de Marcy, abbé de Clairvaux, cardinal-évêque d'Albano et légat pontifical', *Studia Anselmiana*, xliii (1958), 8.

[42] *Chronicon Clarevallense*, PL clxxxv, col. 1251.

of Berry; Cardinal Henry lamented: 'already the cross contends against the cross and the crucified one fights against the crucified'. He complained that Saladin derived profit from these disputes and denounced those who claimed to be Christ's friends as liars and traitors.[43] The cardinal's bitter condemnation of the wars in France may have prompted the Counts of Flanders and Blois to make a dramatic protest: in October 1188, they laid down their arms and refused to use them against fellow Christians until Philip had fulfilled his vow to go to the Holy Land.[44] It was against this background that Clement III requested Henry of Albano to arrange a meeting between Henry II and Philip Augustus at Bonmoulins. This attempt to negotiate a permanent settlement came to nothing, but he managed to persuade the kings to agree to a short truce until January 1189; and when he learned that Richard had done homage to Philip, he excommunicated him as a disturber of the peace. After Cardinal Henry's death, his work was continued by his successor, John of Anagni. In June 1189, John organized a further meeting between the kings at La Ferté-Bernard, and threatened to put France under an interdict if Philip continued to obstruct his negotiations with Henry II.[45]

The legates' appeals for peace were reiterated by other ecclesiastics. Peter of Blois, who was representing the Archbishop of Canterbury at the papal court when news of the fall of Jerusalem reached Gregory VIII, had informed Henry II of the pope's determination to launch a crusade.[46] Upon his return to England, Peter heard the story of the death of Reynald of Châtillon after the battle of Hattin from either Amalric or Geoffrey of Lusignan, and in the *Passio Reginaldi* he portrayed him as a martyr for the faith and exhorted others to follow his example and avenge the loss of Jerusalem. He denounced those who were responsible for the delays in going to the aid of Conrad of Montferrat[47] and in 1188

[43] Henry of Albano, cols. 357–61; Congar, 'Henri de Marcy', 45–52.
[44] Roger of Howden, *Gesta*, ii. 48–9.
[45] Id. *Gesta*, ii. 51, 61, 66–7; *Chronica*, ii. 354–5, 362–3.
[46] Roger of Howden, *Gesta*, ii. 15.
[47] Peter of Blois, *Passio Reginaldi, Opera*, iii. 270–89; B. Hamilton, 'Reynald of Châtillon: The Elephant of Christ', *Studies in Church History*, xv (1978) 107–8.

or 1189 wrote an impassioned appeal in support of the Third Crusade, entitled *De Hierosolymitana peregrinatione acceleranda*. In the course of this he lamented that, although God offered Christians a way of peace and salvation, they chose a path of dissension and death, and gave a warning to those who fought for a transitory kingdom and postponed their pilgrimage that they would not be permitted to enter the Kingdom of God.[48] Peter returned to this theme in a dialogue said to have taken place between Henry II and the Abbot of Bonneval and composed some time before the king's death in July 1189. In this, Henry complained of the treachery of his sons and the continued war with France, and the abbot lamented that no knights journeyed to the East to recover the Holy Sepulchre and the relic of the True Cross from the hands of the idolatrous Muslims.[49] When the English contingent eventually left for the Holy Land in the summer of 1190, Peter was one of the members of Archbishop Baldwin's entourage. But he seems to have been disappointed either by the response to his appeal or by the crusade itself, for when he revised his collection of letters some years after his return, he omitted his exhortation to take the cross.[50]

A similar disenchantment can be seen in the works of Gerald of Wales.[51] In the *Topographia Hibernica*, written between May 1186 and July 1189, Gerald appeared to have no doubts about Henry's sincere desire to go on crusade. He noted that the rebellion of 1173–4 had temporarily upset the king's plans to depart for the East, but predicted that he would soon 'restrain the raging fury of the pagans both of Asia and of Europe'.[52] The *Topographia*'s companion work, the *Expugnatio Hibernica*, was actually written in the shadow of the Third Crusade; in the preface to the second book,

---

[48] Peter of Blois, *Opera*, ii. pp. ix–xii. See also id. *Passio Reginaldi*, iii. 261–3.

[49] Peter of Blois, 'Un écrit de Pierre de Blois réédité', ed. R. B. C. Huygens, *Revue Bénédictine*, lxviii (1958), 97, 102, 106, 112.

[50] This omission may also have been dictated by stylistic considerations. See R. W. Southern, 'Peter of Blois: A Twelfth-century Humanist?', *Medieval Humanism and Other Studies* (Oxford, 1970), 122.

[51] For a summary of Gerald's views on the Third Crusade, see R. Bartlett, *Gerald of Wales, 1146–1223* (Oxford, 1982), 77–86.

[52] Gerald of Wales, *Topographia Hibernica, Opera*, vi. 190, 192.

which was probably composed shortly after his return from Archbishop Baldwin's preaching tour of Wales, Gerald wrote enthusiastically of the preparations for the forthcoming expedition. But by the time he had completed the work, in the early summer of 1189, there were signs of disillusionment. Gerald complained of the delays caused by the wars between Henry II, Richard, and Philip Augustus, and exhorted the kings to follow the example of Frederick I. He also criticized the decision to send Prince John to fight against his fellow Christians in Ireland rather than to campaign against the Muslims in the Holy Land.[53] Gerald returned to the subject of the crusade in his later works and in his description of Baldwin's Welsh preaching tour he even accused the emperor of creating unnecessary delays. He recalled the numbers that had taken the cross and their eagerness to attack the Muslims and lamented:

> if only the crusade had been prosecuted as promptly and with as much haste to match the diligence and devotion of those whom we had collected. By the judgement of God, which is sometimes hidden, but never unjust, it was delayed because of the route taken by the emperor and the dissension between our kings.[54]

In *De principis instructione*, Gerald drew a connection between Henry II's failure to defend the Holy Land and the king's troubled reign, and repeated Patriarch Heraclius' dire warning of the perils of the Last Judgement. In Book III Henry was depicted as a petty schemer who sought to prevent his rivals from leaving on crusade, and his behaviour was contrasted with the crusading zeal of Frederick I.[55] Gerald himself received the cross from Archbishop Baldwin, but he was released from his crusading vow in 1189 because of his poverty and physical weakness.[56]

A number of poets writing in Latin also bewailed the disaster at Hattin and the loss of Jerusalem and urged the faithful, particularly princes and nobles, to take the cross.[57]

---

[53] Id. *Expugnatio Hibernica*, vi. 307–8, 388–9, lvii–viii.
[54] Id. *Itinerarium Kambriae*, vi, pp. xxxiii, 147.
[55] Id. *De principis instructione*, viii. 166, 170–2, 202–11, 244–5, 250–1.
[56] Id. *De rebus a se gestis*, i. 85.
[57] *Carmen Sangallense* in 'Deux poésies latines relatives à la IIIe croisade', ed. Hagenmeyer, *Archives de l'Orient Latin*, i (1881), 585; *Carmina Burana*,

Others were less explicit in their criticism. Berter of Orléans,[58] writing in 1187, drew upon the Lamentations of Jeremiah, the prophet of Israel's misery, to express his grief at the capture of the Holy City. He lamented that the paths to Zion mourned because none attended her sacred feasts and her gates were broken down (Lam. 1: 4). This text had an added significance, for it was used in the service of matins on Holy Saturday, and Berter sought to highlight the Christians' failure to take the path to the Holy Sepulchre by recalling the events of the first Easter, when the three Marys had visited Christ's tomb.[59] In a similar way, an anonymous poet, writing between the fall of Jerusalem and the Third Crusade, drew upon the Book of Exodus to underline the desperate situation in the Holy Land. He observed that the Latin East was groaning under the same yoke as the Israelites had suffered in Egypt (Exod. 1: 13-14) and implied criticism of the crusaders' dilatoriness by bemoaning the vacillations of Moses when God had instructed him to lead the Hebrews out of Egypt (Exod. 3: 11 ff.).[60]

The most outspoken critics of the kings' delays were undoubtedly the troubadours and trouvères. In his early *sirventes*, Bertran de Born, a nobleman who shared the castle of Hautefort in the Périgord with his brother, had encouraged the rivalry between Henry II and his sons[61] and incited Richard and Philip to fight each other,[62] for he relished the

ed. A. Hilka and O. Schumann (Heidelberg, 1930), nos. 48, 49, 50; 'Plange Sion et Iudaea', 'Indue cilicium, sedeas in pulvere, mater', 'Miror cur tepeat', *Analecta hymnica medii aevi*, xxxiii (Leipzig, 1899), 315-20; 'Sede Sion in pulvere', *Analecta hymnica*, xxi (Leipzig, 1895), 164.

[58] J. R. Williams, 'William of the White Hands and Men of Letters', *Anniversary Essays in Medieval History by Students of C. H. Haskins* (Boston, 1929), 372-4, suggested that the poet Berter of Orléans was in fact Archdeacon Berter of Cambrai.

[59] Berter of Orléans, 'Iuxta Threnos Ieremiae', *Oxford Book of Medieval Latin Verse*, ed. F. J. E. Raby (Oxford, 1959), 297-300; D. H. Green, *The Millstätter Exodus* (Cambridge, 1966), 410-11.

[60] *Carmina Burana*, no. 47. See also Green, 27-9.

[61] Bertran de Born, 'D'un sirventes nom chal far lonhor ganda', 'Quan la novela flors par el verjan', *Poésies complètes*, ed. A. Thomas (Toulouse, 1888), 16-18, 56-60. See also *Biographies des troubadours*, ed. J. Boutière and A. H. Schulz (2nd rev. edn., Paris, 1964), 65.

[62] Bertran de Born, 'Pois al baros enoja e lor pesa', 'Al douz nou termini blanc',

pageantry of war and complained that lords were less generous to their vassals in peacetime. But after the disaster at Hattin and subsequent Muslim victories in the Latin Kingdom, he began to urge the kings to settle their disputes and go on crusade. Bertran maintained that Richard had doubled his glory by taking the cross and he exhorted Philip to be worthy of his royal dignity and to emulate his ancestor Charlemagne, who had always been zealous to win fame. He declared himself eager to join Conrad of Montferrat in the defence of Tyre, but explained that the kings' rivalry, as well as his love for his *domna*, had prevented him from fulfilling this desire:

I should like to be over there, in Tyre, I assure you; but I have had to give up this plan, because the counts, dukes, princes, and kings have so delayed their departure. And then I saw my *domna* . . . and my heart weakened; otherwise I would have been with you at least a year ago.

Bertran returned to this theme in another *sirventes*, in which he praised Conrad's achievements and lamented:

I know two kings who are slow to help you (Conrad) . . . King Philip is one for he doubts King Richard and the latter is also suspicious of him . . . they keep deceiving God for they have taken the cross and speak no word of going.[63]

The troubadour Guiraut de Bornelh, who probably accompanied his lord, Adhémar V, Viscount of Limoges, on the Third Crusade, even accused Pope Gregory VIII of being slow to avenge the loss of Christ's sepulchre.[64] And in another *sirventes*, written in the spring of 1188, he lamented that the faithful did not care if God was insulted or shamed; they continued to quarrel amongst themselves whilst the Muslims advanced with ease and conquered Syria. After the conference

'S'en fos aissi senher ni poderos', 'No posc mudar un chantar non esparja', ed. cit. 66–78.

[63] Id. 'Nostre senher somonis el mezeis', 'Folheta, vos mi prejatz que eu chan', 'Ara sai eu de pretz quals l'a plus gran', ed. cit. 79–86.

[64] Guiraut de Bornelh, 'Tals gen prezich'e sermona', *Sämtliche Lieder des Troubadours, Giraut de Bornelh*, ed. A. Kolsen (Halle, 1910–35), i. 428–30. Jeanroy, *La Poésie lyrique*, 57 n. 2, questioned the authenticity of this poem, but Kolsen, ii. 119, accepted the attribution on the basis of literary parallels with Guiraut's other works.

at Gisors, however, Guiraut saw some hope for the future, and in particular praised Richard's crusading zeal.[65]

The troubadour Peire Vidal, a native of Toulouse, also expressed his eagerness to avenge the loss of Christ's sepulchre. He declared that Richard had honoured the name of Poitou by being so prompt to take the cross and denounced Philip as a cowardly and avaricious hypocrite because he was slow to follow his example. But in a later poem Peire found it necessary to remind Richard of his duty to fulfil his crusading vow and he claimed that God had complained to him about his vacillations.[66] In a similar way, the Limousin poet Gaucelm Faidit blamed Richard for delaying his own departure on crusade and emphasized that to be worthy of praise he must actually take part in the expedition.[67]

The troubadour Peirol also protested about the kings' failure to settle their dispute and go on crusade:

I beg the Lord Christ to guide me and to establish quickly peace between the kings, for help is too long delayed and great need is there that the noble and valiant marquess [Conrad] should have more companions.

Peirol appears to have been anxious to accompany his lord, the Dauphin of Auvergne, to the Holy Land. But Love, his antagonist in this poetic debate or *tenso*, chided him for having deserted the service of his *domna* and pointed out that he could do little to aid the Latin Kingdom himself:

Peirol, never by your intervention will the Turk and Arab yield up the Tower of David. Good and weighty counsel do I give you; love and sing often. Will you set forth when the kings make no move? Behold the wars they wage and see how the nobles seek causes to avoid their obligations.[68]

This strain of criticism was also taken up by the trouvères. The castellan of Arras, Huon d'Oisi, denounced Philip as 'le

[65] Guiraut de Bornelh, 'A l'onor Deu torn en mo chan', ed. cit. i. 384-9; ii. 109-11; K. Lewent, *Das altprovenzalische Kreuzlied* (Berlin, 1905), 20-1.

[66] Peire Vidal, 'Si.m laissava de chantar', 'Ges pel temps fer e brau', 'Anc no mori per amor ni per al', *Poésies*, ed. Anglade (Paris, 1913), 68-70, 74, 78-9.

[67] Gaucelm Faidit, 'Mas la bella de cui me mezeis tenh', 'Tant sui ferms e fis vas amor', *Les Poèmes de Gaucelm Faidit, Troubadour du XIIe siècle*, ed. J. Mouzat (Paris, 1965), 439-40, 454-5.

[68] Peirol, 'Quant amors trobet partit', *Peirol, Troubadour of Auvergne*, ed. S. C. Aston (Cambridge, 1953), 8-9, 158-60.

roi failli', because of his slowness to fulfil his crusading vow, and another poet known as Maistre Renaut warned both kings of the perils of the Last Judgement and urged them to avenge the loss of the Holy Sepulchre. An anonymous Anglo-Norman poet asked for forgiveness because he had fought in the wars in France and thus neglected his duty towards the Lord.[69] The most important of these Northern French critics was the Picard, Conon de Béthune, who was a distant relative of Count Baldwin IX of Flanders.[70] A sudden illness or injury seems to have prevented Conon from fulfilling his own desire to go to Jerusalem,[71] but he denounced those barons who had delayed their departure for the East because of the wars between England and France. In one of his poems he declared that God would take revenge upon those who had failed him; one editor has suggested that this was an allusion to the dramatic protest made by the Counts of Flanders and Blois in October 1188.[72] Conon also accused the kings of diverting money collected for the Holy Land to their wars in France, and warned: 'you who tax the crusaders, do not spend in this way the proceeds of the tax, for you will become an enemy of God'.[73] Conon himself was quick to resume the cross; he became one of the leaders of the Fourth Crusade and played an important part in the administration of the Latin Empire of Constantinople.[74]

The extent and variety of this criticism of the kings' delays suggests that it was a reflection of public opinion; and the weight of attacks directed against them must have put a good deal of pressure upon Richard and Philip to abandon their political differences and go to the aid of the Holy Land. In a sense their eventual departure in July 1190 and the Third

---

[69] 'Maugré tous sainz et maugré Dieu ausi', 'Parti de mal e a bien aturné', 'Pour lou peuple resconforteir', *Chansons de croisade*, ed. J. Bédier and P. Aubry (Paris, 1909), 59–63, 67–71, 77–81.

[70] Conon de Béthune, *Les Chansons*, ed. A. Wallenskold (Paris, 1921), pp. iii–iv.

[71] See Huon d'Oisi, 'Maugré tous sainz', *Chansons de croisade*, 59; Conon de Béthune, 'Ahi! amours com dure departie', ed. cit. 6–7.

[72] 'Bien me deusse targier', *Chansons de croisade*, 42–3, 46. See above, p. 54.

[73] *Chansons de croisade*, 45–6. See also Gerald of Wales, *De principis instructione, Opera*, viii. 326.

[74] See R. W. Wolff, 'The Latin Empire of Constantinople, 1204–61', *History of the Crusades*, ii. 211–14.

Crusade itself might be described as a victory for public opinion.

Only Fulk de Marseille maintained that the delays were justifiable. In a *sirventes* written soon after the defeat at Hattin, Fulk had praised Richard for being so prompt to take the cross and, in a veiled reference to Philip, denounced those who stayed at home and attacked the lands of crusaders.[75] And, as a member of the royal entourage, on the eve of the king's embarkation for the East, he was anxious to counter any criticism of Richard's late departure. He therefore excused his vacillations on the grounds that the time had been spent profitably, ensuring that he was equipped as befitted a king rather than a count.[76]

The objections raised by contemporary critics were repeated by a variety of later chroniclers and observers. In his verse history of the Third Crusade, Ambroise lamented that Satan had found a way to disrupt the peace negotiated at Gisors in 1188,[77] and several German chroniclers contrasted the crusading zeal of Frederick I with the vacillations of Richard and Philip; while the emperor set out for the Holy Land, they continued their wars, fearful that if one went on crusade the other would invade his lands.[78] Somewhat surprisingly, Ralph Niger was also critical of the kings' slowness to avenge the defeat at Hattin. In his treatise *De re militari*, he had urged Philip to postpone his departure for the Holy Land, because of the threat posed by the growth of heresy in the West.[79] But his attitude had changed dramatically by the time he wrote his longer chronicle, some time after 1194. In this Ralph paid tribute to the courage of Reynald of Châtillon— 'beatus Reinaldus'—after the battle of Hattin and emphasized the perilous state of the Latin Kingdom. He was critical of Henry II because of his failure to fulfil his earlier promises

[75] Fulk de Marseille, 'Consiros, cum partitz d'amor', *Le Troubadour Folquet de Marseille*, ed. S. Stronski (Cracow, 1910), 106-8. In *Das altprovenzalische Kreuzlied*, 101-3, Lewent attributed this poem to Aimeric de Belenoi, but Stronski, 18*-23*, argued that it was more likely to be the *chanson* mentioned by Fulk in 'A! quan gens vens et ab quan pauc d'afan', (51, ll. 39-40), dated 1190.

[76] Fulk de Marseille, 'A quan gens vens', ed. cit. 50-1.

[77] Ambroise, ll. 135-9, 160-6; *Itinerarium regis Ricardi*, 141.

[78] *Annales Marbacenses*, 164; *Historia peregrinorum*, 128-9; *Historia de expeditione Friderici*, 22-3.

[79] Ralph Niger, DRM 67-8, 187-8, 193, 199; Flahiff, 'Deus non vult', 167-8.

to go on crusade, and lamented that the renewed discord between England and France had delayed the urgent business of the cross.[80]

Richard and Philip Augustus eventually left for the Holy Land in July 1190, but their behaviour and disputes during the expedition prompted some contemporaries to question their commitment to crusading. Two historians lamented that the kings' renewed rivalry had been detrimental to the overall success of the Third Crusade,[81] and there was bitter criticism of Philip because he set sail for the West in July 1191 without fulfilling his undertaking to recapture the Holy Sepulchre.[82] The troubadour Peire Vidal described the French king's conduct as unworthy of his high station in life and Fulk de Marseille urged Philip to return to the East, for if he failed to resume the campaign against the Muslims his shame would be doubled.[83] When Richard left Acre in October 1192, he apparently promised to return as soon as circumstances permitted,[84] he repeated this undertaking after his release from captivity in February 1194.[85] Almost immediately he became involved in the wars in France, but in November 1194 the legate Cardinal Melior arranged a truce,[86] and Fulk urged Richard to use this opportunity to hasten to the East. Henry VI was thought to be using the money obtained from Richard's ransom to finance his own crusade, Fulk warned the king that if he delayed any further the emperor would receive all the credit:

What then are our barons doing and the English king, whom may God preserve? Does he think that he has accomplished his task? There

---

[80] Ralph Niger, *Chronica universalis*, extr. MGH SS xxvii, 336-7. For the dating of this work, see id. *DRM* 13-14; Flahiff, 'Ralph Niger', 112-13, 122; R. Pauli, 'Die Chroniken des Radulphus Niger', *Nachrichten von der Gesellschaft der Wissenschaften zu Göttingen* (1880), 572-3, 584-4.

[81] James of Vitry, *Historia Hierosolimitana*, ed. J. Bongars, *Gesta Dei per Francos* (Hanau, 1611), i. 122; *Itinerarium regis Ricardi*, 332-3.

[82] Ambroise, ll. 5245-56; *Itinerarium regis Ricardi*, 236-7; Richard of Devizes, 58.

[83] Peire Vidal, 'A per pauc de chantar no.m lais', ed. cit. 102; Fulk de Marseille, 'Chantars mi torn ad afan', ed. cit. 82.

[84] *Itinerarium regis Ricardi*, 442. See also Roger Wendover, *Flores historiarum*, ed. H. G. Hewlett (London, 1886-9), i. 218.

[85] Roger of Howden, *Chronica*, iii. 233.

[86] Ibid. 257.

will be a very ugly deception if he has borne the expense and another takes the prize. For the emperor is making efforts that God may recover his land (and) he will indeed be the first to bring help to it.[87]

There may also have been some implied criticism of the kings' renewed dispute in the didactic religious poem *Les Vers de la mort*, composed by Hélinant, a monk at Froidmont between 1193 and 1197. In the course of this work Hélinant denounced the wars in France and reminded 'toz faus croisiez' of the perils of the Last Judgement.[88] The suggestion that Richard and Philip had still not fulfilled their previous crusading vows, because the Holy Sepulchre remained in Muslim hands, seems, however, to have been confined to this small group of writers. And, although in the late 1190s there was a series of papal appeals to the kings to abandon their wars and go on crusade, they were always accompanied by an exhortation to take the cross.[89]

In the early thirteenth century there was similar criticism of Frederick II's repeated failure to take part in the Fifth Crusade. Frederick had taken the cross after his coronation at Aachen in July 1215,[90] but he made no immediate preparations to fulfil his vow and remained in the West when the crusaders set sail for the Holy Land in the summer of 1217. He reaffirmed his desire to join the army at Damietta in January 1219 and undertook to leave by the following June, however it soon became clear that this would not be possible; in May Frederick wrote to the pope asking for permission to postpone his departure until September. He was anxious that Germany should be well governed in his absence and to secure his son's succession to the throne in the event of his death on crusade, but this proposal met with resistance from the German princes. Honorius III reluctantly authorized a further delay until March 1220, but threatened Frederick with excommunication if he had not left by this

---

[87] Fulk de Marseille, 'Chantars mi torn', ed. cit. 81-2, 176-7, 181. See also William of Newburgh, ii. 486.

[88] Hélinant de Froidmont, *Les Vers de la mort*, stt. xiii, xx, xxxii, ed. F. Wulff and E. Walberg (Paris, 1905), pp. xiii, xv–xvi, xxvii.

[89] Roger of Howden, *Chronica*, iii. 200–2; Ralph of Diceto, ii. 132–5; Innocent III, PL ccxiv, cols. 308–12, 329–30.

[90] *Chronicon Sancti Jacobi Leodiensis* extr. RHGF xviii. 632; *Chronica regia Coloniensis et continuationes*, ed. G. Waitz, MGH Scr. rer. Germ. (Hanover, 1880), 236.

date and exhorted him to emulate the example of his crusading grandfather Frederick I. The pope granted yet another postponement until May 1220, but by this stage he had virtually admitted defeat and commented that if the emperor himself would not fulfil his vow, then at least he should not deter others from doing so.[91] At the Diet of Frankfurt the German princes eventually agreed to the coronation of Prince Henry, but Frederick was still faced with serious political problems in other parts of his realm; before he left on crusade he was determined to settle affairs in Lombardy and to restore peace to Sicily, which had been in a state of virtual anarchy since his departure in 1212.[92] As proof of his good intentions, at his coronation in Rome in November 1220, Frederick took the cross a second time and promised to set sail for Egypt in the following August. Meanwhile he sent an advance-party under Louis of Bavaria.[93] In the following months, the emperor continued to stress his sincere desire to go on crusade, but his attention was focused upon the problems of Sicily and once again the crusaders at Damietta waited in vain for his arrival.[94] In the end they began their advance up the Nile under the leadership of the legate Pelagius. An imperial fleet commanded by the Chancellor of Sicily, Walter of Palear, and Count Henry of Malta actually set sail for the East in June 1221, but it did not arrive until late August,[95] too late to save the army from disaster at Mansurah and to prevent the surrender of Damietta. Honorius had already complained to Frederick that his repeated delays had placed the army in danger; and when news reached the West of the fall of Damietta, he declared that all Christendom was reproaching him for not forcing the emperor to go to Egypt.[96]

The pope was not the only contemporary to complain

[91] *HD* i. 584-6, 691-3, 746-7, 783-4; MGH Epistolae saeculi XIII e regestis pontificum Romanorum, sel. G. H. Pertz and C. Rodenberg (Berlin, 1883-94), i. 70; Donovan, 76-8.

[92] For the political background, see Van Cleve, *Frederick II*, 107-53.

[93] *HD* ii. 82-3; Oliver of Paderborn, *Historia Damiatina, Die Schriften*, 256-7; Richard of San Germano, 340.

[94] Roger Wendover, ii. 262; Ralph of Coggeshall, *Chronicon Anglicanum*, ed. J. Stevenson (London, 1875), 189.

[95] *HD* iii. 40; MGH Epistolae saeculi XIII, i. 124.

[96] MGH Epistolae saeculi XIII, i. 122, 128-30.

about Frederick's failure to discharge his crusading obligations. Writing shortly after the Fourth Lateran Council, the Italian moralist Thomasin von Zirclaira urged the emperor to follow the example of his grandfather Frederick I and his uncle Frederick of Swabia and, paraphrasing Innocent III's bull *Quia maior*, he exhorted the faithful to take the cross.[97] The most interesting example of this type of criticism is however to be found in a treatise on rhetoric entitled *Parisiana Poetria*, composed by the Englishman known as John of Garland, a master of grammar and literature at the University of Paris and one of the founder members of the University of Toulouse. The first draft of this was written in *c.*1220; as one of his *exempla* John quoted a model letter purportedly addressed by the pope to Frederick II, which described the enthusiastic response to the preaching of the Fifth Crusade. In language reminiscent of papal crusading bulls, John of Garland made Honorius exhort the emperor to take the cross and threaten with anathema those who stirred up wars and hindered the army's departure:

our soul would be base and contrary to reason if, either from fear of the secular power or from the weight of the burden put on us, we should permit the army of the cross, now ardently hastening from here to our spiritual fatherland, to fade into ashes . . . But now nation rises up against nation and seditions wake in diverse places, impeding the advance to the Promised Land . . . we hold excommunicate all those who raise storms of persecution . . . disturbing the peace.

In his model reply Frederick was made to advocate John's ideal of a united front against the Muslims. He declared his obedience to the pope and his desire for peace in the West and commanded the German princes to assemble at Cologne to discuss plans for the crusade.[98]

The most outspoken critics of the emperor's vacillations were again the troubadours.[99] In a *sirventes* dated some time between 1215 and 1220, Guilhem Figueira praised Frederick's decision to take the cross and sacrifice himself for Christ,

[97] Thomasin von Zirclaira, ll. 11798–813; Rocher, 303, 708–13, 716–18.

[98] John of Garland, *Parisiana Poetria de arte prosaica, metrica et rithmica*, ed. T. Lawler (New Haven, Conn., 1974), pp. xv, 142–4, 264.

[99] For poems concerning Frederick II, see De Bartholomaeis, 'Osservazioni sulle poesie provenzali', 97=125.

but he urged him to make sure that this good beginning had a worthy conclusion, in other words that he fulfilled his vow.[100] In the following years several other poets reminded the emperor of his undertaking and exhorted him to hasten to the Holy Land. The troubadour Elias Cairel, who probably accompanied his lord Boniface of Montferrat on the Fourth Crusade, lamented that whilst the Western princes devoted their energies to wars amongst themselves, the Muslims advanced with ease, and he called upon Frederick in particular to avenge the loss of the Holy Sepulchre.[101] In spite of his initial enthusiasm, Peirol does not appear to have taken part in the Third Crusade. But in the summer of 1221 he went on pilgrimage to the Holy Land and whilst he was in the East may have witnessed the surrender of Damietta. He ascribed some of the blame for this reversal of Christian fortunes to Frederick's apathy:

I saw the emperor take many an oath last year which he now seeks to evade . . .

Emperor, Damietta awaits you and night and day the White Tower weeps for your eagle [standard] which a vulture has cast down therefrom; cowardly is the eagle that is captured by a vulture! Shame is thereby yours and honour accrues to the Sultan and besides the shame you all suffer such hurt in that he is ever diminishing there the domain of our faith.[102]

Only the German minnesinger Walther von der Vogelweide attributed the delays to the troubles caused by the emperor's opponents. In a poem probably written for the Diet of Frankfurt in April 1220, he urged the German princes to let Frederick depart for Egypt and pointed out that his absence could only be to their advantage:

If you wish, I will send the king a thousand miles away . . . beyond Trani. The hero wishes to go on Christ's expedition; whoever hinders him in this has acted against God and Christendom.[103]

[100] Guilhem Figueira, 'Totz hom qui ben comensa e ben fenis', ed. cit. 49–52.

[101] Elias Cairel, 'Qui saubes dar tan bo conselh denan', *Der Trobador Elias Cairel*, ed. H. Jaeschke (Berlin, 1921), 164–5. See also id. 'So que.m sol dar alegransa', 186 and 'Un sirventes historique d'Elias Cairel', ed. De Bartholomaeis, *Annales du Midi*, xvi (1904), 492–3.

[102] Peirol, 'Pas flum Jordan our vist e.l monimen', ed. cit. 16–17, 161–3. See also above, p. 59.

[103] Walther von der Vogelweide, 'Ir fürsten, die des küneges gerne waeren

When he received news of the fall of Damietta, Frederick reiterated his desire to go to the East; he discussed plans for a new crusade with Honorius III at a series of meetings in 1222 and 1223. In March 1223 the emperor renewed his crusading vow and promised to leave for the East by June 1225,[104] but his departure was delayed by further troubles in Italy with the Lombard League.[105] In July 1225 the pope agreed to another postponement until August 1227, but when Frederick failed to meet this deadline he was excommunicated.[106]

As before, the emperor's repeated delays aroused complaints from the troubadours. Writing in the Languedoc between 1225 and 1228, Elias de Barjols exhorted the emperor to fulfil his obligations to God by attacking his enemies the Muslims;[107] and this plea was echoed several times by Fulk de Romans, a poet at the North Italian court of the Malaspina family. In his *sirventes* Fulk stressed the perilous state of the Latin Kingdom and lamented that the faithful and especially Frederick were slow to send assistance. He warned these laggard crusaders of the perils of the Last Judgement, and urged them to summon up their courage and serve the Lord by freeing the Holy Places from Muslim domination.[108] Once again only Walther von der Vogelweide seems to have defended the emperor's vacillations: since the archangels Michael, Gabriel, and Raphael had done nothing against the Muslims, what could one expect from a mere mortal, Frederick?[109]

The weight of public opinion directed against them appears

âne', *Die Gedichte*, ed. K. Lachmann, rev. C. von Kraus and H. Kuhn (Berlin, 1965), 38. For doubts about the authenticity of this poem, see F. Maurer, *Die politischen Lieder Walthers von der Vogelweide* (Tübingen, 1954), 72–4.

[104] Richard of San Germano, 342–3; *HD* ii. 241.

[105] Van Cleve, *Frederick II*, 179–88.

[106] Richard of San Germano, 344, 348. See also Donovan, 106–11.

[107] Elias de Barjols, 'Ben deu hom son bon senhor', *Le Troubadour Elias de Barjols*, ed. Stronski (Toulouse, 1906), 231; De Bartholomaeis, 'Osservazioni', 104–5.

[108] Fulk de Romans, 'Aucel no troub chantan', 'Quan lo dous temps ven', 'En chantan volh que.m digatz', 'Quan cug chantar', *Die Gedichte des Folquet von Romans*, ed. R. Zenker (Halle, 1896), 51, 60–3, 69.

[109] Walther von der Vogelweide, 'Der anegenge nie gewan', ed. cit. 111. For another interpretation of this poem, see Walther von der Vogelweide, *Werke*, ed. J. Schaefer (Darmstadt, 1972), 511.

to have helped to persuade Richard and Philip to abandon their private wars and leave for the Holy Land. But Frederick II did not set sail for Jerusalem until 1228, that is thirteen years after he had first taken the cross. By this time he had been excommunicated by Pope Gregory IX;[110] he was still under the papal ban when he met Sultan al-Kāmil and negotiated the return of the Holy City to Christian rule. As we have seen, the principal reason for the emperor's slowness to fulfil his crusading vow was the troubled state of Northern Italy, Sicily, and Germany. But, although there was clearly widespread support for the Fifth Crusade, the improved situation in the Latin East also meant that the critics' arguments did not have the same force or effect. The particular circumstances of the disaster at Hattin seem to have created a unique atmosphere of crusading zeal in which Richard and Philip were compelled to pay heed to the critics' demands.

[110] *HD* iii. 24–30. See below, p. 176.

CHAPTER III

Sin and its consequences

THE crusades were holy wars and as such were believed to be sanctioned and even commanded by God. It was thought that he intervened in and decided the outcome of battles and in this context the church found it difficult to explain a defeat: at a popular level there was a tendency to accuse God of deserting his people. Apologists found that the most satisfactory way out of this dilemma was to attribute a reverse to a divine judgement upon man's innate unworthiness even when acting as God's instrument; in other words to place the blame upon the crusaders themselves.[1] According to the popes, preachers, poets, and chroniclers, the Lord was angered by men's sins—the Latin formula generally adopted was *peccatis exigentibus hominum* —and as a punishment allowed them to be defeated by the Muslims. But God was merciful and if they were repentant he would forgive them their transgressions; with this restoration of divine grace the crusaders would be victorious over their enemies. Apologists stressed that God did not desire the death of a sinner but rather his conversion and life (Ezek. 33: 11); they regarded the crusade as a means of putting the faithful to the test. God could have sent legions of angels to defeat the Muslims (Matt. 26: 53), but he preferred to test men to see if they were willing to serve him: he wished to give them an opportunity to win salvation.[2] The defeats and natural disasters experienced by the crusaders were seen as

---

[1] Riley-Smith, 'An Approach', 9-10 and 'Peace Never Established: The Case of the Kingdom of Jerusalem', *TRHS*, xxviii (1978), 89, 98-9; Stickel, 190-217.

[2] Bernard, *Opera*, viii. 313; *Historia de expeditione Friderici*, 8-10; *Carmina Burana*, no. 48, st. 5; Innocent III, PL ccxiv, cols. 263-5; Aimeric de Péguilhan, 'Ara parra qual seran enveyos', *Poems*, ed. W. P. Shepard and F. M. Chambers (Illinois, 1950), 85-6; Humbert of Romans, *De praedicatione sancte crucis*, ch. 15. See also Albrecht von Johansdorf, 'Die hinnen varn', *MF*, 185; Thomasin von Zirclaira, ll. 11499, 507.

further trials sent by God;[3] Fulcher of Chartres remarked that those besieging Antioch on the First Crusade were tried and purified of their sins like metal in a furnace (Ps. 11: 7).[4]

The origins of the concept peccatis exigentibus hominum

The origins of the concept *peccatis exigentibus hominum* are to be found in the Old Testament, a major source for crusade thinkers.[5] Here history was placed within a religious framework and God was portrayed as an all-powerful and righteous figure whose hand was to be seen in all events. Men submitted themselves unquestioningly to his will and they drew lessons from the past. They recognized that God rewarded good and punished evil, and questioned man's worthiness rather than God's justice.[6] In the Old Testament a pattern of sin, repentance, and forgiveness was established. The Hebrews escaped from Egypt with God's aid, but, because they transgressed, he permitted only two of them to reach the Promised Land (Num. 32: 12). As a punishment for breaking their covenant with the Lord, their descendants had to endure the Babylonish captivity. (4 K. 17: 22-3). At the same time God was merciful; when his people were penitent he forgave them and guided them back to Jerusalem (Ezra 1). The Lord was thought to have used the Assyrians to test and discipline the Hebrews (Judith 8: 26-7) and the just were often compared with metal purified in a furnace. (Ps. 11: 7, Mal. 3: 3, Wisd. 3: 6).

Classical and early Christian historians also saw the past in moral terms[7] and some of their works were influential in the Middle Ages: for example, in the introduction to his *Historia*

---

[3] Odo of Deuil, 132; Oliver of Paderborn, *Historia Damiatina*, 191-3; John of Joinville, *Histoire de Saint Louis*, ed. N. de Wailly (Paris, 1868), 144.

[4] Fulcher of Chartres, 226. See also *Itinerarium regis Ricardi*, 92; Ambroise, ll. 3495-504; Henry of Livonia, *Chronicon Lyvoniae*, ed. Pertz, MGH Scr. rer. Germ. (Hanover, 1874), 20; Tangl, 89.

[5] P. Alphandéry, 'Les citations bibliques chez les historiens de la première croisade', *Revue de l'histoire des religions*, xcix (1929), 139-58; Rousset, 'L'idée de croisade chez les chroniqueurs d'Occident', *Storia del medioevo. Relazioni del X congresso*, iii. 556-8.

[6] P. L. Berger, *The Social Reality of Religion* (London, 1969), 80-8.

[7] S. Mazzarino, *The End of the Ancient World*, trans. G. Holmes (London, 1966), 40-3, 56-62.

Anglorum the twelfth-century chronicler Henry of Huntingdon praised Homer because he presented virtues and vices
in his *exempla*, endeavouring to attract men to good and dissuade them from evil:[8] and Sallust's accounts of the Jugur-
thine War and Catiline's conspiracy, which described the
moral decline of the Roman republic, were to be found in
many libraries in the late eleventh century.[9] Sallust was also
influential in another way, for his works formed part of the
cultural heritage of St Augustine and were among the sources
used in *De civitate Dei*.[10] In this Augustine argued that the
Lord controlled the beginning, the progress, and the end of
wars; he maintained that God willed that the good should
suffer as well as the wicked in order to test their devotion.
His most important statement for our purposes, however,
concerned the relationship between sin and the just war.
Augustine declared that:

even when a just war is waged it is in defence of his sin that the other
side is contending and victory, even when victory falls to the wicked,
is a humiliation visited on the conquered by divine judgement either to
correct or to punish their sins.[11]

Even if contemporaries had not read *De civitate Dei*, they
would have inherited the 'concept' *peccatis exigentibus
hominum* directly from the Old Testament. This historiographical tradition was certainly well established by the
eleventh century. For example, the phrase *peccatis exigentibus*
occurs several times in the letters of Pope Gregory VII, as
an explanation for the various setbacks and difficulties
suffered by the church;[12] it was also used by medieval chroniclers such as Orderic Vitalis[13] and the historians of the earlier

[8] Henry of Huntingdon, *Historia Anglorum*, ed. T. Arnold (London, 1874),
1-2.

[9] B. Smalley, 'Sallust in the Middle Ages', in R. R. Bolgar (ed.), *Classical
Influences on European Culture, 500–1500* (Cambridge, 1971), 165-6.

[10] P. R. L. Brown, *Augustine of Hippo* (London, 1969), 311; Augustine, *De
civitate Dei*, Corpus Christianorum, Series Latina, xlvii–xlviii (Turnhout, 1955),
i. 5; ii. 18.

[11] Ibid. xix. 15. (cf. id. i. 1, 8, 9; xvii. 2 and H. A. Deane, *The Political and
Social Ideas of St Augustine* (New York, 1963), 157, 309-10.

[12] Gregory VII, *Registrum*, ed. E. Caspar (Berlin, 1920), 54, 299, 372, 471,
527; id. *Epistolae vagantes*, ed. Cowdrey (Oxford, 1972), 134.

[13] See C. J. Holdsworth, 'Ideas and Reality: Some Attempts to Control and
Defuse War in the Twelfth Century', *Studies in Church History*, xx (1983), 75-6.

campaigns against the Muslims—the Norman wars in Southern Italy, the Byzantine expeditions to Asia Minor, and the Spanish *Reconquista*. They attributed Christian defeats to human sinfulness and depicted the army doing penance and praying before a military engagement.[14] In fact the connection between sin and a military reverse might be described as a commonplace of medieval historiography. There was, however, one important difference between these early holy wars and the crusades, namely that the latter were unambiguously stated to be authorized by God.[15] In this context it was even more essential to find an explanation for a defeat and the way in which various groups, particularly the crusading historians and priests accompanying the army, used the formula *peccatis exigentibus hominum* to account for the many trials and reverses endured by the Christians merits close study.

Sin and the failure of crusades

This problem was recognized by the earliest historians of the First Crusade—the clerks Fulcher of Chartres, Raymond of Aguilers, and Peter Tudebode[16] all of whom took part in the expedition. Their accounts were intended to point out the lessons to be drawn from reverses and victories; they demonstrated how repentance could bring about a restoration of divine grace: 'although God's army because of its transgressions suffered the whip of the Lord, through his mercy it triumphed over all the pagans'.[17] But these ideas were not confined to clerical circles; there is some evidence that they had begun to filter through to the rest of the crusading host.[18] The leaders of the army seem to have been convinced that God fought on behalf of the

[14] Rousset, *Les Origines et les caractères de la première croisade* (Neuchâtel, 1945), 29-39.

[15] See Riley-Smith, *What were the Crusades?*, 15-17.

[16] Until recently Peter Tudebode was regarded as a plagiarist who took all his information from the *Gesta Francorum*, but it has now been shown that his work has an independent value. See Peter Tudebode, *Historia de Hierosolymitano itinere*, ed. J. H. and L. L. Hill (Paris, 1977), 15-18.

[17] Raymond of Aguilers, 35.

[18] See Rousset, *Les Origines*, 25-6; E. O. Blake, 'The Formation of the "Crusade idea"', *Journal of Ecclesiastical History*, xxi (1970), 21-4.

crusaders[19] and the author of the *Gesta Francorum*, who was probably a knight in Bohemond's contingent, described the sense of despair after a defeat and the call to repentance.[20] The formula *peccatis exigentibus hominum* is also to be found in the histories of the First Crusade written by learned clergymen in the West such as Robert of Rheims, Guibert of Nogent, Albert of Aix, and Baldric of Dol in the early twelfth century.[21]

According to one version of his sermon at Clermont, Urban II drew a connection between human sinfulness and the Muslim occupation of the Holy Land[22] and this explanation was adopted by contemporary chroniclers to account for setbacks throughout the expedition itself. In July 1097, the Christians met the forces of the Selçük Sultan Kılıç Arslan at Dorylaeum. According to Fulcher of Chartres, the crusaders were surrounded by the Muslims and began to despair; but then they realized that these trials were a divine judgement upon their sins; so they confessed and the clergy begged God to show mercy upon his people. After this act of penance, the Lord apparently willed that the Christians should triumph over their enemies.[23]

This pattern of repentance, forgiveness, and victory took a more definite shape during the siege of Antioch. In the course of the first siege, which lasted from October 1097 to June 1098, the crusaders fell victim to hunger and disease and there were some desertions. The author of the *Gesta* regarded these misfortunes as a divine judgement upon the crusaders' sins,[24] but Raymond and Fulcher went further and underlined the connection between repentance and success. According to their accounts, an earthquake and a mysterious red glow in the sky were thought to be indications of divine wrath and the clergy instituted a programme of reform. It was believed that God showed mercy on the army; in June the city was betrayed into Christian

---

[19] *Die Kreuzzugsbriefe*, 159, 168-74.

[20] *Gesta Francorum*, pp. xi-xiii.

[21] See Riley-Smith, *The Crusades*, 16; Blake, 24-5.

[22] Baldric of Dol, *Historia Jerosolymitana*, RHC Occ. iv. 13.

[23] Fulcher of Chartres, 125-7. See also Raymond of Aguilers, 45-6; *Gesta Francorum*, 20-1; Peter Tudebode, 54.

[24] *Gesta Francorum*, 34. See also Peter Tudebode, 69.

hands.[25] The Muslims, however, retained the citadel, and the crusaders had to mount a second siege. They soon found themselves short of food and trapped between the garrison and the relieving force led by Kerbogha, governor of Mosul; again they began to despair of victory. At this time of crisis Peter Bartholomew revealed the secret burial-place of the Holy Lance, and the Provençal priest Stephen of Valence had a vision in which he claimed that Christ had appeared to him and urged the army to reform. The Lord apparently reminded Stephen of his support in the past, told him that the crusaders' sins were the cause of their present suffering, and promised that if they returned to him he would send them help within five days.[26] This vision was the first of a series of divine admonitory messages recorded by the historians of the First Crusade; its effect seems to have been to point out the lessons to be drawn from a setback. The author of the *Gesta* described the restoration of morale in the army and the ritual of penance which followed. God was thought to have restored his favour to the Christians and made them triumph over Kerbogha.[27] This connection between repentance and victory was stressed by later historians of the expedition, such as Albert of Aix, who gave detailed accounts of the various reform measures instituted by the clergy.[28]

After their victory at Antioch, the crusaders marched to Ma'arrat-an-Nu'man. Their first attack upon the city was unsuccessful; once again there were said to be signs of despair. At this point Peter Bartholomew had another admonitory vision. According to Raymond of Aguilers, Peter claimed that St Peter and St Andrew had appeared and reminded him that transgressors against the Lord's commands would be punished: God had granted the crusaders a victory at Antioch, but now they had offended him, and only if they

[25] Fulcher of Chartres, 222-3, 230-1; Raymond of Aguilers, 54. See also *Die Kreuzzugsbriefe*, 159.

[26] Peter Tudebode, 99-100; *Gesta Francorum*, 57-8; Raymond of Aguilers, 72-4; Fulcher of Chartres, 244-6.

[27] *Gesta Francorum*, 67-70; Peter Tudebode, 110-13; Raymond of Aguilers, 82-3; Fulcher of Chartres, 257.

[28] Guibert of Nogent, 205; Albert of Aix, *Historia Hierosolymitana*, RHC Occ. iv. 421; Baldric of Dol, 75.

repented would he permit them to recapture the city. When the crusaders heard this they apparently prayed and gave alms, and their second assault was successful.[29] Peter Tudebode's version of this vision was somewhat different. He maintained that St Andrew urged the crusaders to turn from evil and give a tenth of all that they possessed to the church and the poor. But his conclusion was the same: the crusaders heeded God's warning and soon afterwards Ma'arrat-an-Nu'man was captured.[30] Admittedly Peter Bartholomew was later discredited as a false prophet. Nevertheless the initial response to his vision reflects the army's attitude towards a defeat.

A similar series of events occurred during the siege of Jerusalem in the summer of 1099. When the crusaders first arrived before the Holy City, a hermit on the Mount of Olives had predicted that it would soon fall to them, but in fact their first assault failed. During these months the Christians suffered from the climate, shortages of food, and enemy ambushes; there were some desertions. Once again Raymond of Aguilers attributed these difficulties to the crusaders' refusal to obey God's instructions to reform; Bishop Adhémar of Le Puy, who had perished during an epidemic at Antioch, was said to have appeared to the priest Peter Desiderius and to have commanded the army to make a procession around the walls of Jerusalem. It was thought that God was appeased by this act of penance and, when the crusaders mounted a second siege, granted his people a victory.[31]

The chroniclers of the First Crusade had occasion to use the formula *peccatis exigentibus hominum* to explain only temporary setbacks. But it was soon employed to justify the three catastrophic defeats and the overall failure of the crusade of 1101. Fulcher of Chartres wrote that the Poitevin army was defeated at Heraclea because of its sins, and maintained that Count William only escaped because a merciful God 'chastening has chastised but has not delivered over to

---

[29] Raymond of Aguilers, 95-8.

[30] Peter Tudebode, 121-4.

[31] Raymond of Aguilers, 127, 137, 140-1, 144-5, 149-51. See also Peter Tudebode, 137-41; *Gesta Francorum*, 90-1. For later accounts, see J. France, 'An Unknown Account of the Capture of Jerusalem', *EHR* lxxxvii (1972), 777; Albert of Aix, 470-1.

death' (Ps. 117: 18).[32] In the same way Albert of Aix regarded the Muslim victory over the Lombards at the battle of Mersivan as a divine judgement,[33] and God was said to have willed that, because of their folly, the Christians should be defeated at the battle of Ramla by those whom they had vanquished.[34] An alternative explanation put forward by the German chronicler Ekkehard of Aura was that the Byzantine Emperor had betrayed the Christians to the Muslims;[35] significantly, when this idea was taken up by some later historians a connection was drawn between Greek treachery and the crusaders' transgressions: the Greeks were described as divine agents, and it was suggested that God had countenanced the destruction of the crusading armies in Asia Minor as a means of punishing the Christians for their sins.[36]

The popularity of the formula *peccatis exigentibus hominum* also prompted chroniclers to use it in other times of crisis to account for seemingly inexplicable events; for example, when on Easter Saturday 1101 the Holy Fire failed to kindle the lamps in the Holy Sepulchre. Fulcher of Chartres dismissed this incident in one sentence, but sources dependent upon him, such as Guibert of Nogent and Bartolf of Nangis, together with Ekkehard of Aura, attributed the phenomenon to God's anger at men's sins.[37] All these chroniclers had written accounts of the First Crusade; they stressed the connection between repentance and the restoration of divine grace. The Patriarch of Jerusalem apparently advised the people to seek God's forgiveness; he was said to have been so pleased by their conversion that there was a second outpouring of the Holy Fire, which ignited a multitude of lamps in the church.[38] Fulcher of Chartres, the only historian of the

[32] Fulcher of Chartres, 432-3.

[33] Albert of Aix, 570.

[34] Fulcher of Chartres, 438-40. See also Bartolf of Nangis, *Gesta Francorum Iherusalem expugnantium*, RHC Occ. iii. 533-4.

[35] Ekkehard of Aura, *Hierosolymita*, RHC Occ. v. 30. See also Richard of Poitiers, *Chronicon*, extr. RHGF xii. 412.

[36] Matthew of Edessa, *Chronique*, extr. RHC Doc. arm., i. 56-7; William of Tyre, *Historia rerum in partibus transmarinis gestarum*, RHC Occ. i. 417-18; Orderic Vitalis, v. 332-40.

[37] Fulcher of Chartres, 395-6; Bartolf of Nangis, 524-6; Guibert of Nogent, 256; Ekkehard of Aura, *Hierosolymita*, 36. See also Matthew of Edessa, 54-5.

[38] B. McGinn, 'Iter Sancti Sepulchri: The Piety of the First Crusaders', in

First Crusade who remained in the Latin East, believed that the settlers continued to fight in God's service; when, for example, King Baldwin was defeated by the Muslim rulers of Mosul and Damascus in 1113, he described this as a great shame caused by men's sins.[39] In fact this became the traditional way of explaining a defeat in the Latin East.[40] Thus it is not surprising that when Edessa fell to Zengi in 1144 Pope Eugenius III attributed the disaster to 'nostris et ipsius populi peccatis exigentibus'.[41]

Various attempts were made to explain the sudden reversal of Christian fortunes at Damascus on the Second Crusade. Some chroniclers accused the Syrian barons of treachery, arguing that in an attempt to protect their own position they had accepted bribes from the Muslim ruler of the city and persuaded the crusaders to retreat.[42] Others placed the blame on the treacherous Greeks,[43] on natural disasters such as floods and famine,[44] or the large number of non-combatants; and, as we have seen, efforts were made to ensure that future expeditions were militarily viable.[45] But once again the most common and acceptable explanation for the defeat of the Christian army seems to have been a divine judgement upon human sinfulness. Chroniclers throughout Europe lamented that, because of their transgressions, many crusaders had perished and the survivors had returned home ignominiously; all their efforts had been in vain because God was not with them.[46] Indeed Abbot Suger's secretary William of St Denis

B. K. Lackner and K. R. Philp (eds.), *Essays on Medieval Civilization* (Arlington, Tex., 1978), 33-8.

[39] Fulcher of Chartres, 569; Riley-Smith, 'Peace Never Established', 94.

[40] See Fulcher of Chartres, 603, 622, 756; William of Tyre, 485, 531-2.

[41] Eugenius III, 'Text die Kreuzzugsbulle Eugens III.', ed. P. Rassow, *Neues Archiv der Gesellschaft für ältere deutsche Geschichtskunde*, xlv (1924), 302. See also Bernard, *Opera*, viii. 312.

[42] *Chronicon Nicholai Ambianensis*, extr. RHGF xiv. 22; *Chronicon coenobii Sancti Medardi Suessionensis*, extr. RHGF xii. 278; Robert of Torigni, *Chronica*, ed. R. Howlett (London, 1892), 155; *Chronica regia Coloniensis*, 84.

[43] *Annales Sancti Pauli Virdunensis*, MGH SS xvi. 501; *Annales Romoaldi Archiepiscopi Salernitani* MGH SS xix. 425; Odo of Deuil, 12-14, 132; *Annales Magdeburgenses*, MGH SS xvi. 188.

[44] *Annales Palidenses*, MGH SS xvi. 83; *Casus monasterii Petrishusensis*, MGH SS xx. 674; Odo of Deuil, 48.

[45] See above, pp. 25-8.

[46] *Annales Rodenses*, MGH SS xvi. 719; Otto of Freising, *Gesta Friderici imperatoris*, ed. A. Hofmeister, MGH Scr. rer. Germ (Hanover, 1912), 65; Ralph

declared that the remnants of the army had only reached the West because the Lord was merciful.[47] The formula *peccatis nostris exigentibus* was also used by King Conrad III of Germany in a letter addressed to Eugenius III lamenting the failure of the expedition. In his reply the pope counselled Conrad to bear his tribulations humbly, for God sent them to test him and to bring him to repentance.[48]

Because of his advocacy of the crusade, the brunt of popular disillusionment fell upon St Bernard.[49] In his defence three fellow Cistercians put forward their own interpretations of the disaster, based upon the idea of a divine judgement upon human sinfulness. Bishop Otto of Freising lamented the tragic outcome of the expedition, but drew a distinction between what was good for the body and what was good for the soul; although the crusade had not produced any material advantages, Otto pointed out that it had brought about the salvation of many souls.[50] A similar thesis was advanced by St Bernard's biographer Geoffrey of Auxerre. He lamented the heavy casualties suffered by the Second Crusade, but commented that those who perished had been saved from further sin.[51] This theme was also taken up by Abbot John of Casa Maria. In a letter addressed to St Bernard, he declared that God had punished the crusaders because they had reverted to their evil ways. But he added that the Lord soon turned their wickedness into his mercy and described a vision in which St John and St Paul had appeared and informed him that those who died on the crusade had gone to heaven to fill the gaps left by the fallen angels.[52]

Niger, *Chronica universalis*, 335; *Appendiculum ad Sigebertum anonymi Blandiniensis*, extr. RHGF xiv. 20; *Gesta abbatum Sancti Bertini Sithiensium continuatio*, 664.

[47] William of St Denis, *Dialogus*, 105-6, 109.

[48] *MGH Diplomata regum et imperatorum Germaniae*, ix (Cologne, Vienna, and Graz, 1969), 358; Otto of Freising, *Gesta Friderici*, 93-4. See also Wibald of Corvey, 245.   [49] See below, p. 191.

[50] Otto of Freising, *Gesta Friderici*, 65, 90-2.

[51] 'Vita Sancti Bernardi et res gestae', PL clxxxv, col. 309.

[52] Bernard, *Opera*, PL clxxxii, cols. 590-1. John here makes use of an idea from Augustine, *De civitate Dei*, xxii. 1. See also Constable, 'A Report of a Lost Crusading Sermon by St. Bernard on the Failure of the Second Crusade' in *Studies presented to J. F. O'Sullivan*, 49.

St Bernard's own apologia for the Second Crusade was included in his treatise *De consideratione* and was probably composed between 1149 and 1152, at the request of Eugenius III. In it the Abbot of Clairvaux lamented that so many Christians had perished, and commented that God had neither spared his own people nor his own name; he was so angered by men's sins that he had perhaps forgotten his mercy. St Bernard stressed that the Lord's judgements were always true, but admitted that this judgement was so deep that he who was not scandalized by it deserved to be called a saint.[53] He sought to console the faithful, who were disillusioned by this reverse, by recalling how God had judged his people in the past. St Bernard took as his first example the exodus of the Hebrews from Egypt. Moses had promised to lead them to a better land, but although he obeyed God's commands, both he and the Hebrews failed to reach it, for they were rebellious and unbelieving and contended against Moses and the Lord; because of their iniquity, many Hebrews perished along the way. St Bernard drew a parallel between their fate and the suffering endured by the crusaders and concluded that they also made no progress because they were always looking backwards. He emphasized that God did not break his word when he punished them, for his justice could never prejudice his promises, and in this context he quoted an example from the Book of Judges. The Lord had commanded the Hebrews to fight the tribe of Benjamin and when they advanced into battle they relied upon his aid; but although their cause was just they were defeated twice. In spite of these setbacks they remained constant and the third time they were victorious (Judg. 20). St Bernard contrasted the Hebrews' steadfast behaviour with the murmurings of the crusaders after their defeat and expressed the hope that they would heed this example and resume the campaign against the Muslims.[54]

These biblical *exempla* were also used by several later apologists as a means of reminding the faithful of the sometimes

[53] A continuator of Sigebert of Gembloux's chronicle declared that it would be difficult to find such a severe judgement in any history or annal of the Christian era. *Continuatio Gemblacensis*, MGH SS, vi. 390.
[54] Bernard, *Opera*, iii. 410-14.

severe judgements of the Lord. For example, in his treatise
De re militari, Ralph Niger described the exodus of the
Hebrews from Egypt and pointed out that God willed that
only two Hebrews should survive the journey as a punishment for their sins (Num. 32: 12).[55] At about the same
time, Peter of Blois recalled the disastrous outcome of
the Second Crusade. He commented that the Lord had
punished severely those whom he had found wanting and
exhorted Christians to emulate the Hebrews' loyalty in
the face of defeat and to take part in the forthcoming
expedition against the Muslims.[56] The steadfastness of the
Hebrews was also noted by Innocent III in a letter urging
the faithful to join the Fourth Crusade.[57] And this theme
was taken up again by Humbert of Romans, writing in
the aftermath of Louis IX's death at Tunis. Like St Bernard,
Humbert was anxious to answer popular doubts about
the advisability of crusading and he used the Book of
Judges to explain the hidden judgements of the Lord
whereby he permitted misfortunes to befall his people.
Humbert argued that the Lord willed that the Hebrews
should be defeated by the tribe of Benjamin as a punishment
for their sins and claimed that this suffering had increased
their devotion: after their defeat they had prayed to the
Lord and fasted and, because they had shown that they
were penitent, when they advanced a third time he granted
them a victory.[58]

De consideratione was undoubtedly a popular work,
quoted both by contemporaries and by later apologists.[59]
But there is no evidence to support the thesis that St Bernard
was responsible for the development of the concept *peccatis
exigentibus hominum* and that its later popularity can be
attributed to his influence.[60] As we have seen, the formula
was established as part of the terminology used by chroniclers

[55] Ralph Niger, *DRM*, 147–8, 153, 161.

[56] Peter of Blois, *Opera*, i. 349–50.

[57] Innocent III, PL ccxiv, col. 264.

[58] Humbert of Romans, *Opus tripartitum*, 192–3, 197–8. See also below,
p. 88.

[59] See Gerhoh of Reichersberg, *De investigatione Antichristi*, 381–2.

[60] See Throop, 71, 180–1; Stickel, 193; Riley-Smith, 'Peace Never Established', 99.

of the crusades and Latin East early in the twelfth century. Later writers such as Humbert of Romans described a sequence of sin, divine intervention, repentance, and victory in the same way as historians of the First Crusade. Admittedly the formula was used more widely after the failure of the Second Crusade, but this was because contemporaries believed that it offered the only adequate explanation for the retreat from Damascus: its popularity is indicative of the impact of this reverse rather than the power of St Bernard's advocacy.

A divine judgement upon human sinfulness was also thought to be the most satisfactory explanation for Saladin's victory over the forces of the Latin Kingdom at the Horns of Hattin in July 1187. Although this was not a crusading defeat as such, it is worth studying the reaction to the disaster in the Latin East and West, for there were some interesting develop- ments in the use of the concept *peccatis exigentibus hominum*. In his bull *Audita tremendi*, Pope Gregory VIII blamed the reverse upon the sins of Christendom as a whole: 'non solum peccatum habitatorum illius sed et nostrum et totius populi Christianorum'. He observed that God had punished his people severely because of their iniquity, and urged them to amend themselves and to take the cross as proof of their repentance.[61] At the same time, the pope instructed the clergy to implement various reforms in the church as a mark of their contrition.[62] This plea was re- iterated by crusading apologists, preachers, and historians. Like Gregory, Cardinal Henry of Albano interpreted the dif- ficulties in Palestine as a punishment sent by God and associated the success of the forthcoming crusade with the reform of the church as a whole. In his famous letter *Publicani et peccatores* Henry exhorted clerks to improve their way of life, and when he preached the Third Crusade at the assembly at Mainz he urged the German laity to take this opportunity to amend themselves and to perform an act of satisfaction for their sins by taking the cross.[63] In his apologia for Reynald of Châtillon, Peter of Blois remarked

---

[61] *Historia de expeditione Friderici*, 6-10.

[62] Roger of Howden, *Gesta*, ii. 19; *Sacrorum conciliorum nova et amplissima collectio*, ed. G. D. Mansi (Florence and Venice, 1759-98), xxii, cols. 534-5.

[63] Henry of Albano, cols. 247-52, 355-7; Congar, 'Henri de Marcy', 87.

upon the severity of the Lord's judgement, but accepted that Saladin's victories were a means of testing the faithful and drew a distinction between the just and the evil: whereas the just bore these tribulations patiently and were brought to repentance, the evil ones persisted in their errors.[64] Two contemporary chroniclers also made a connection between human sinfulness and the Muslim conquest of the Latin Kingdom;[65] and, after lamenting the fall of Jerusalem, the satirist Walter Map commented that such was men's iniquity that God's vengeance had touched not only them but Christ himself.[66]

Clerical apologists had long argued that a defeat was a divine judgement upon human sinfulness. But, after the disaster at Hattin, this explanation seems to have been adopted by other groups as well. Poets writing in Latin described the Muslims as the new Philistines and the Christians as the new Israelites, and compared the capture of the Holy Cross after the battle of Hattin with the loss of the Ark of the Covenant: in the same way as the Lord had punished the Hebrews for their transgressions, he now permitted the Christians to be defeated by the Muslims. Like St Bernard, the poets regarded the crusade as an opportunity for salvation and they enjoined the faithful to take the cross as an act of penance, warning the Muslims that their victories would soon be reversed.[67] These themes were also to be found in vernacular poetry, in the crusading songs of the Northern French trouvères and German minnesingers. For example, an anonymous Anglo-Norman poet lamented that the Turks had driven God from his land 'pur nos pechiez'.[68] And, although the jongleur Ambroise complained that the faithful had been slow to go to the relief of the Holy City, he admitted that if God had not punished his people severely for their transgressions, then few would have come to him at the Last Judgement.[69]

[64] Peter of Blois, *Passio Reginaldi*, *Opera*, iii. 263-8.
[65] See *Itinerarium regis Ricardi*, 182-3; *Historia de expeditione Friderici*, 5.
[66] Walter Map, 42.
[67] Berter of Orléans, 'Iuxta Threnos Ieremiae', *Oxford Book of Medieval Latin Verse*, 297-300; 'Miror cur tepeat', 'Plange Sion et Iudaea', *Analecta hymnica*, xxxiii. 315, 319-20; *Carmina Burana*, no. 48.
[68] 'Parti de mal e a bien aturné', *Chansons de croisade*, 71.
[69] Ambroise, ll. 11-17, 29-31, 1355-78, 2558-65.

It seems likely that these ideas had spread through the influence of crusading apologists and preachers; close parallels have been drawn between the poems of the minnesinger Albrecht von Johansdorf and the sermons of the main preachers of the cross in Germany, Cardinal Henry of Albano and the Bishops of Strasburg and Würzburg.[70] Like them Albrecht attributed the defeat at Hattin to divine wrath, and urged Christians to make amends for their sins.[71]

Nevertheless, if some contemporaries believed that Christendom as a whole was to blame for Saladin's victories, others laid particular emphasis upon the iniquities of the Christians in the Latin Kingdom. In their appeals for aid, the Syrian Franks acknowledged that the disaster at Hattin was a divine judgement 'peccatis nostris exigentibus'[72] and the citizens of Jerusalem appear to have regarded their sufferings during the siege as a chastisement sent by God.[73] James of Vitry, Bishop of Acre from 1216 to 1228, was particularly critical of the behaviour of the inhabitants of the Latin Kingdom; he declared that such was God's anger at their transgressions that he permitted them to fall into the hands of their enemies.[74] Similar accusations were made by a number of chroniclers. The Templar who wrote the early part of the *Itinerarium peregrinorum* described Saladin as the scourge of God's vengeance;[75] William of Newburgh, who derived most of his information about the Latin East from the *Itinerarium*, observed that, although at the time of the First Crusade the Holy Land had welcomed the Christians, now the Lord wished to expel them from his land because of their sins.[76] In fact the fate of the corrupt inhabitants of the Holy City was held up as an example and warning to the faithful.[77] According to a late thirteenth-century collection of *exempla*, after the fall of Jerusalem to Saladin a pilgrim marvelled that

[70] See Wolfram, 111-14.
[71] Albrecht von Johansdorf, 'Ich und ein wîp, wir haben gestriten', *MF* 181-4.
[72] Magnus of Reichersberg, *Chronicon*, MGH SS xvii. 507-8.
[73] *L'estoire d'Eracles*, 88.
[74] James of Vitry, *Historia Hierosolimitana*, 1118-19.
[75] *Itinerarium peregrinorum*, 247. See also Roger Wendover, ii. 370-1.
[76] William of Newburgh, i, pp. xxvii-xxviii, 254-5. See also Rostand of Cluny, *Tractatus de translatione capitis Sancti Clementi*, PL ccix, cols. 905-9.
[77] See Caesar of Heisterbach, *Dialogus miraculorum*, i. 185-8.

the Lord allowed the Holy Places to be profaned by the Muslims; but a voice from heaven replied that the sins of the Christians were a far greater profanation.[78] The violence of this criticism reflected the natural tendency to blame those on the spot for the Muslim victories; but it also highlights the search for an explanation for the continued failure of the campaigns in the Holy Land.[79]

The most interesting example of the use of the formula *peccatis exigentibus* in the aftermath of the battle of Hattin can be found in Ralph Niger's treatise *De re militari*. Ralph appears to have been particularly impressed by the extravagant behaviour of the Patriarch Heraclius, who headed an embassy to the West in 1184; he contrasted the latter's ostentation with the parlous state of the Latin Kingdom. Like other contemporaries, Ralph attributed Saladin's victories to a divine judgement upon the vices of the inhabitants of Jerusalem, but he went further and questioned whether God wanted a crusade to be launched. Ralph observed that the Lord had permitted disasters to befall the Hebrews in order to bring them to repentance and suggested that the crusades might interfere with God's plans to punish his people in the East. He pointed out that the Lord controlled the distribution of territories (Ps. 23: 1) and only he would decide when the Muslim domination of the Holy Land should cease.[80] Ralph's argument represented a radical development of the 'traditional concept' of *peccatis exigentibus*, but it seems unlikely that it attracted much support. There is a possibility that similar views were advanced by Stephen Langton, in his life of Richard I: however, only fragments of this have survived, incorporated in the work of the fourteenth-century chronicler Ranulf Higden.[81] *De re militari* itself does not appear to have been widely read and is to be found in only two thirteenth-century manuscripts.[82]

Like their predecessors, the historians of the Third and Fourth Crusades continued to point out the connection

[78] *Catalogue of Romances*, iii. 480.
[79] Riley-Smith, 'Peace Never Established', 96–9, 102.
[80] Ralph Niger, *DRM* 92, 162, 185–7, 193–4, 196–7, 220.
[81] Ranulf Higden, *Polychronicon*, ed. C. Babington and J. R. Lumby (London, 1865–86), viii. 118–20; Powicke, *Stephen Langton* (Oxford, 1928), 21–2.
[82] Ralph Niger, *DRM*, 17.

between repentance and victory. For example, the members of Frederick I's crusade were said to have attributed their suffering in Asia Minor to their sins[83] and after the failure of the first assault upon Constantinople in 1204, the clergy led the crusaders in a ritual of penance. The success of the second attack was attributed to a restoration of divine grace.[84]

The fact that defeats were attributed to human sinfulness meant that each new expedition was preceded by a call to repentance and in his bull *Vineam Domini*, issued in 1213, Innocent III followed the example of Gregory VIII and associated the successful recovery of the Holy Land with the reform of the church as a whole.[85] This link between the crusade and ecclesiastical reform was underlined in Innocent's opening sermon at the Fourth Lateran Council,[86] and a similar connection was drawn by Gregory X at the Second Council of Lyons.[87]

Chroniclers throughout Europe turned to the traditional formula *peccatis exigentibus hominum* in 1221 to explain the sudden reversal of the fortunes of the Fifth Crusade at Damietta.[88] In his history of the expedition, Oliver, later Bishop of Paderborn, referred to the workings of divine providence and the hidden judgements of the Lord, who ordained that the Christians should capture Mount Tabor, Saphet, and Damietta, but also willed that they should be defeated by the Muslims as a punishment for their sins. And he described the sense of despair after the surrender of the army and the charity shown to the starving crusaders by the Sultan al-Kāmil, commenting:

At one and the same time the just judgement of divinity appeared and the moderation of mercy was shown in the form of opportune

---

[83] *Historia de expeditione Friderici*, 83–4; *Historia peregrinorum*, 163–4.

[84] Geoffrey of Villehardouin, *La Conquête de Constantinople*, ed. E. Faral (Paris, 1938–9) ii. 38; Robert of Clari, 71–2 (see also id. 106).

[85] Tangl, 84–5.

[86] Innocent III, PL ccxvii, cols. 78, 673–80.

[87] *COD* 309–10. See also Gregory X, no. 160.

[88] Richard of San Germano, 341: *Chronica regia Coloniensis*, 252; *Chronicon Turonense*, extr. RHGF xviii. 301–2; William of Andres, 761; *Annales Reineri*, MGH SS xvi. 678–9; *Annales Marbacenses*, 174; *L'estoire d'Eracles*, 349–52; Luke of Tuy, *Chronicon mundi*, ed. Schott, *Hispaniae illustratae*, iii. 113.

aid. The enormity of our evil deeds . . . compelled the vengeance of divine decision, but the natural fount of goodness, whose property is always to have mercy and to be sparing, justly mitigated the sentence of severity.[89]

Some years later Pope Honorius III observed that God had been provoked and his grace turned to anger, but he reassured Christians that, although the loss of Damietta had delayed the recapture of the Holy Land, God's strength was not thereby diminished. As soon as he had chastised his people for their sins he would obtain full revenge for all the injuries which he had suffered at the hands of the Muslims.[90]

A divine judgement upon men's sins also seemed to be the most satisfactory explanation for the defeat of the crusading forces at Mansurah in 1250 and the capture of King Louis IX. According to Matthew Paris, the French king had aroused God's wrath because he had plundered the poor and the church, and in the *Chronica maiora* Louis was made to lament the error of his ways: 'If I alone could suffer the shame and adversity and my sins did not rebound upon the whole church, I could endure with equanimity, but woe is me, through me all Christendom has fallen into confusion.'[91] Admittedly Matthew was not an impartial observer—his attitude towards Louis was influenced by his bitter resentment of the clerical tenth levied to finance the French expedition.[92] But there is other, more reliable evidence that the king regarded the collapse of the crusade as a judgement upon his own transgressions. For example, after his release from captivity Louis addressed a public letter to churchmen and nobles in France appealing for aid and in this he used the formula *peccatis nostris exigentibus* to explain the destruction of his army.[93] According to John of Joinville the king believed that God sent men trials as warnings so that they might become aware of their sins and repent[94] and when

---

[89] Oliver of Paderborn, *Historia Damiatina*, 274-5 (cf. ibid. 165-6, 188-9, 213-18, 245-6, 280-2).

[90] MGH Epistolae saeculi XIII, i. 153, 174. See also Honorius III, no. 855.

[91] Matthew Paris, *CM* v. 170-2, 466.

[92] See below, p. 138.

[93] *Epistola Sancti Ludovici regis de captione et liberatione sua*, ed. F. Duchesne, *Historiae Francorum Scriptores* (Paris, 1636-49), v. 429.

[94] John of Joinville, 227-8.

he returned to France he practised his religious devotions with a new intensity, as if they were a form of penance.[95]

Notwithstanding Louis's own expressions of guilt, most contemporaries seem to have laid the blame for the failure of the crusade upon the sins of the army as a whole. Like historians of previous expeditions, John of Joinville attributed the capture of Damietta to God's favour, and he declared that the Lord had withdrawn his grace from the Christians because they had sinned. Henceforward he had ordained that the Muslims should be victorious. This argument was reinforced by an incident said to have taken place after Louis's release from captivity. According to Joinville, the king sent his Master of Ordnance, John the Armenian, to Damascus. There he met an old man, who on learning that he was a Christian apparently remarked:

> You Christians must be hating each other very much; for I once saw the leper King Baldwin IV of Jerusalem defeat Saladin, though he had only three hundred men at arms whilst Saladin had three thousand. Now you have been brought so low by your sins that we take you in the fields just as if you were cattle.

The old man pointed out that God punished the Christians for the smallest fault because they were his children and had been given teachers so that they might learn to distinguish between right and wrong. Some years later, just before his departure for the West, the papal legate warned John of Joinville that God would exact great vengeance for the sins committed in Acre: in fact the city would only be washed clean by the blood of its inhabitants. And when John wrote his history in the early fourteenth century this prophecy seemed to have been at least partly fulfilled by the Muslim sack of Acre.[96]

In a similar way, in his treatise *De triumphis ecclesiae*, John of Garland drew a connection between the conduct of the army and the disaster at Mansurah,[97] and this theme was

---

[95] See W. C. Jordan, *Louis IX and the Challenge of the Crusade* (Princeton, 1979), 127-30.

[96] John of Joinville, 58, 158-9, 219.

[97] John of Garland, *De triumphis ecclesiae*, ed. T. Wright (London, 1856), 135, ll. 7-20; L. J. Paetow, 'The Crusading Ardor of John of Garland', in *Essays Presented to Dana C. Munro* (New York, 1928), 220-1.

also taken up by the Franciscan, Gilbert of Tournai. He may have accompanied Louis on his Egyptian crusade and at the king's request in 1259 he composed a treatise on the duties of a prince, entitled *Eruditio regum et principum*. In this Gilbert bewailed the suffering of the Christian forces and the imprisonment of the king and commented that God had punished both the just and the impious in order to test their faith and make them worthy of a heavenly crown.[98] In his *Collectio de scandalis ecclesiae*, written in the aftermath of Louis IX's abortive Tunisian Crusade and submitted to the Second Council of Lyons, Gilbert again made the connection between human sinfulness and a crusading defeat, lamenting: 'because of our transgressions the enemies of the cross of Christ who hate the Lord raise up their heads and those who hate Sion exult.'[99]

The most detailed exposition on this theme is however to be found in Humbert of Romans's treatise, *Opus tripartitum*. In it Humbert sought to reassure those disillusioned by the continued failure of the campaigns in the East, and in particular to answer the criticisms of those who questioned the adequacy of the conventional formula *peccatis exigentibus hominum* as an explanation for the misfortunes of the saintly Louis.[100] Like St Bernard, he quoted a number of examples from the Bible which showed that God allowed adversities to befall both the good and the evil and stressed that to suffer, and not to merit suffering, was to lead the life of a saint. Humbert claimed that Louis IX had rejoiced when he was captured after the battle of Mansurah, for at the Last Judgement he would be able to say to Christ that he had suffered for his sake. He pointed out that the Lord sent these tribulations to test the faithful and urged Christians to emulate the loyalty of the Hebrews in the face of defeat, assuring them that in the end God always granted his people a victory.[101] In fact, contemporaries found that there was no

---

[98] Gilbert of Tournai, *Eruditio regum et principum*, ed. A. de Poorter (Louvain, 1914), pp. vi, 15.

[99] Id. *Collectio*, 39. Close parallels have been drawn between this and Peter of Blois's reaction to the battle of Hattin. See Stroick, 434.

[100] For the reaction to Louis IX's defeat, see Stickel, 196-8, 214-15.

[101] Humbert of Romans, *Opus tripartitum*, 192-3, 197-8, 205. See also id. *De praedicatione sancte crucis*, ch. 15 and above p. 80.

other satisfactory way of explaining why God's enemies continued to triumph over the faithful fighting in a war authorized by God in the Holy Land. And, although some sought a material explanation for the fall of Acre, in 1291, most chroniclers turned yet again to the traditional formula.[102]

Historians of the Spanish *Reconquista* and the crusades against pagans, heretics, and Christian lay powers in the West also regarded military reverses as a divine judgement upon human sinfulness. For example, William of Puylaurens believed that this was the most adequate explanation for Raymond VII's gradual reconquest of the Languedoc after the settlement reached by the Fourth Lateran Council;[103] and the chronicler of the Livonian campaign commented that God tested his people through various tribulations.[104] When the forces of the Italian tyrant Ezzelino of Romano defeated the papal army, captured Brescia, and took the papal legate Philip of Ravenna prisoner in 1258, some apparently found it hard to accept that divine providence willed that the good should be thus afflicted, whilst the impious prospered. But a Paduan chronicler, whose own city had been the victim of some of Ezzelino's excesses, reiterated that men's failings were responsible for these disasters and attributed the eventual capture of the tyrant to a restoration of divine grace.[105]

In the preceding pages, I have described the use of the formula *peccatis exigentibus hominum* by crusading apologists, historians, preachers, and poets. But from the very beginning there is also evidence that the clergy accompanying the army pointed out the lessons to be drawn from reverses and the connection between repentance and victory and exhorted the crusaders to beseech God's forgiveness through a penitential ritual. According to the medieval doctrine of penance, man owed God an obligation not to sin and in refusing obedience he 'dishonoured' him. This act alienated the sinner from the church and if he wished to be reconciled he must show that he was repentant. He should be contrite

[102] See Schein, 'The West and the Crusade', 82, 92, 98, 102, 106; Stickel, 193-5, 202-4.

[103] William of Puylaurens, *Cronica*, ed. J. Duvernoy (Paris, 1976), 94-6.

[104] Henry of Livonia, 20.

[105] *Annales Sanctae Iustinae Patavini*, MGH SS xix. 171-2, 174-5.

and vow to avoid sin and, as proof of his intention, he should give God something greater than the 'honour' which he had lost; he should confess and perform an act of satisfaction. In his doctrine of atonement, St Anselm stressed that this was not to appease God's wrath but rather to vindicate his justice, since, if he forgave man's sins without imposing any penalties, the order of the universe might be violated; he pointed out that, although the satisfaction offered by man in penance was inadequate, it was made worthy by Christ's supreme act of sacrifice.[106] According to the Old Testament, the Hebrews had besought God's mercy through a ritual of prayers, fasting, almsgiving, and processions (Josh. 6, Judg. 20: 26. Judith 4: 9-15) and their example was followed by the early Christians and the medieval church, particularly at times of danger or crisis.[107] In the context of the medieval doctrine of penance this ritual was regarded as an act of satisfaction.

The first reference to a penitential ritual on the crusades can be found in Fulcher of Chartres's description of the battle of Dorylaeum. According to this account, at the height of the conflict the priests vested in white begged God to show mercy and help his people defeat the Muslims; 'weeping they sang and singing they wept', and believing that death was imminent many crusaders confessed their sins.[108] Fulcher is the only early source to mention this particular act of penance,[109] but in the course of the First Crusade a definite pattern of ceremonies seems to have developed. During the first siege of Antioch the clergy led the crusaders in processions, prayers, and almsgiving and they encouraged them to seek God's forgiveness by means of a three-day fast.[110] At the same time, the members of the army apparently consulted together and decided to expel women from the camp,[111] and later historians described a detailed programme

[106] J. Pelikan, *The Growth of Medieval Theology, 600–1300* (Chicago, 1978), 111–14, 140–3.

[107] T. Bailey, *The Processions of Sarum and the Western Church* (Toronto, 1971), 93–6, 112, 115.

[108] Fulcher of Chartres, 195–7.

[109] For a later account, see Robert of Rheims, 761.

[110] Raymond of Aguilers, 54. See also Fulcher of Chartres, 230–1.

[111] Fulcher of Chartres, 223.

of reform instituted by Bishop Adhémar of Le Puy in which a man and woman caught in the act of adultery were whipped.[112] During the second siege Christ was said to have appeared to Stephen of Valence and to have promised the crusaders help if they would amend their behaviour. Once again the army spent three days fasting and in processions from one church to another; then the crusaders confessed their sins, gave alms, received communion, and arranged for masses to be celebrated. When the army actually advanced into battle against Kerbogha, the priests put on their holy vestments and stood on the city walls with crosses in their hands, invoking God's aid in the words of a prayer used by the Hebrews (Ps. 27).[113] Later, at Maʻarrat-an-Nuʻman, the clergy stood behind the siege-tower, praying and beseeching God to defend his people and grant them a victory over the Muslims.[114] The culmination of these penitential rituals was of course the march around the walls of Jerusalem. Our most detailed source for this is Peter Tudebode, who claimed to have taken part in it himself. This procession, led by barefooted priests clad in holy vestments and carrying crosses, wound its way from Mount Sion to the church of St Stephen, then to the Mount of Olives, where a sermon was preached by Arnulf of Chocques, and finally to the monastery of St Mary in the valley of Josaphat. A later historian, Guibert of Nogent, compared it with the march of the Hebrews around the walls of Jericho (Josh. 6).[115] By the end of the First Crusade a fixed sequence of events seems to have been established[116] and this was followed by later crusaders and inhabitants of the Latin East at other times of adversity.[117]

Hence when the Holy Fire failed to appear in 1101, the clergy exhorted the people of Jerusalem to confess their sins and, since God had promised to hear the petitions of the

---

[112] See for example Bartolf of Nangis, 498–9; Albert of Aix, 278–9.

[113] *Gesta Francorum*, 67–8; Peter Tudebode, 110–11; Raymond of Aguilers, 81; Robert of Rheims, 828.

[114] *Gesta Francorum*, 78–9; Peter Tudebode, 123. See also Raymond of Aguilers, 97; Robert of Rheims, 847.

[115] Peter Tudebode, 137–8; Guibert of Nogent, 226. See also Raymond of Aguilers, 144–5; *Gesta Francorum*, 90; France, 777.

[116] For the penitential ritual before the battle of Ascalon in 1099, see *Gesta Francorum*, 94; Peter Tudebode, 144–5; Raymond of Aguilers, 155–6.

[117] For similar ceremonies on the crusade of 1101, see Albert of Aix, 568.

faithful in the Temple of Solomon (3 Kgs. 8: 30), King Baldwin led a penitential procession to its supposed site, the Dome of the Rock.[118] This ritual was repeated before the battle of Jaffa in 1105. According to Fulcher of Chartres, those who remained in Jerusalem proceeded from one church to another, and both the old and the young gave themselves up to fasting and prayers.[119] The defenders of the Holy City performed even more elaborate penitential rituals during the Muslim siege in 1187. According to one account, the clergy bearing precious relics led a procession around the walls of the city and women shaved their heads and bathed in cold water as a mark of contrition.[120]

In a similar way, the members of the German contingent on the Third Crusade were enjoined to confess, give alms, and receive communion before the siege of Iconium; and Frederick I instituted a programme of reform in which those guilty of fornication were punished severely.[121] This connection between human sinfulness and a military reverse was made again on the Fourth Crusade. After the failure of the first assault on Constantinople, the Bishops of Halberstadt, Troyes, and Soissons urged the crusaders to confess and take communion. Moreover, as at Antioch, 'it was commanded that the light women be sought out and expelled from the host and sent far away'.[122]

At times of crisis during the Fifth Crusade the clergy led further penitential rituals. Priests praying and singing psalms accompanied the crusaders when they attacked the fortress of Mount Tabor;[123] and, at one stage during the siege of the chain-tower at Damietta, the Patriarch of Jerusalem apparently lay in the dust with a fragment of the True Cross before him, praying for divine aid.[124] In November 1218, the papal

[118] Ekkehard of Aura, *Hierosolymita*, 36; Guibert of Nogent, 256; Bartolf of Nangis, 524-5; McGinn, 'Iter Sancti Sepulchri', 34-5.

[119] Fulcher of Chartres, 494.   [120] *L'estoire d'Eracles*, 87-8.

[121] Arnold of Lübeck, *Chronica Slavorum*, MGH SS xxi. 171; *Historia de expeditione Friderici*, 60, 83-4; *Historia peregrinorum*, 147-8, 163-4.

[122] Robert of Clari, 71-2 (cf. id. 41-2); Geoffrey of Villehardouin, ii. 38 (cf. id. i. 152).

[123] Oliver of Paderborn, *Historia Damiatina*, 165-6, Ep. iii. 289-90.

[124] Oliver of Paderborn, *Historia Damiatina*, 183-5, Ep. iii. 294-5; James of Vitry, *Lettres*, 106-7; *Gesta crucigerorum Rhenanorum*, ed. R. Röhricht, *Quinti belli sacri scriptores* (Geneva, 1879), 41-2; *Gesta obsidionis Damiate*, ibid. 76.

legate Cardinal Pelagius also commanded the army to fast and pray, after the sinking of a ship manned by the Templars.[125] And this procedure was repeated before the crusaders began their disastrous advance up the Nile.[126] As on previous expeditions, certain reforms were introduced into the crusaders' camp, and at Damietta prostitutes were expelled from the host and threatened with a public whipping and branding should they ever return.[127]

According to John of Joinville, penitential rituals were also performed on Louis IX's first crusade. On the outward voyage, the effects of adverse currents apparently frightened the crusaders and they appealed to a priest for aid. He advised them to process on three successive Saturdays around the masts of the ship, imploring God to grant them relief. They followed these instructions and on the third Saturday the ship reached Cyprus safely. A similar incident occurred after the king's arrival at Damietta. Louis was apparently becoming anxious because there had been no news of his brother, the Count of Poitiers, who commanded the reserves of the army. When he noticed this Joinville reminded the papal legate of what had happened during the outward voyage and the latter ordered the crusaders to process on each of the three following Saturdays, in this instance from his quarters to a church in the city. Before the third Saturday the count had arrived in the camp. Like his predecessors, Louis IX was also concerned about the moral conduct of the army. Hence after the capture of Damietta he dismissed a number of crusaders because they had consorted with prostitutes and at Caesarea he disciplined a knight who had been arrested in a brothel.[128]

Penitential rituals also seem to have been performed at times of crisis during the Spanish *Reconquista*[129] and on the crusades against pagans and heretics in Europe.[130] For example, at the height of the siege of Moissac, on the Albigensian

[125] Ibid. 81; John of Tulbia, *De Domino Iohanne rege Ierusalem*, ibid. 122-3.
[126] Oliver of Paderborn, *Historia Damiatina*, 257.
[127] James of Vitry, *Lettres*, 139.
[128] John of Joinville, 46, 60, 63-4, 180-1.
[129] See Roderick of Toledo, 133.
[130] For rituals on the Livonian Crusade and the expedition against the Stedingers, see Henry of Livonia, 25; *Annales Stadenses*, 362.

Crusade, the Archbishops of Rheims and Toul led a procession of barefooted priests, vested in white and bearing precious relics, and before the battle of Muret the clergy encouraged the army to confess and receive communion: when the crusaders actually advanced against the Southern forces, the priests entered the church and prayed and besought God to grant them a victory.[131]

These ceremonies were intended to express sorrow for the sins committed by the crusaders themselves. But from the late twelfth century onwards penitential rituals were also performed by the faithful in the West as a means of seeking God's forgiveness for the sins of Christendom as a whole and to pray for the success of future expeditions. Hence when news reached Rome of Saladin's victories, Gregory VIII and his successor Clement III ordered the clergy and laity to take part in a general act of supplication, including prayers and fasting.[132] And there were also elaborate processions in Rome in 1212, as a preliminary to the Spanish crusade against the Almohads, which culminated in the battle of Las Navas de Tolosa.[133] The most detailed liturgical instructions were issued by Innocent III in his bull *Quia maior*, dated 1213. In this the pope ordered the faithful to take part in monthly processions, men and women walking separately, and he decreed that public prayers should be offered begging God to free the Holy Land from Muslim domination. During the daily celebration of mass, immediately after communion, men and women were to prostrate themselves humbly while the priest chanted an antiphon, and at the conclusion of the ceremony a special prayer was to be offered for the release of the land consecrated by the blood of Christ.[134] Pope Honorius III instituted further processions after the crusaders' departure for the East in 1217,[135] and in 1260 and 1261, the Councils of Paris and Préaux authorized intercessory prayers beseeching God's mercy for their brethren in the

---

[131] Peter of Vaux de Cernay, ii. 47–8, 146, 149, 152–3; William of Puylaurens, 82, 86. See also Peter of Vaux de Cernay, i. 272.

[132] Roger of Howden, *Gesta*, ii. 19; *Sacrorum conciliorum collectio*, xxii. cols. 534–5; Arnold of Lübeck, 170.

[133] Innocent III, PL ccxvi. cols. 698–9.

[134] Tangl, 95–6.

[135] Honorius III, no. 885.

Holy Land and the Latin Empire of Constantinople.[136] This idea of a general supplication in the face of the growing threat from the Tartars and Muslims was also to be found in the treatises submitted to the Second Council of Lyons. As we have seen, Humbert of Romans urged Christians to follow the example of the Hebrews, who had placated God's anger by means of fasting, alms, and processions,[137] and Gilbert of Tournai suggested that a duty of prayers should be imposed upon the whole church. He pointed out that when Moses stood on the hill and held up the rod of God in his hand, the forces of Israel were victorious over Amalek, and when he let down his hand the latter prevailed (Exod. 17: 8-14). In a similar way the walls of Jericho crumbled when the people shouted and the priests blew their trumpets. (Josh. 6: 20)[138] Fidenzio of Padua's memoir was mainly concerned with the military tactics and possible means of recovering the Holy Land, but he also made some observations about the conduct of the army and reminded the crusaders that they should rely as much upon prayers as upon their own strength.[139]

The intention of crusaders

Having impressed upon the crusaders the connection between human sinfulness and a military reverse, clerical apologists urged them to behave as befitted those who had undertaken God's work. They described the virtues of the *miles Christi*, who alone would receive the reward of eternal salvation, and chief amongst these was the right inward disposition, or 'right intention'.[140] According to the pilgrimage tradition, a major source of crusading ideology, the physical *imitatio Christi* was of little value unless it was also accompanied by an internal, spiritual *imitatio*, which took the form of a moral regeneration and was a mark of true repentance. The crusaders

---

[136] Odo Rigaud, 389; William of Nangis, *Gesta Sancti Ludovici*, RHGF xx. 412.

[137] Humbert of Romans, *Opus tripartitum*, 198, 204.

[138] Gilbert of Tournai, *Collectio*, 40. Parallels have been drawn between this and Peter of Blois's letter to the Bishop of Orléans. See Stroick, 435.

[139] Fidenzio of Padua, 40-1.

[140] See Blake, 25-30.

were reminded that only those who possessed this 'right intention' would derive any benefit from the perilous journey to the Holy Land:[141] thus Peter the Venerable warned Abbot Theobald of St Columba at Sens, who had vowed to go on the Second Crusade, to shun levity, curiosity, and the love of vain praise;[142] and in his apologia for the Templars, St Bernard emphasized the importance of the spiritual condition of the sinner in the eyes of God. He argued that the crusader's undertaking would be in vain if he did not possess internal contrition and true repentance;[143] and complained to Suger of two knights who had just returned from the Holy Land, intending to resume their evil ways: 'notice with what dispositions they must have set out on the road to Jerusalem when they return in this frame of mind! How rightly can it be said . . . "thou hast struck them and they have not grieved" ' (Jer. 5: 3).[144]

The fullest treatment of 'right intention' is to be found in Ralph Niger's treatise *De re militari*. Like other chroniclers, Ralph had attributed the collapse of the Second Crusade to a divine judgement upon men's sins;[145] he advised those who planned to join the Third Crusade to make sure that they underwent a spiritual pilgrimage to the heavenly Jerusalem, as well as a physical pilgrimage to the earthly city, for all their labours would be in vain if they were not purified themselves. Ralph believed that the Bible recounted the events of the only true pilgrimages and warned pilgrims that, if they did not draw lessons from them, God would see that they perished in the desert like many of the Hebrews. (Num. 14: 37–8). He maintained that it was better to follow the way of faith, grace, and justice than to go on any bodily pilgrimage, and that anyone who failed to build Jerusalem, the vision of peace, within himself would derive no benefit from his journey to its earthly counterpart. Ralph warned

---

[141] Gaucelm Faidit, 'Del gran golfe de mar', st. iv, ed. cit. 474–5; John of Joinville, 45–6.

[142] Peter the Venerable, *Letters*, i. 358–60.

[143] Bernard, *Opera*, iii. 223, 237–8, viii. 315. See also Henry of Albano, cols. 249–52, 356–7; Constable, 'The Second Crusade as Seen by Contemporaries', *Traditio*, ix (1953), 251.

[144] Bernard, *Opera*, viii. 339. See also Caesar of Heisterbach, *Dialogus miraculorum*, i. 12.   [145] Ralph Niger, *Chronica universalis*, 335.

that the pilgrim should examine his conduct and make sure that he had performed an adequate act of satisfaction before he set out. Even then he should be wary, for evil spirits laid traps for men along the way.[146]

There is another interesting discussion of 'right intention' in John of Garland's rhetorical treatise *Parisiana Poetria*, written at the time of the Fifth Crusade. In this work John included an exhortation to the faithful to take the cross and described an allegorical battle—*psychomachia*—which took place within the soul of the crusader; a struggle between the armies of the virtues and vices. He concluded that the crusader would be victorious in his real battle against the Muslims only if the virtues were triumphant within him.[147]

This emphasis upon the crusader's inward disposition can also be found in the works of the vernacular poets. For example, the German minnesinger, Hartmann von Aue, who took part either in the Third Crusade or in the German expedition of 1197, reiterated that, if one was to be worthy of the cross and win a reward of eternal happiness, then one must have a pure heart.[148] And in a poem dated *c.*1213, the troubadour Aimeric de Péguilhan declared that God summoned only the bold and the good to fight in the Latin East.[149] The poet and crusader Theobald of Champagne urged men to amend themselves before they took the cross, for the Lord would permit only those with a just and loyal heart to conquer his homeland.[150]

According to the apologists, the true crusader did not just bear the cross as an outward symbol upon his clothes: it was also imprinted upon his heart, mind, or body.[151] Fulcher of Chartres wrote of those who had taken the cross at Clermont: 'Since they thus decorated themselves with this mark of their faith, in the end they obtained from the symbol the reality itself. They marked themselves with the (outward) sign so that they might attain the (inner) reality.'[152] And several

[146] Id. *DRM* 92-3, 147, 179, 182-3, 218-19.
[147] John of Garland, *Parisiana Poetria*, 68-73, 244-5.
[148] 'Dem kriuze zimet wol reiner muot', *MF* 412.
[149] Aimeric de Péguilhan, 'Ara parra qual seran enveyos', ed. cit. 85-6.
[150] 'Au tans plein de felonie', *Chansons de croisade*, 182.
[151] See above, p. 38.
[152] Fulcher of Chartres, 140-2.

other chroniclers recorded the miraculous appearance of the cross upon men's flesh during the preaching of the First Crusade or in the course of the expedition itself.[153] Writing in the aftermath of the battle of Hattin, Ralph Niger cautioned men who hastened to sew the cross upon their clothes, for their efforts would be in vain unless they also fought with spiritual arms and made this plain in their works,[154] and the same imagery was used by the minnesinger Hartmann von Aue.[155] In a sermon preached upon the Festival of the Exaltation of the Cross in 1189, Alan of Lille observed that the sign of the internal cross was penance, and exhorted crusaders to mark this symbol upon their hearts, for without it the external cross became worthless and futile.[156] This theme was taken up again in two medieval proverbs:

> Crux in mantellis non est purgatio pellis.
>
> Crux vestimenti dat premia nulla ferenti—
> Hoc animo senti—nisi sit prius insita menti.[157]

And in the thirteenth century, such popular imagery was adopted by Innocent III. In a letter dated 1212, the pope complained of false crusaders who postponed their departure for the East because they only bore the symbol of the cross upon their clothes.[158]

Since a divine judgement upon human sinfulness seemed to be the only adequate explanation for God's apparent desertion of his people, it is hardly surprising that the crusaders found themselves the subject of much criticism. Chroniclers drew a connection between the absence of 'right intention' and a military reverse and pointed out the lessons to be drawn from previous expeditions. This anxiety to account for a defeat seems to have acted as a stimulus to criticism of the army's conduct. Certain themes of criticism

---

[153] Bernold of St Blasien, 464; Ekkehard of Aura, *Hierosolymita*, 19; Fulcher of Chartres, 169-70; Raymond of Aguilers, 102.

[154] Ralph Niger, *DRM* 94.

[155] See above p. 97 n. 148 and Thomasin von Zirclaira, ll. 11607-78.

[156] Alan of Lille, 'Sermo de cruce domini', *Textes inédits*, ed. M. T. d'Alverny, Études de philosophie médiévale, lii (Paris, 1965), 281-2.

[157] *Proverbia sententiaeque Latinitatis medii aevi*, ed. H. Walther, Carmina Medii Aevi Posterioris Latina, II (Göttingen, 1963-7), nos. 3824, 3827.

[158] Innocent III, PL ccxvi, cols. 729-30. See also Reinmar der Fiedler, 'Ez ist in . . . vil swaere', *Minnesinger*, ii. 162.

seem to have been particularly popular and were repeated by chroniclers throughout the twelfth and thirteenth centuries.

One common accusation levelled against the crusaders was that they were guilty of pride, and certain chroniclers maintained that this overconfidence had been the cause of previous Christian reverses. For example, Fulcher of Chartres exhorted men to place their trust in God rather than in arms, strength, or numbers, and attributed the defeats of Count William of Poitou and King Baldwin, at the battles of Heraclea and Ramla on the 1101 crusade, to a divine judgement upon their arrogance.[159] A similar explanation was advanced by contemporaries for the sudden collapse of the Second Crusade. In a sermon preached after Louis VII's return from the East, St Bernard was said to have remarked that the expedition failed because of the pride of the army,[160] and a number of chroniclers observed that the retreat from Damascus was God's way of humbling the proud (Isa. 2: 12-17); the Lord willed that the Christians should suffer and perish because they had trusted in their own strength rather than in his power and mercy.[161] As we have seen, William of St Denis drew parallels between the crusade and the Greek campaign of Xerxes, and, whilst he believed that both expeditions had failed because of the unwieldy nature of the armies, he also placed some of the blame for their defeat upon the overconfidence of the leaders.[162] The crusaders' arrogance was thought to be reflected in their conduct of the expedition.[163] Thus Louis

[159] Fulcher of Chartres, 433, 438-9, 454.

[160] Constable, 'A Report of a Lost Sermon', 49-52. This sermon is attributed to Bernard, but this seems doubtful for it only occurs in a late 13th-c. manuscript and belongs to a collection of *exempla* gathered by an itinerant friar after 1254. See *Catalogue of Western Manuscripts in the Old Royal and King's Collections, British Museum*, ed. J. P. Gilson and G. F. Warner, i (London, 1921) 185.

[161] Otto of Freising, *Gesta Friderici*, 92; Vincent of Prague, 663; Odo of Deuil, 22, 90; *Casus monasterii Petrishusensis*, 674; *Annales Magdeburgenses*, 188; *Annales Egmundani*, MGH SS xvi. 456; Geoffrey of Vigeois, *Chronicon*, extr. RHGF xii. 436; *Vita Ludovici summatim complectens*, ibid. 286. See also John of Ford, *Life of Wulfric of Haselbury*, ed. M. Bell, Somerset Record Society Publications, XLVIII (Frome, 1933), 112.

[162] See above, p. 28 n. 6.

[163] *Liber de compositone castri Ambaziae et ipsius dominorum gesta*, ed. L. Halphen and R. Poupardin, *Chroniques des comtes d'Anjou* (Paris, 1913), 24.

VII was criticized for refusing to take the Greeks' advice about which route the French army should follow through Asia Minor;[164] and in a letter to Abbot Suger, the king admitted that he had set out recklessly and that consequently some of the responsibility for the failure of the crusade lay with him.[165] In a similar way King Conrad of Germany was accused of ignoring the Byzantine Emperor's recommendations;[166] according to Odo of Deuil, when he related his misfortunes to Louis VII he placed much of the blame for the destruction of his army upon his own shoulders:

> when I conducted a numerous and wealthy army from my realm, if I had rendered the proper thanks to the giver of good things, perhaps he would have preserved what he had given . . . if confident of victory over the Turks, I had not been puffed up because of my large force, but had placed my hope humbly in the Lord of hosts, God would not have subdued an arrogance which did not exist.[167]

The most successful element of the Second Crusade was undoubtedly the English and Flemish contingent, which captured Lisbon; and the contrast between its achievements and the reverse at Damascus led two chroniclers to comment: 'God resisteth the proud, but to the humble he giveth grace'.[168] (Jas. 4: 6, 1 Pet. 5:5). This dictum was repeated by two historians of the Fifth Crusade[169] and the connection between pride and the loss of Damietta was also highlighted by Oliver of Paderborn.[170]

In a similar way, William of Puylaurens attributed the initial success of the Albigensian Crusade to divine aid and maintained that the crusaders themselves were to blame for their defeats after 1215, for they had neglected the Lord. William reminded his readers that God had used the Egyptians as a means of punishing the Hebrews for their sins and would ensure that the Christians also drank the very dregs of his cup of wrath.[171] The anonymous continuator of *La Chanson*

---

[164] *Chronicon Mauriniacense*, extr. RHGF xiv. 88. See also Odo of Deuil, 58.

[165] Suger, *Epistolae*, RHGF xv. 496.

[166] *Annales Herbipolenses*, 4–5. See also *Annales Egmundani*, 456.

[167] Odo of Deuil, 90, 98–100.

[168] Henry of Huntingdon, 280–1; William of Newburgh, i. 66.

[169] *Gesta obsidionis Damiate*, 103; John of Tulbia, 132.

[170] Oliver of Paderborn, *Historia Damiatina*, 213. See also Burchard of Ursperg, *Chronicon*, MGH SS xxiii. 381.

[171] William of Puylaurens, 94–6.

de la croisade albigeoise put his criticisms of the army's behaviour into the mouths of the crusaders themselves. Thus at the height of the siege of Beaucaire in 1217, he made Simon of Montfort ask his barons why God permitted his enemies to be victorious; Alan of Roucy replied that the Lord had withdrawn his favour from the crusaders because of Simon's pride and arrogance and he repeated these charges in answer to a similar question during the siege of Toulouse. Another French knight, Robert of Picquigny, gave the same explanation for Raymond VII's success.[172]

This strain of criticism was taken up again by a poor knight or sergeant on Theobald of Champagne's crusade. He complained that, rather than attack any Muslim strongholds, the leaders had devoted their energies to the pursuit of rivalries amongst themselves and commented that the Lord had punished them for their arrogance, for the army which had left France so full of promise had returned home ignominiously.[173] And Matthew Paris attributed the disaster at Mansurah to God's exasperation with the pride of Louis IX's brother Robert of Artois, who had led the advance against the Muslims.[174]

The same pattern of repetition emerges from an analysis of criticism of avarice, which seems to have been a popular explanation for a defeat from the time of the First Crusade. For example, Albert of Aix ascribed the surprise defeat of the forces of Emicho of Leiningen at the siege of Wieselberg in 1096 to a divine judgement, because they had massacred Jews out of greed rather than a sense of divine justice;[175] and Fulcher of Chartres declared that the Lord willed that the Christians should suffer at Dorylaeum because they were corrupted by avarice.[176] This connection between greed and a military reverse was made again by the historian of the Fourth Crusade, Robert of Clari. He complained that after the siege of Constantinople the leaders had seized the wealth

---

[172] *La Chanson de la croisade albigeoise*, ed. E. Martin-Chabot (Paris, 1931–60), ii. 130; iii. 28, 66–8. (Cf. ibid. iii. 24, 172, 302.)

[173] 'Ne chant pas que que nus die', *Chansons de croisade*, 230–5. See also *L'estoire d'Eracles*, 550.

[174] Matthew Paris, *CM* v. 165.

[175] Albert of Aix, 295.

[176] Fulcher of Chartres, 196.

of the city for themselves and ignored the mass of the army and suggested that their defeat at Adrianople in 1205 was the Lord's vengeance for this.[177] William of Puylaurens seems to have been particularly anxious to find an explanation for the victories of Count Raymond VII after the Fourth Lateran Council, and, in addition to accusing the crusaders of pride, he lamented that they had become slaves to their own cupidity. William pointed out that they had conquered the South with God's aid, but, when they divided it amongst themselves, they forgot that which pertained to Christ; and as a punishment for this the Lord withdrew his favour from their endeavours.[178] The historian of the Fifth Crusade, Oliver of Paderborn, advanced a similar explanation for the loss of Damietta.[179]

The third main criticism of the crusaders was that they had committed fornication and adultery, and again it was suggested that their indisciplined behaviour had been responsible for several military reverses. A divine judgement upon the army's incontinence was put forward as yet another explanation for the misfortunes of the crusaders in Hungary in the early stages of the First Crusade, in particular the unexpected defeat of Emicho of Leiningen's forces at the siege of Wieselberg;[180] and chroniclers reverted to this argument to explain setbacks throughout the expedition. For example, according to Fulcher of Chartres, at the height of the first siege of Antioch, the Christians decided to expel women from the camp, 'lest by chance defiled by the sordidness of riotous living they should displease the Lord'; and the crusaders apparently regarded their suffering during the second siege as a further divine punishment, for, 'as soon as they had entered the city, many of them had mingled with unlawful women'.[181] Fulcher, however, may not be a reliable witness, for at the time he was with Baldwin of Boulogne at Edessa; if one reads the accounts of the chroniclers who were with the army at Antioch—Raymond of Aguilers, Peter Tudebode,

[177] Robert of Clari, 79-80, 95-6, 106.
[178] William of Puylaurens, 94-6.
[179] Oliver of Paderborn, *Historia Damiatina*, 277-8.
[180] Ekkehard of Aura, *Chronicon universale*, MGH SS vi. 208; Bernold of St Blasien, 464; *Annales Sancti Disibodi*, MGH SS xvii. 16; Albert of Aix, 295.
[181] Fulcher of Chartres, 223, 243.

and the author of the *Gesta Francorum*—this criticism is associated with Stephen of Valence's vision. In this Christ apparently reminded Stephen of his support in the past, attributed the crusaders' present suffering to their 'filthy lusts, which they satisfied with both Christian and loose pagan women', and promised them help if they reformed.[182] A similar sequence of events occurred during the siege of Ma'arrat-an-Nu'man. After the failure of the first assault, St Peter was said to have appeared to Peter Bartholomew and to have accused the crusaders of offending God by committing adultery; once again their victory was ascribed to their repentance.[183] A number of chroniclers also described the reversal of Christian fortunes at Damascus on the Second Crusade as a divine judgement upon the immorality of the army.[184] These accusations were repeated by historians of later crusades. The corruption of the army after the capture of Damietta was advanced as yet another reason for the failure of the Fifth Crusade;[185] and William of Puylaurens claimed that the Lord was so angered by the wantonness of the members of Foucaud of Berze's contingent on the Albigensian Crusade, who kept concubines and carried off other men's wives by force, that he willed that they should be defeated by the Count of Toulouse.[186] Gilbert of Tournai advanced a similar explanation for the collapse of Louis IX's first crusade.[187] The fact that chroniclers levelled the same criticisms against the crusaders, often offering a variety of explanations for a particular reverse, again suggests that they were searching for a satisfactory explanation for defeats in wars supposedly willed by God.

The presence or absence of 'right intention' was also thought to be manifested in the crusaders' outward conduct. For example, Albert of Aix praised his hero Godfrey of Bouillon because after the capture of Jerusalem he apparently chose to process around its walls wearing the dress of a humble

---

[182] *Gesta Francorum*, 58; Raymond of Aguilers, 72–4; Peter Tudebode, 99.

[183] Raymond of Aguilers, 97.

[184] William of Newburgh, i. 66; Gislebert of Mons, 516; Vincent of Prague, 663.

[185] Oliver of Paderborn, *Historia Damiatina*, 252.

[186] William of Puylaurens, 108–10.

[187] Gilbert of Tournai, *Eruditio regum*, 14. See also John of Joinville, 60.

pilgrim and to give thanks to God for this victory in the Holy
Sepulchre whilst the other leaders were sacking the city.[188]
During the twelfth century a definite pattern seems to have
been established in acts of outward devotion, and both
Louis VII and Richard I visited local shrines before they
departed for the East.[189] The Emperor Frederick I was com-
mended because he resembled a pilgrim both in his external
dress and his internal disposition;[190] but the culmination of
this image of a *miles peregrinus* was undoubtedly Louis IX.
He was said to have received the staff and scrip at Saint
Denis and then to have journeyed as a barefoot pilgrim from
Notre-Dame in Paris to the abbey of St Antoine.[191] Before
he left for the East in 1248, he confirmed the privileges
of several religious foundations and probably attended
an exposition of the relics of the Passion at the Sainte
Chapelle.[192] Louis's biographer, John of Joinville, portrayed
himself in the same mould. He apparently received the staff
and scrip from the Abbot of Cheminon and on his journey
to the port of embarkation he visited several local shrines.[193]

A display of moderation in dress and demeanour was
thought to be a clear external manifestation of 'right intention'.
Hence when the Council of Troyes commissioned St Bernard
to draw up a Rule for the recently founded Order of the
Temple in 1128, he placed great emphasis upon the prohibition of elaborate arms and clothing.[194] And in his
apologia *De laude novae militiae* he drew a contrast between
the more worldly preoccupations of the laity and the objectives
of the new knighthood: whereas the secular knight wore
bejewelled armour and advanced into battle on a richly
caparisoned horse, the Templar preferred to place his trust
in strong weapons and a swift rather than a handsomely

---

[188] Albert of Aix, 481.

[189] See Odo of Deuil, 16–18; Ambroise, ll. 287–8; *Itinerarium regis Ricardi*, 147.

[190] *Itinerarium peregrinorum*, 278.

[191] Matthew Paris, *CM* v. 22; William of St. Panthus, *Vie de Saint Louis*, ed. Delaborde (Paris, 1899), 22, 40; *Chronicon Lirensis monasterii*, extr. RHGF xxiii. 469. See also E. R. Labande, 'Saint Louis pèlerin', *Revue d'histoire de l'église de France*, lvii (1971), 13–15.

[192] See Jordan, *Louis IX*, 108–10.

[193] John of Joinville, 43–5.

[194] *La Règle du Temple*, ed. H. de Curzon (Paris, 1886), ch. 18, 51–3.

decorated horse.[195] At the same time there was sumptuary legislation for ordinary ecclesiastics[196] and these rulings seem to have influenced attitudes towards the crusaders.

The first real codification of crusading practices is to be found in Eugenius III's bull *Quantum praedecessores*, issued in December 1145: prominent in which were sumptuary laws. Like St Bernard, Eugenius attributed the loss of Edessa in 1144 to men's sins and urged the French to seek God's forgiveness by taking the cross. Henceforward they should not concern themselves

with costly garments, external appearances, dogs, hawks, or other things which are signs of licentiousness . . . those who do such holy work . . . shall with all their strength devote their attention and diligence to arms, horses, and other things with which they may fight against the Muslims.[197]

It is significant that, when the bull was reissued in March 1146,[198] the only important alteration in the text concerned the prohibition of extravagance; now crusaders were forbidden to wear furs—*variis aut grisiis*[199]—or to bear gold or silver arms.[200] And it has been suggested that this additional ruling was the result of St Bernard's personal influence at the curia during the Franco-papal negotiations about the crusade early in 1146.[201] Significantly there was no sumptuary

[195] Bernard, *Opera*, iii. 216, 220-1.

[196] See Bernard's letter to Fulk of Lincoln, *Opera*, vii. 21-2; Peter the Venerable, *Statuta*, ed. Constable, Corpus consuetudinum monasticorum, VI (Siegburg, 1975), 55; *Councils and Synods with Other Documents Relating to the English Church*, i, ed. D. Whitelock, M. Brett and C. N. L. Brooke, (Oxford, 1982), 2, 676, 680, 683, 778.

[197] Otto of Freising, *Gesta Friderici*, 55-8.

[198] See Berry, 'The Second Crusade', 466-9.

[199] An anonymous poet writing in 1146 exhorted others to follow the example of Louis VII, who abandoned 'furs of vair and gris' after he had taken the cross. See 'Chevalier mult estes guariz', *Chansons de croisade*, 9. Indeed this form of renunciation may have been associated with the crusades as early as 1101. In his poem 'Pos de chantar m'es pres talenz', st. ix, *Les Chansons de Guillaume IX, duc d'Aquitaine*, ed. Jeanroy (Paris, 1913), 29, William IX of Poitou declared; 'So do I give up joy and delight and vair and gris and sable.' Topsfield, 40, argues that this poem was written in 1111 or 1112 when William was lying wounded after the siege of Taillebourg. J. L. Cate, 'A Gay Crusader', *Byzantion*, xvi (1942-3), 517, however, maintains that it referred to his departure on crusade in 1101.

[200] Eugenius III, 'Text der Kreuzzugsbulle', 304.

[201] E. Caspar, 'Die Kreuzzugsbullen Eugens III.', *Neues Archiv der Gesellschaft für ältere deutsche Geschichtskunde*, xlv (1924), 290-3.

clause in Eugenius' letter to the Italians dated October 1146,[202] and a reference to the March version of the bull can be found in St Bernard's letter to Duke Vladislav of Bohemia. The Abbot of Clairvaux's interest in sumptuary legislation was also highlighted in a letter addressed to the members of the German contingent.[203] These rulings seem to have influenced other groups of crusaders: on their own initiative the English members of the Lisbon expedition drew up a similar code of practice with regulations about dress.[204] In his reflections upon the Second Crusade, Odo of Deüil praised the wisdom and usefulness of the papal directives and commented that those who had ignored them had acted 'foolishly and unprofitably'.[205]

The March version of *Quantum praedecessores* was reissued in 1165 by Alexander III,[206] and seems to have become the source for future crusading enactments. In his bull *Audita tremendi*, issued after the defeat at Hattin, Gregory VIII exhorted crusaders to behave as if they were performing an act of penance rather than pursuing vainglory: and, following *Quantum praedecessores*, he advised them to be modest in their bearing and habit and not to journey to the Holy Land in costly garments with dogs and birds, but rather to take only that which could be of use against the Muslims.[207] Similar provisions were incorporated in Henry II's and Philip Augustus' rulings for the Third Crusade. The Council of Le Mans decreed that no crusader might appear in vair, gris, sable, or scarlet; and gambling was forbidden, as were dinners of more than two courses.[208] These injunctions were reiterated by the preachers of the crusade. For example, at the assembly at Mainz, Cardinal Henry of Albano urged the German crusaders to act so that 'dress . . . and behaviour confess the

---

[202] 'Papsturkunden in Malta', ed. P. Kehr, *Nachrichten von der Königlichen Gesellschaft der Wissenschaften zu Göttingen, philologisch-historische Klasse* (1899), 389–90.

[203] Bernard, *Opera*, viii. 433, 436.

[204] *De expugnatione Lyxbonensi*, ed. C. W. David (New York, 1936), 56.

[205] Odo of Deuil, 8, 94.

[206] Alexander III, *Opera*, PL cc, col. 386.

[207] *Historia de expeditione Friderici*, 10. See also *Regesta Pontificum Romanorum*, comp. Jaffé, no. 16013.

[208] Roger of Howden, *Chronica*, ii. 336–7. For similar rulings issued by the kings at Messina see id. *Gesta*, ii. 130–1.

faith which our tongue professes'.[209] According to William of Newburgh, for some time after he had taken the cross Hugh of Puiset, Bishop of Durham, lived in unaccustomed severity;[210] and Archbishop Baldwin of Canterbury lamented that the members of the Third Crusade at Acre failed to behave as befitted their status, but frequented taverns and gambling houses.[211]

In the aftermath of Hattin, Gregory VIII and Clement III also instituted various measures of reform for the clergy and members of lay society, including prohibitions against gambling, hunting, feasting and luxurious clothes.[212] And, following the Christian defeat by the Moors at the battle of Alarcos in 1195, the Council of Montpellier ordered the clergy and laity in the diocese of Narbonne to shun vain things and to wear simple garments as a mark of repentance, in the hope that this emendation would cause God to have mercy on his people and release them from Muslim domination.[213]

Sumptuary clauses remained a feature of crusading enactments in the pontificate of Innocent III. Like his predecessors, the pope exhorted the members of the Fourth Crusade to walk in the Lord's way, shunning the paths of the vain and those who passed their time in feasting and drinking,[214] and the papal legate Abbot Arnaud of Cîteaux was apparently anxious that those who took the cross for the Albigensian expedition should abandon wine, extravagant meals, and fine clothes.[215] In the thirteenth century a connection came to be drawn between the army's failure to follow the papal directives and a military reverse. The Fourth Lateran Council had enjoined crusaders to exercise moderation in food and clothing,[216] but this ruling seems to have been ignored. Two contemporary chroniclers remarked that after the capture

---

[209] *Historia de expeditione Friderici*, 13.

[210] William of Newburgh, i. 275; ii. 438.

[211] *Epistolae Cantuarienses*, ed. W. Stubbs (London, 1865), 328-9; *Itinerarium peregrinorum*, 356-7.

[212] Roger of Howden, *Gesta*, ii. 19; *Sacrorum conciliorum collectio*, xxii. cols. 534-5; Arnold of Lübeck, 170. See also Henry of Albano's appeal to the clergy, cols. 247-9.

[213] *Sacrorum conciliorum collectio*, xxii, col. 670.

[214] Innocent III, PL ccxiv, col. 312.

[215] *La Chanson de la croisade albigeoise*, i. 20.　　　　[216] *COD* 267.

of Damietta the members of the Fifth Crusade had given
themselves up to drunkenness and feasting; they suggested
that this was one reason for the ultimate failure of the
expedition.[217] When Louis IX took the cross in 1244, he
apparently put aside his regal robes and assumed more
sombre garments.[218] But, although the First Council of
Lyons had repeated the provisions of 1215 and urged noble
crusaders to 'abstain from all useless and superfluous expenditure on banquets and other festivities',[219] the king's
example does not seem to have been followed. John of
Joinville denounced the barons because they misused the
booty from Damietta, spending it on lavish banquets at
which vast amounts of food were consumed, and he described
Louis's grief and anger when he saw his brother the Count
of Anjou gambling on board the ship taking him to the Holy
Land.[220] When the king returned to France he apparently
continued to shun the vanities of his early life as a mark
of penance:

the king led so devout a life that he never again wore furs of vair or
gris or scarlet or gilt stirrups or spurs. His clothing was of undyed or
grey woollen cloth . . . He was so temperate at table that he ordered
no special dishes for himself (and) . . . he mixed his wine with water.[211]

The relationship between the conduct of the army and a defeat
was also pointed out by Fidenzio of Padua. In his treatise
written after the Second Council of Lyons, he reminded
crusaders of the fate of previous expeditions and warned
them that they would be victorious only if they were chaste
and sober, and avoided any form of excess.[222]

---

[217] Oliver of Paderborn, *Historia Damiatina*, 252, 237-8; *L'estoire d'Eracles*,
348-9.
[218] *Grandes chroniques de France*, ed. J. Viard, (Paris, 1920-53), vii. 118;
William of Nangis, 356.   [219] COD 298.
[220] John of Joinville, 60, 144.
[221] Ibid. 239-40. See also William of St Panthus, 111; Jordan, *Louis IX*,
129, n. 158.   [222] Fidenzio of Padua, 35-6, 38-40.

PART II
CRITICISM OF CRUSADES

CHAPTER IV

Papal and royal taxation

THE high cost of provisioning and transporting an army in the Central Middle Ages meant that royal and papal taxation became the main source of finance for the crusades. For various reasons these impositions aroused criticism throughout Western Europe.

Claims for exemption

Certain religious orders objected to taxation in principle and claimed exemption from both royal and papal levies. For example, the Cistercians refused to pay the Saladin tithe of 1188;[1] and when Innocent III asked them for a fiftieth in 1199,[2] as their contribution to the first clerical income-tax, a deputation of abbots was sent to Rome to remind the pope of the order's privileges. By the time the abbots reached the curia, Innocent had already withdrawn his demand, apparently as a result of a visit from a monk named Reinier. The latter claimed to have had a vision in which the Virgin Mary had appeared and told him to warn the pope not to despoil her beloved sons, the Cistercians; it was rumoured that Innocent heeded this admonition and confirmed the monks' immunity from taxation.[3] As a token of good will, the order then agreed to make a collection of two thousand marks for the Fourth Crusade; in 1203 the Chapter-General instructed abbots whose houses had still not paid their contribution to do so within a specified time or suffer a penalty.[4] The Cistercians,

[1] *Annales de Waverleia*, 245.

[2] Innocent III, PL ccxiv, col. 827. The Premonstratensians, Grandimontines, and Carthusians were also asked for a fiftieth.

[3] Ralph of Coggeshall, 130–3; *Annales de Waverleia*, 253; *Chronicon monasterii Campensis*, ed. G. Eckertz, *Fontes adhuc inediti rerum Rhenanarum* (Cologne, 1864–70), ii. 345–6; Caesar of Heisterbach, *Dialogus miraculorum*, ii. 7–8.

[4] *Regesta Pontificum Romanorum*, comp. A. Potthast (Berlin, 1874–5), no.

Cluniacs, Grandimontines, and Premonstratensians were also exempted from the twentieth authorized by the Fourth Lateran Council in 1215;[5] this privilege was reaffirmed by the First Council of Lyons in 1245.[6] Some French royal officials, however, appear to have been over-zealous in their collection of the crusading tenth. The *bailli* in the Mâconnais, Baldwin of Pian, confiscated the goods of the Abbot of Cluny when he refused to contribute. Having failed to obtain redress from the Regent Queen Blanche, the monks appealed to their overlord the pope. Innocent IV confirmed their immunity and urged the crusading King Louis IX to discipline his official.[7] The English Cistercians also appear to have persuaded Henry III to grant them exemption from the taxes associated with his Sicilian venture and in 1256 Pope Alexander IV repeated their immunity from all financial levies.[8] Further negotiations were held between the Chapter-General and the papacy in the 1260s; although the monks eventually agreed to make a composition for Charles of Anjou's expedition to Southern Italy, in return they demanded a reaffirmation of their privileges.[9]

The other body which claimed exemption from taxation was the Spanish church. Its prelates objected to the papal levies on the grounds that all the resources within the Iberian peninsula should be devoted to the *Reconquista*, rather than diverted to the Latin East.[10] In 1212 Kings Peter II of Aragon and Alfonso VIII of Castile had won a great victory over the Almohads at the battle of Las Navas de Tolosa. But the cost of the campaign had impoverished the Spanish clergy,[11] and

1435; *Statuta Ordinis Cisterciensis*, i no. 51, 274; no. 27, 290. See also *Statuta*, i no. 32, 424. For further details of the dispute between the papacy and the and the Cistercians, see Brown, 'The Cistercians', 69-73.

[5] *COD* 269. The religious orders to be exempted were specified in later papal letters. See Honorius III, nos. 101-2, 652, 1921, 2088, 2090, 2558.

[6] *Maius chronicon Lemovicense*, RHGF xxi. 766.

[7] Innocent IV, nos. 5597-9. For further details of this incident, see Jordan, *Louis IX*, 80, 121-2.

[8] Matthew Paris, *CM* v. 553-7; *Annales de Waverleia*, 348.

[9] *Statuta Ordinis Cisterciensis*, iii no. 2, 18; no. 7, 60; no. 24, 72-3; no. 13, 107; no. 7, 116.

[10] See P. A. Linehan, 'Religion, Nationalism and National Identity in Medieval Spain', *Studies in Church History*, xviii (1982), 188-92.

[11] See 'Chronique latine inédite des Rois de Castille (1236)', ed. G. Cirot, *Bulletin hispanique*, xiv (1912), 335.

the situation was exacerbated in 1213 when Innocent III revoked the crusading indulgence for non-Spaniards fighting the Moors and gave priority to the Fifth Crusade.[12] The Spanish representatives at the Fourth Lateran Council begged the pope to restore the crusading indulgence to the *Reconquista*;[13] but Innocent refused to divert any aid from the East and instructed the prelates to contribute to the triennial twentieth levied to finance the expedition to Egypt.[14] Not surprisingly this ruling figured prominently in the Spanish chroniclers' accounts of the Council;[15] when they returned home the clergy seem to have used every means at their disposal to frustrate the collection of the tax. Innocent had entrusted this task in Spain to the regional Masters of the Military Orders and the cantor and archdeacon of Zamora; but, because of the scale of the undertaking, they were dependent upon local co-operation, which was not forthcoming. Some bishops alleged that they were not responsible for summoning diocesan synods to approve the levy and others that they were not obliged to pay in cash; November 1216, the deadline which Innocent III had set for payment, passed without any result. In December his successor Honorius III answered a series of objections posed by the chapter of Compostela; in the following February he ordered the bishops to expedite the collection of the twentieth.[16] Once again the situation was complicated by the progress of the *Reconquista*. In the summer of 1217 a Frisian-German expedition, under the joint command of Counts William of Holland and George of Wied, had combined in a successful attack upon the Muslim stronghold of Alcácer do Sal. The leaders were anxious to continue the campaign against the Moors and begged the pope to grant them the proceeds of the twentieth in the Spanish kingdoms and restore the crusading indulgence for non-Spanish members of the army.[17] Honorius, however, remained

---

[12] Tangl, 94.

[13] See Honorius III, Appendix I, no. 7.   [14] *COD* 268-9.

[15] See Luke of Tuy, 113; Gil de Zamora, 'Biografías de San Fernando y de Alfonso el Sabio', publ. F. Fita, *Boletín de la Real Academia de la Historia*, v (1884), 312.   [16] Honorius III, nos. 132, 337.

[17] MGH Epistolae saeculi XIII, i. 27-8, 32-4. See also Riant, *Expéditions et pèlerinages des Scandinaves en Terre Sainte* (Paris, 1865), 324-9.

determined not to divert any resources from the Fifth Crusade. Although in January 1218 he granted Archbishop Rodrigo of Toledo legatine authority in the kingdoms of Léon, Castile, and Aragon, in connection with the new Christian offensive, he made further attempts to persuade the Spanish clergy to contribute towards the twentieth. When these failed, the pope appointed two canons of St Peter, Master Cintius and his chaplain Huguccio, as new collectors.[18] Still the twentieth remained seriously in arrears, and in the end Honorius was forced to agree to the prelates' demands and restore the crusading indulgence for those fighting in Spain. Moreover, perhaps influenced by recent disastrous harvests,[19] he granted Archbishop Rodrigo half the proceeds of the twentieth in the dioceses of Toledo and Segovia; in the following year he made over the entire uncollected balance to the legate for the *Reconquista.*[20]

It was not long, however, before the Spanish church was again required to contribute towards the cost of the Fifth Crusade.[21] Honorius had received reports of Rodrigo's peculation; although the charges levelled against the archbishop did not actually concern the twentieth, the pope seems to have suspected that its proceeds had also been misused. He therefore decided to withdraw his grant, justifying his action on the grounds that the legate's proposed campaign against the Moors had never materialized.[22] Not surprisingly these plans to collect the twentieth met with stern resistance from certain Spanish bishops, who refused to contribute even after the surrender of Damietta to the Muslims in August 1221. In fact, Archbishop Sparago of Tarragona had still not collected the arrears of the twentieth due in his province in January 1222, and the Archbishop of Compostela was said to owe eight hundred pounds.[23] In October 1225 Honorius sent yet another collector, Pelayo,

[18] Honorius III, nos. 1042, 1116, 1547, 1634.

[19] See *Gesta Episcoporum Leodiensium*, MGH SS xxv. 119; Linehan, *The Spanish Church and the Papacy in the Thirteenth Century* (Cambridge, 1971), 8.

[20] Honorius III, nos. 1864, 1930-1, 2488.

[21] Linehan, 'Documento español sobre la quinta cruzada', *Hispania sacra*, xx (1967), 181; J. G. Gaztambide, *Historia de la bula de la cruzada en España* (Vitoria, 1958), 134-6.

[22] Honorius III, nos. 2515-17, 2525; Linehan, *The Spanish Church*, 8-10.

[23] *Le Liber Censuum de l'église romaine*, ed. Fabre and Duchesne (Paris, 1905-52), i. 14*; Honorius III, no. 3729.

Bishop-elect of Lydda, to Spain with the commission to take charge of the balance of the tax due from the provinces of Braga and Compostela and the sees of León and Oviedo. But there is no indication that he was more successful in countering local opposition than his predecessors had been.[24]

In spite of severe financial difficulties, the Spanish clergy appear to have been anxious to contribute towards the papal campaigns against Frederick II in 1228 and 1240, because they feared that their own rulers might be tempted to follow his example and deny the liberties of the church.[25] But they remained opposed to any form of taxation for the crusades in the East, and there was further clerical resistance to the levies authorized by the First Council of Lyons in 1245, namely a twentieth for the campaign in the Holy Land and a subsidy for the Latin Empire of Constantinople.[26] In 1247 the Abbey of Montearagón protested that the papal collectors had no jurisdiction within its walls, and the clergy of the dioceses of Braga and Coimbra in Portugal declared that they were unable to contribute because of the difficulties in the kingdom.[27] Innocent IV had appointed the Franciscan Desiderius to co-ordinate the collection of the taxes throughout the Iberian peninsula, but, as in 1215, the absence of local co-operation made his officials' work almost impossible. One of Desiderius' agents threatened the dean and chapter of Toledo with excommunication if they had not paid the levies by Easter 1248; but these dire warnings seem to have been ignored and in March yet another collector was sent from Rome.[28] Once again the reason for the prelates' intransigence seems to have been that the papal request for aid coincided with a crucial stage in the *Reconquista*. In 1248, Ferdinand III of Castile had captured Seville, and at the same time the Kings of Aragon and Portugal won important victories in Valencia, Faro, and Silves.[29] Against this background of events it is hardly surprising that the

---

[24] Honorius III, nos. 5693, 5888; Linehan, op. cit. 19.

[25] For further details of the papal levies in 1240 and 1244, see Linehan, op. cit. 102, 112, 159-61, 191-3.

[26] *COD* 295, 299.

[27] Innocent IV, nos. 2388, 3561.

[28] Linehan, op. cit. 195-7.

[29] Gaztambide, 183-5.

clergy were reluctant to divert any resources to the East; in November 1248 the pope actually agreed to suspend the collection of the twentieth in Aragon so that the church might contribute towards the cost of King James's campaign.[30] In May 1249 the Castilians' sense of grievance turned to violence. When Master Manfred de' Roberti attempted to recover some property of the Roman church, and possibly some receipts of the subsidy which Bishop Vicente of Guarda had deposited with the Master of the Order of Alcántara, the brothers drew their swords and drove him off. It was only in 1255 that they were brought to justice and made to pay.[31] In an effort to collect at least some of the proceeds of the twentieth, in 1252 the papal nuncio Peter of Piperno granted defaulters such as the Archbishop of Tarragona and the Bishops of Pamplona and Segovia a further period of grace; and in the following year Innocent IV authorized the Bishop of Zamora to absolve clerks in his diocese who had been excommunicated for non-payment and to accept a reduced contribution. In May 1254 yet another nuncio, Brother Velascus, was sent to Spain with instructions to collect what was still owed; but his commission was invalidated when the pope died in December, and many accounts remained unsettled: for example, the 1,500 *aurei* 'of the twentieth and subsidy' owed by Archbishop Pedro of Tarragona were not paid until 1259, eight years after his death.[32]

As a former Patriarch of Jerusalem, Innocent's successor Urban IV was particularly anxious to send aid to the East; in 1262 he requested another subsidy from the Spanish church in order to finance the reconquest of the Latin Empire of Constantinople. Urban obviously expected to encounter resistance to this latest demand, for he advised the papal collector Raymond of Paphos to prepare the ground carefully: to seek the support of Alfonso X of Castile and then to impress upon the prelates the strategic importance

[30] Linehan, op. cit. 126, n. 6.

[31] Linehan, op. cit. 197, suggests that a similar incident may have been responsible for the general interdict which Manfred imposed upon the diocese of Calahorra.

[32] Innocent IV, nos. 5982, 6083, 6537, 7474, 8308; Linehan, op. cit. 198–200.

of the Latin Empire for the Holy Land. But before Raymond could present his case, the Castilian bishops appealed directly to the pope. They sent Urban lists of grievances or *gravamina*, which are especially interesting because they highlight the reasons behind earlier Spanish opposition to papal taxation. In the *gravamina* the bishops enumerated their past and present services to the Christian cause; they claimed that the Spanish victory at Las Navas de Tolosa had saved Europe from the Muslims and reminded the pope that this lengthy campaign had been a severe burden upon the church's resources. The prelates also underlined the disastrous effects of the recent famine and drought, and in this context, they denounced the frequent exactions of the papal nuncios, alleging that the Emperor Baldwin II of Constantinople had already received 40,000 *aurei* from them with seemingly little result.[33] The chapter of Toledo made a similar appeal on behalf of their province, which was forwarded to Rome by Bishop Pedro Lorenzo of Cuenca, who appended a letter of his own. In it Pedro argued that the pope would not have imposed such levies had he been aware of the desolation of the Spanish church; and proposed that the Castilian clergy should be exempted from future papal taxation on the grounds that it diverted much-needed resources from the *Reconquista.*[34] Urban seems to have paid no heed to these pleas, and in October 1263 sent another collector to Spain with instructions that, if aid was not forthcoming, it should be taken 'by compulsion'.[35]

At the same time the pope asked the Aragonese and Portuguese churches for another aid for the Holy Land; and in June 1264 he sent a long letter to all Spanish prelates describing the damage done to the church by the Muslims, heretics, and Staufen and requesting their urgent assistance. This levy was never collected. In the early summer the predictions of the Bishop of Cuenca about the fragility of Castile's frontier were proved correct: the Muslim King of Granada rose in revolt against Alfonso X. In order to

[33] E. Benito Ruano, 'La Iglesia española ante la caída del Imperio Latino de Constantinopla', *Hispania sacra*, xi (1958), 12–17; Linehan, 'The *Gravamina* of the Castilian church in 1262–3', *EHR* lxxxv (1970), 730–4, 746–7.

[34] Linehan, 'The *Gravamina*', 734–8, 747–9.

[35] Urban IV, *Registres*, ed. J. Guiraud (Paris, 1901), no. 740.

meet this new threat, Urban's successor Clement IV abandoned
the policy of making the peninsula contribute towards the
campaigns in the East. Henceforward he granted ecclesiastical
revenues to the Spanish prelates for use in the *Reconquista.* [36]

As we have seen, the religious orders objected to all forms
of taxation and the Spanish church resented the diversion of
resources from the *Reconquista.* But lay and ecclesiastical
critics elsewhere seem to have been mainly concerned with
the harshness and frequency of royal and papal demands,
coming as they did on top of taxes and subsidies for other
purposes. [37]

Royal taxation

The first royal crusading tax was levied in 1146 by Louis VII
of France to finance the Second Crusade. According to the
English chronicler Ralph of Diceto this took the form of
a general levy; but one must be wary of Ralph's testimony
since he used the same term, 'descriptio generalis', to refer
to the means by which the king supplied his army besieging
the town of Verneuil in 1173. [38] In fact it is more likely that
the tax resembled a feudal aid. There were complaints about
its severity from ecclesiastics associated with the crown. [39]
John, Abbot of Ferrières, appealed to the regent, Abbot
Suger, for more time to fulfil his obligations; [40] and the
Abbot of Saint-Benoît-sur-Loire begged the king to moderate
his demands because of recent poor harvests. The abbot
eventually reached a compromise with Louis about the
sum that was due, but even then he apparently found it
necessary to melt down some silver and gold in order to make
up the full amount. [41] The Bishop of Le Puy agreed to make
a contribution, in return for a confirmation of his privileges

[36] Linehan, *The Spanish Church*, 206-11; Clement IV, nos. 15-16, 19.

[37] For a list of papal impositions, see W. E. Lunt, *Financial Relations of the Papacy with England to 1327* (Cambridge, Mass. 1939), appendix I.

[38] Ralph of Diceto, i. 256-7, 372.

[39] See R. P. Grossman, 'The Financing of the Crusades' (unpubl. thesis, Chicago, 1965), 61-70. This tax may also have been levied by lesser lords such as the Count of Soissons. See Eugenius III, *Opera*, PL clxxx, col. 1118.

[40] Suger, 496.

[41] *Recueil des chartes de l'abbaye de Saint-Benoît-sur-Loire*, ed. M. Prou and A. Vidier (Paris, 1900-7), i. 340-2.

in the area; but significantly, even at this early stage, he
sought an assurance that this aid would neither prejudice
the rights of his church nor set a precedent for future impositions.[42] We have no record of the sum raised by the tax; but
it obviously failed to satisfy Louis's needs, for he wrote
several times from the East exhorting Suger to collect the
unpaid assessments or to arrange alternative means of
finance, namely loans.[43] Even so the Abbot of Mont-Saint-
Michel, Robert of Torigni, complained of the spoliation of
the poor and the church, and ascribed the failure of the
expedition to a divine judgement.[44] This explanation for the
reverse at Damascus was also adopted by other historians;
John of Salisbury, writing c.1169, observed:

in our own time . . . many princes went on . . . pilgrimage, but the most
wretched outcome . . . taught the lesson that gifts offered from theft
and wrongdoing are not pleasing to God.[45]

The first income-tax for the crusade in the Holy Land was
levied by the Kings of England and France in 1166, the year
after Alexander III's general exhortation to take the cross.[46]
According to the decree promulgated in the Angevin
domains the rate of assessment was to be twopence in the
pound sterling in the first year and one penny in each of the
four succeeding years; and this time the tax was to be paid by
the laity as well as the clergy.[47] Because of the relative
silence of the sources, some historians have questioned
whether this levy was ever collected.[48] But a number of contributions must have been received, for Robert of Torigni
reported that the kings clashed over the identity of the men
who should take the money to Jerusalem.[49] This imposition

[42] *Études sur les actes de Louis VII*, ed. A. Luchaire (Paris, 1885), no. 185.

[43] Suger, 487–8, 495–6, 509. See also William of St Denis, 'Vie de Suger',
ed. Lecoy de la Marche, *Œuvres de Suger* (Paris, 1867), 395.

[44] Robert of Torigni, 154.

[45] John of Salisbury, *Letters*, ii. 632–4. See also Geoffrey of Vigeois, 436.

[46] Robert of Torigni, 227; *Chronicon Petroburgense*, ed. T. Stapleton (London,
1849), 3; Smail, 11–12.

[47] Gervase of Canterbury, i. 198–9.

[48] Smail, 12; F. A. Cazel, 'The Tax of 1185 in Aid of the Holy Land', *Speculum*,
xxx (1950), 385–92.

[49] Robert of Torigni, 230, 249; Kedar, 'The General Tax of 1183 in the
Crusading Kingdom of Jerusalem: Innovation or Adaptation', *EHR* lxxxix (1974),
343.

of a tax levied upon income rather than property set an important precedent, but there is no evidence that it aroused any opposition; and the success of the experiment prompted Henry II and Philip Augustus to levy a second income-tax in 1185, in response to Patriarch Heraclius of Jerusalem's appeal for aid.[50] According to the monastic chronicler Gervase of Canterbury, Henry promised to contribute 50,000 silver marks towards the defence of the Latin Kingdom,[51] but it is unlikely that such a large sum was ever collected.[52] In a letter to the suffragans of the Archbishop of Canterbury, Peter of Blois described the perilous situation in the Latin East and the urgent need for aid,[53] and, although the Patriarch's personal behaviour and extravagant retinue aroused some criticism,[54] there do not seem to have been any complaints about the severity of the tax itself.

There was, however, an outspoken and hostile reaction to the third income-tax levied for the crusades, the so-called Saladin tithe, which was authorized by the Councils of Geddington and Le Mans in 1188.[55] This tax took the form of a tenth levied for one year on the income of clerks and laymen who had not taken the cross; Gervase of Canterbury claimed that the total sum raised in England was £130,000–£70,000 from Christians and £60,000 from the Jews.[56] Gervase's estimate is probably a deliberate exaggeration, intended to highlight the plight of his own church (Christchurch, Canterbury).[57] But there is no doubt that the heavy incidence of the tax and the method of assessment aroused bitter resentment both in England and France. In previous levies the amount due had been a matter for a man's conscience. Now it was made dependent upon the judgement of his neighbours. Collectors were appointed in each parish and given authority to investigate suspected cases of dishonesty; and, if they believed that anyone had given less than

[50] William of Newburgh, i. 247; Rigord, 46–8; Recueil des actes de Philippe Auguste, ed. Delaborde (Paris, 1916–43), i. 152–3.

[51] Gervase of Canterbury, i. 325.

[52] See Chronicon anonymi Laudunensis canonici, extr. RHGF xviii. 705; Mayer, 'Henry II', 731–4.

[53] Ralph Niger, DRM 186–7, 193–4.   [54] Peter of Blois, Opera, i. 309.

[55] Roger of Howden, Gesta, ii. 30–1; Gervase of Canterbury, i. 409.

[56] Gervase of Canterbury, i. 422.

[57] For the background to Gervase's history, see Gransden, 253–60.

he ought, they were instructed to refer the matter to the judgement of four or six law-worthy men. A similar method was adopted in the towns and those who rebelled and refused to agree to their revised assessment were apparently imprisoned until they had submitted.[58]

In England, Ralph of Diceto, now Dean of St Paul's, protested that the tithe terrified both the clergy and the laity by its violence;[59] and the historian of Durham, Geoffrey of Coldingham, wrote that it arose from the root of cupidity.[60] The chronicler Ralph of Coggeshall even suggested that the renewed wars in France were a divine punishment for the kings' rapacity.[61] According to Gervase of Canterbury, Archbishop Baldwin was widely condemned because it was rumoured that the tithe had been adopted on his advice.[62] But most contemporaries seem to have blamed Henry II himself for the harshness of the levy. Ralph Niger contrasted the king's exactions with the moderate demands of the Emperor Frederick I and warned prospective crusaders that God would not favour a pilgrimage financed by the spoliation of the poor.[63] Gerald of Wales related an incident said to have taken place when Henry was at Portsmouth. The king was apparently approached by a noble lady, Margaret of Bohun, who feared for his safety because the Saladin tithe had caused him to forfeit the blessing of his people. Her comments angered Henry, who replied that if he returned from France he would give his subjects reason to curse him. Gerald commented that God punished the king for this exaction by an unexpected death.[64] Lying behind this opposition seems to have been a concern that consent to the levy would establish a dangerous precedent for the future. But in spite of their vociferous protests, the English critics

---

[58] Roger of Howden, *Gesta*, ii. 31, 33.

[59] Ralph of Diceto, ii. 73. See also *Annales de Waverleia*, 245.

[60] Geoffrey of Coldingham, *Liber de statu ecclesiae Dunelmensis*, ed. J. Raine, Historiae Dunelmensis Scriptores Tres, Surtees Society, IX (London, 1839), 13. See also *Itinerarium peregrinorum*, 278.

[61] Ralph of Coggeshall, 25.

[62] Gervase of Canterbury, i. 422–3. For Gervase's attitude towards the archbishop, see Gransden, 253–4.

[63] Ralph Niger, *Chronica universalis*, 338 and *DRM* 213, 215.

[64] Gerald of Wales, *De principis instructione, Opera*, viii. 253. See also William of Newburgh, i. 282.

failed to obtain any remission from the Saladin tithe and their worst fears were realized in 1207, when King John raised a tax for a purpose other than the crusade—his projected French campaign.[65]

In Scotland opposition was more successful. King William offered Bishop Hugh of Durham a lump sum of 4,000 or 5,000 merks to cover both the tithe and the restoration of the border castles which he had surrendered to Henry II in 1174. This composition was accepted by the English envoys, but when the king consulted the Scottish barons and clergy they refused to give their consent. In the face of their determined opposition it proved impossible to collect the tithe, and Bishop Hugh decided to withdraw.[66]

In France the resistance to the tithe was led by the clergy. The Archbishop of Canterbury's secretary, Peter of Blois, corresponded with many prominent French ecclesiastics; although he was himself a keen advocate of the Third Crusade and had welcomed the tax of 1185, he urged them to resist this latest royal demand. In a letter to the Bishop of Orléans, Peter declared that it was outrageous that the 'champions of the church despoil her, instead of enriching her with the fruits of victory'; and he maintained that Philip should ask nothing of the French clergy except their prayers. Peter expressed his fear that the tithe would become a habit and the church fall into 'shameful servitude', and exhorted the Bishop of Chartres and Dean of Rouen not to allow themselves to be swayed from their resolve and to continue to oppose the tax even in the face of the king's wrath.[67] The Saladin tithe was also criticized by Stephen, later Bishop of Tournai. In a letter addressed to Pope Clement III he complained of the severity of the levy and appealed to the Bishop of Soissons to release the hard-pressed canons of La Ferté-Milon from this latest imposition.[68] One French chronicler even suggested that these exactions had impeded the expedition's chances of success.[69]

---

[65] For further details, see S. K. Mitchell, *Studies in Taxation under John and Henry III* (New Haven, Conn., 1914), 84–92.

[66] Roger of Howden, *Gesta*, ii. 44–5. See also id. *Chronica*, ii. 338–9; William of Newburgh, i. 304.   [67] Peter of Blois, *Opera*, i. 76–8, 309, 346–8, 368–9.

[68] Stephen of Tournai, *Lettres*, ed. J. Desilve (Paris, 1893), 194–5, 222–3.

[69] Robert of Auxerre, *Chronologia*, extr. RHGF xviii. 257. See also Peter of Blois, *De Hierosolymitana peregrinatione acceleranda, Opera*, iii, pp. xii, xviii.

In a poem composed in 1188 or 1189 the trouvère Conon de Béthune proclaimed his intention of hastening to the Holy Land, for he refused to stay in France 'with these tyrants who have taken up the cross so that they may tax clerks, citizens, and soldiers', and lamented, 'more have taken the cross out of greed than faith'.[70]

Henry II appears to have been able to ignore the bitter protests of the English clergy and laity and his officials collected the tithe throughout the kingdom. But the same was not true of Philip Augustus. Because of his weaker position on the throne, he was forced to issue an ordinance of abolition which acknowledged some of the critics' demands:

> The tithe for the recovery of the Holy Land has been levied once . . . Lest the enormity of this deed should set a precedent, we have decided, on the petition of both princes and churchmen, by a law valid in perpetuity, that no future exactions shall be made by reason of it or for any other similar cause . . . it seemed to us that God would be offended rather than conciliated by a sacrifice offered to him at the price of the tears of the widows and the poor.

Moreover, Philip forbade his counsellors to impose another such tax on pain of damnation; this prohibition was repeated in the testament which he composed on the eve of his departure for the East.[71]

The Saladin tithe was also collected by the French nobility and close parallels can be drawn between the royal capitulation and the submission of certain barons. For example, Count Theobald of Blois reassured the Abbey of St Père of Chartres that the tax had only been levied upon its lands because of the perilous state of the Latin Kingdom of Jerusalem and promised that it would not be taken as a precedent for the future.[72] A similar assurance was given to the local chapter of St Peter by Count Henry of Troyes.[73]

The Saladin tithe seems to have created an atmosphere of suspicion and hostility towards royal crusade taxation in both England and France; but, in the years that followed,

---

[70] 'Bien me deusse targier', *Chansons de croisade*, 45, st. iii.

[71] *Recueil des actes de Philippe Auguste*, 306, 419.

[72] *Cartulaire de l'abbaye de Saint-Père de Chartres*, ed. M. Guérard, Collection des cartulaires de France, II (Paris, 1840), 661-2.

[73] *Cartulaire de l'abbaye de Saint-Pierre de Troyes*, ed. G. Lalore, Collection des principaux cartulaires du diocèse de Troyes, V (Paris, 1880), 65.

French resistance continued to be more effective than English opposition. Admittedly, Philip Augustus managed to extort more money from the French church in 1194, on the grounds that it was necessary to defend his kingdom and to liberate Jerusalem from the Muslims; on this occasion, however, even the royal chronicler Rigord commented: 'some who do not know the king's purpose will attribute it to his greed and ambition'.[74] Further royal attempts to levy money for the Holy Land met with stubborn resistance. In 1201 both Philip and John agreed to grant Innocent III a fortieth of their revenues and those of their vassals, in order to finance the Fourth Crusade.[75] But, whilst this tax appears to have been successfully levied in the Angevin domains, there is no evidence that it was ever collected in France.[76] The only time when the English critics appear to have achieved any major concessions was when Henry III authorized a compulsory poll-tax for the crusade in 1222.[77] Because of the strength of opposition the king was forced to make contribution voluntary, and there were changes in the classes subject to the levy. Even so, in the end at least some of the proceeds were collected.[78]

Criticism of the tenth which Innocent IV granted Louis IX for his first crusade will be discussed later in the context of papal taxation.[79] But there was also bitter opposition to the other financial expedients which the French king employed to raise money for his expedition, particularly the aids which he requested from the towns in the royal domain, 'pro auxilio viae transmarinae'.[80] Louis had given assurances that these contributions would not be taken as a precedent for future levies;[81] but, according to a survey of 1260, many towns were heavily in debt as a result of repeated royal

[74] Rigord, 128-9. See also E. M. Hallam, *Capetian France, 987-1328* (London, 1980), 164; G. M. Spiegel, ' "Defence of the Realm": Evolution of a Capetian Propaganda Slogan', *Journal of Medieval History*, iii (1977), 124.

[75] *Recueil des actes de Philippe Auguste*, ii. 240-1; Roger of Howden, *Chronica*, iv. 187-9.

[76] See Cheney, *Innocent III and England*, 247-8.

[77] *Annales de Waverleia*, 496.

[78] For further details, see Mitchell, 141-2.   [79] See below, pp. 136-8.

[80] Jordan, *Louis IX*, 82-105, especially 95-9.

[81] *Archives administratives de la ville de Reims*, ed. P. Varin (Paris, 1839-48), i (2), nos. 216, 218, 220.

demands. The citizens of Noyon, Montdidier, Cerny, La Neuville-Roi, Crandelain, Chauny, and Roye gave officials a detailed statement of their past expenditure, and in this they complained that the king had authorized five aids within the space of twelve years—for the purposes of his first crusade in 1248, for his ransom in 1250, for the Hainaut campaign in 1253, for the marriage of his daughter in 1255, and for the peace with England in 1259.[82] These municipal accounts reveal the deep-seated resentment felt by the towns-people, and against such a background it is hardly surprising that, when Louis requested an aid for his second crusade in 1267, a number of towns refused to contribute. In fact there were serious disturbances in several localities and a royal collector was killed at Chorges.[83] In the end most towns were either persuaded or forced to pay their assessment. But a few continued to protest and appeals against the levy were still being heard by the Parlement of Paris in 1270.[84]

Louis's example was followed by his brother Alphonse of Poitiers. Although few details have survived, he seems to have requested an aid from the towns in his domain in 1248, in order to finance his Egyptian campaign, giving an assurance that it would not set a precedent for the future.[85] Alphonse offered similar guarantees when he asked for another aid in the 1260s,[86] and in an effort to forestall criticism advised his envoys to hold a series of meetings with the townspeople to negotiate their contribution.[87] In spite of this some areas declined to pay, or offered inadequate

[82] *Layettes du trésor de chartes*, ed. J. B. Teulet, Delaborde, *et al.* (Paris, 1863-1909), iii. 4598, 4609, 4654, 4662. See also C. Stephenson, 'The Aids of the French Towns in the Twelfth and Thirteenth Centuries', ed. B. Lyon, *Medieval Institutions* (New York, 1954), 29-32.

[83] *Les Olim ou registres des arrêts rendus par la cour du roi*, ed. A. Beugnot, i (Paris, 1839), 835-6. For opposition from the nobility, see HGL viii, cols. 1669-70.

[84] *Les Olim*, i. 848-9. For similar cases, see ibid. 799, 840, 843.

[85] *Correspondance administrative d'Alfonse de Poitiers*, ed. A. Molinier (Paris, 1894-1900), i. no. 7474; *Layettes*, iii. no. 3775.

[86] *Correspondance administrative*, i. nos. 814-15; ii. 202, 206; *Enquêtes administratives d'Alfonse de Poitiers*, ed. P. Fournier and P. Guébin (Paris, 1959), 278.

[87] *Correspondance administrative*, ii. nos. 1962, 1968; T. N. Bisson, 'Negotiations for Taxes under Alfonse of Poitiers', *XIIe Congrès international des sciences historiques: Études présentées à la commission internationale pour l'histoire des assemblées d'états, Vienne, 1965*, (Paris and Louvain, 1966), 77-102.

compositions.[88] The towns of Montferrand and Riom were finally persuaded to contribute under threat of additional levies,[89] but others remained obdurate. Alphonse was still trying to collect his 4,000 livres from Riom in 1270, and it was eventually left to the Parlement of Paris under Philip III to enforce payment.[90] When Louis's other brother, Count Robert of Artois, asked for an aid from his towns, royal commissioners had to be sent in to force the citizens to pay.[91]

Yet again one can see a marked contrast between the reactions to royal taxation in France and England. After the poll-tax of 1222, the next crusading tax authorized by Henry III was the twentieth of 1269, intended to finance the Lord Edward's crusade.[92] At first this measure aroused opposition from the beneficed clergy of the province of Canterbury, but in the end the king received the tax from all classes in the kingdom, including the towns, and a fair proportion had even been collected before Edward's departure in 1270.[93]

Papal taxation

The main contribution towards the cost of the crusades in the thirteenth century came, however, from the direct taxation of the church by the pope. In January 1199 Innocent III, following the example of his predecessor Clement III,[94] called upon all the prelates of Christendom to contribute to a subsidy for the Fourth Crusade. This appeal for voluntary aid evoked a poor response; so, in December, he decided to impose a tax of a fortieth for one year upon clerical incomes.[95] This was the first clerical income-tax and, although Innocent promised that it was an exceptional levy, there were fears that it would establish a precedent. In fact the

[88] *Correspondance administrative*, i. no. 689; Stephenson, 23–6.
[89] *Correspondance administrative*, i. nos. 224, 725–8, 739, 743, 1163, 1191.
[90] Ibid. no. 1197; *Les Olim*, i. 406–7.
[91] J. Favier, 'Les finances de Saint Louis', *Septième Centenaire*, 135.
[92] Gervase of Canterbury, ii. 250.
[93] *Letters from the Northern Registers*, ed. Raine (London, 1873), 24–5, 38–9. For further details, see Mitchell, 295–9.
[94] See Gerald of Wales, *De principis instructione, Opera*, viii. 237.
[95] Innocent III, PL ccxiv, cols. 263–6, 310, 737–8, 828–32.

English justiciar, Geoffrey FitzPeter, may have tried to prevent the Council of Westminster from taking place in 1200, in case the archbishop used it as an opportunity to initiate a discussion of the papal demand;[96] and, at an assembly of the clergy at St Albans in 1207, the king issued a mandate objecting to the removal of the church's wealth from England. In this John referred specifically to the annual levy known as Peter's pence; but the implication was that he had other demands in mind.[97] The exceptional delays in the collection of the fortieth were a further indication of clerical resistance. In 1201 Innocent instructed Archbishop Hubert Walter to see that the tax was diligently collected,[98] but the legate John of Ferentino was probably charged with the pursuit of debtors in 1206[99] and the pope was still dissatisfied with returns in 1207. Early that year Innocent wrote to the Bishops of Ely and Norwich complaining of delays in the payment of the fortieth and ordered them to make sure that the money was handed over to the Templars in London. Some clerks and monks, however, still refused to contribute and in May Innocent sent a second letter to the bishops, answering various queries about the fortieth and instructing them to make certain that laggard ecclesiastics paid their contributions.[100] The pope's plans to collect the arrears were frustrated by the Bishop of Norwich's absence from England and the Interdict, which lasted from 1208 to 1213. And in c.1217 Archbishop Stephen Langton received some assessments which had been levied in the diocese of Exeter before 1206.[101]

The fortieth also seems to have aroused opposition in other parts of Europe. In 1200 Innocent III reminded the French clergy that, although they had promised his legate at the Council of Dijon that they would contribute a thirtieth of their incomes towards the cost of the crusade, they had

---

[96] See Roger of Howden, *Chronica*, iv. 128; Cheney, *Hubert Walter*, 65–6.

[97] *Councils and Synods*, ed. Powicke and Cheney, ii (Oxford, 1964), 9–10.

[98] Roger of Howden, *Chronica*, iv. 166–7.

[99] See Cheney, *Innocent III and England*, 39.

[100] Id. 'Master Philip the Notary and the Fortieth of 1199', *EHR* lxiii (1948), 348–50.

[101] Walter Bronescombe and Peter Quivil, Bishops of Exeter, *Register*, ed. C. Hingeston-Radulph (London, 1889), 293.

not yet paid the fortieth which he had originally requested. He appointed the Bishops of Paris and Soissons and the Abbots of St Victor and Vaux de Cernay to supervise the collection of the arrears. Innocent was obviously concerned to ensure that there should be no further delays and he lamented: 'Already you (the French clergy) are reproached by the laity whom you exhort to succour Christ's patrimony . . . prodigal with others' goods, thrifty, or to be more accurate avaricious, with your own.'[102] But in spite of his efforts, the passive resistance of the clergy remained a problem and some receipts from the Italian church were still due in 1208.[103]

The difficulties experienced in collecting the fortieth may have persuaded Innocent not to demand another general tax in 1213. Instead, in his bull *Quia maior*, he exhorted the clergy to send voluntary contributions for the forthcoming expedition and ordered that trunks should be set up in the churches to receive alms from the laity.[104] But even this measure aroused violent criticism from the German minnesinger Walther von der Vogelweide. He had supported each of the three main candidates for the German throne, Philip of Swabia, Otto of Brunswick, and Frederick II, in turn during the Interregnum which followed Henry VI's death; but he resented the papacy's interference in this dispute. Playing upon the German word *stoc*, meaning stick or trunk, Walther accused Innocent of plotting to ruin the German people and embezzling the money which they had donated for the Fifth Crusade:

How the pope now laughs . . . when he says to his Italians, '. . . I have brought two Germans under one crown so that they will destroy and lay waste the empire. Meanwhile we will fill our coffers. I have driven them to my collecting-box (*stoc*); all that they have belongs to me; their German silver is flowing into my Italian casket. You priests eat chicken and drink wine and let the Germans hunger and fast.'

In another spruch Walther appears to have denounced Innocent as the new Judas; in a third he sought advice on whether to retain his wealth, for poverty could be an advantage:

[102] 'Gesta Innocentii', PL ccxiv, cols. cxxxiii f., cxxxviii.
[103] Innocent III, PL ccxv, col. 1503. See also Innocent's letter to the Patriarch of Jerusalem and the Masters of the Military Orders dated July 1208, ibid. cols. 1427-8.   [104] Tangl, 93, 96.

The priests' discussion is of no interest to me. Unless there is something in the coffer they will not be able to find anything there. Let them search high and low, I have nothing in it.

In a fourth poem Walther made the pope admit his cunning and scheme to enrich himself and his cardinals, and he lamented:

I believe that little of the silver will come to help God's land, for priests seldom share great treasure. Sir stick, you have been sent here to harm us and are seeking foolish men and women from the German people.[105]

No other contemporary criticism of this papal request for aid has survived; but, according to the Italian moralist Thomasin von Zirclaira, Walther's fierce denunciation of papal avarice led many astray.[106]

The next clerical income-tax was the triennial twentieth, authorized by the Fourth Lateran Council in 1215.[107] This time Innocent III issued no guarantee that similar taxes would not be levied in the future and there were complaints about the severity of this imposition from monks and clerics throughout Europe. In France, Abbot Gervais of Prémontré protested that those who had to pay the twentieth, without deducting from the assessment the ordinary and general taxes, could barely afford to do so unless they had an assured living.[108] And, in his reflections upon the loss of Damietta, Abbot William of Andres lamented that the great suffering of the church, 'which had been grievously wounded', had been in vain.[109] Not surprisingly, papal officials experienced serious problems collecting this tax. Several French clerks were accused of fraudulent assessment and some contributions were still due in 1220.[110] Innocent's successor Honorius III also seems to have had some difficulty levying the tax

---

[105] Walther von der Vogelweide, 'Ahî, wie kristenlîche, nû der bâbest lachet', 'Wir klagen alle und wizzen doht niht waz uns wirret', 'Der künec mîn hêrre lêch mir gelt ze drîzec marken', 'Sagt an hêr Stoc hât iuch der bâbest her gesendet', ed. cit. 35, 44-6. See also id. *Werke*, 504, 509.

[106] Thomasin von Zirclaira, ll. 11191-5, 11223. See above, p. 10.

[107] *COD* 268-9.

[108] Gervais of Prémontré, 8.

[109] William of Andres, 761.

[110] Honorius III, nos. 993, 2847, 3145, 3148, 3307.

in Italy;[111] and, although the Scandinavian clergy agreed to contribute, several years later they asked if they might render their payments in kind because of the impoverishment of their church.[112] In addition there seems to have been some resistance to the twentieth in Germany and Hungary, for, in spite of repeated papal warnings and appeals, some receipts were still due in 1219.[113] In fact the only country not to object to the tax was England. This anomaly can be explained by the fact that, from 1216, its government was in the hands of two papal legates, one of whom had been the head of the apostolic Camera. They threatened defrauders with excommunication, and by 1220 some twenty thousand marks had been sent to Rome on behalf of the English clergy.[114]

There does not appear to have been any opposition to the tenth which Innocent III imposed upon French ecclesiastics in 1209, in order to finance the Albigensian Crusade, or indeed to the voluntary subsidy which he requested from laymen for the same purpose.[115] There was, however, prolonged resistance to the triennial tenth which his successor Honorius III levied upon the French clergy in 1221, to aid Amaury of Montfort. The Archbishops of Sens, Rheims, and Bourges, who were in charge of the administration of the tax, held a series of councils in order to obtain the clergy's consent.[116] But this does not seem to have satisfied all those concerned and the chapters of the province of Rheims refused to contribute on the grounds that the archbishop and his suffragans had not consulted them about the levy. Pope Honorius rejected their appeal, but to ensure speedy payment of the tax these chapters were allowed to make a composition, rather than pay the full assessment. Some still remained obdurate and by December 1223 the twentieth was seriously in arrears. Honorius appointed four commissioners

---

[111] Ibid. no. 1547.

[112] *Diplomatarium Suecanum*, ed. J. G. Liljegren, i (Stockholm, 1829), nos. 171, 197, 830.

[113] *Regesta Pontificum Romanorum*, comp. Potthast, nos. 5959, 5966; Honorius III, no. 3523.

[114] See Cheney, *Innocent III and England*, 267–8.

[115] Innocent III, PL ccxv, col. 1470; ccxvi, cols. 98–9.

[116] Honorius III, nos. 3423, 3427, 3574, 3644, 3860.

to collect the unpaid receipts in the provinces of Sens, Rouen, and Rheims, but his agents do not appear to have had much success, for some of the tax was still due in 1225 when the papal legate Conrad, Bishop of Porto, died.[117] The situation was exacerbated when the Council of Bourges authorized a second tenth, in order to finance Louis VIII's expedition to the Languedoc. According to one chronicler, the representatives of the French chapters put forward various objections, but the king and the papal legate refused to listen to their arguments and the clerks left the assembly secretly cursing this business of the cross.[118] Although the first instalment of the tenth seems to have been paid, after the king's death in November 1226 a violent controversy broke out in the French church as to whether the clergy were bound to pay the balance. Not surprisingly the resistance was led by the clerks of the provinces of Rheims, Rouen, Sens, and Tours; in 1227 they were threatened with excommunication by the legate Cardinal Romanus because they had still not paid their full contributions.[119]

The next general income-tax, yet another tenth, was levied in 1228 to finance Gregory IX's campaign against Frederick II. Admittedly, this was not a crusade, but it is worth studying the clergy's reaction to the tax, for it formed the background to their later opposition to the levies for the papal crusades against the Staufen. The tenth seems to have been collected successfully in Sweden, Eastern Europe, and Northern Italy, and after the conclusion of the Albigensian Crusade the French ecclesiastics agreed to reassign the remaining proceeds of the 1226 levy.[120] The main area of resistance was England. According to the chronicler William of Andres, during the administration of the papal legate Stephen of Anagni, more than sixty thousand marks were sent from England to replenish the papal coffers in Rome[121]

[117] Honorius III, nos. 3959, 4607, 4613, 4620, 4621, 5337. For further details, see R. Kay, 'The Albigensian Twentieth of 1221-3: an Earlier Chapter in the History of Papal Taxation', *Journal of Medieval History*, vi (1980), 307-16.

[118] 'Chronicon Turonense', RHGF, xviii. 314.

[119] *Layettes*, v. nos. 324, 325.

[120] *Regesta Imperii, 1198-1272*, comp. J. F. Böhmer, rev. J. Ficker and E. Winkelmann (Innsbruck, 1894), nos. 6751, 6808; *Annales de Dunstaplia*, *Annales monastici*, iii. 114; MGH Epistolae saeculi XIII, i. 295-6.

[121] William of Andres, 768.

and the severity of this latest imposition aroused bitter complaints, particularly from the St Albans' chroniclers, Roger Wendover and Matthew Paris.[122] Roger protested that the clerics' contribution was calculated even on unharvested crops, forcing some prelates to pawn holy chalices and other sacred vessels in order to honour their assessment, and remarked that maledictions were voiced against the legate throughout the kingdom. According to Matthew many priests were ruined by the exactions of the moneylenders who accompanied Stephen, and Ralph, Count of Chester, was said to have forbidden either the religious or secular clergy on his estates to contribute because he was unwilling for his lands to be reduced to servitude.[123] At the same time, the barons apparently refused to grant Gregory IX's request for a voluntary subsidy from English laymen, because they were reluctant to mortgage their lands to the papacy.[124]

Roger and Matthew may have deliberately exaggerated the harshness of Stephen's administration in order to underline their criticisms of papal taxation.[125] But there are other indications that the English clergy were becoming increasingly resentful of repeated papal demands. This seems to be the most likely explanation for the non-collection of the thirtieth which Gregory requested in 1238 for his proposed expedition to the Latin Empire of Constantinople.[126] And there was certainly bitter resistance in 1239 when the pope asked for a fifth of the revenues of foreigners beneficed in England and a subsidy from the native clergy for his first crusade against Frederick II. The dispute between the papacy and the Staufen had both created a need for revenue and reduced the number of possible sources; there were protests about the impoverishment of the English church from several monastic chroniclers. According to Matthew Paris, Henry III's counsellors begged him not to give his consent to this

---

[122] See above, pp. 13–14.
[123] Roger Wendover, ii. 377; Matthew Paris, *CM* iii. 188–9. See also *Annales de Waverleia*, 305.
[124] Roger Wendover, ii. 375–6; Lunt, op. cit. 190–4.
[125] Mitchell (178, n. 288) questioned whether the levy was as severe as the chroniclers suggest: the valuation of one of the deaneries in Salisbury was £89. 3s. 4d. in 1216, £80 in 1226, and £100 in 1229.
[126] Gregory IX, nos. 4605–7. See also Lunt, 194–7.

latest papal imposition and in his version of their speech Matthew made them use one of his favourite metaphors from the Psalms:

Why do you permit England to become the booty and spoil of those coming across like a vineyard without a wall (Psalm 79: 13), open to every traveller and subject to destruction by wild beasts, when you have an effective privilege that such exactions may not be made in this kingdom?

But the king was reluctant to oppose the pope, and in 1240 he granted the legate, Cardinal Otto, permission to collect the subsidy. The latter first put the matter before a clerical assembly at Reading in May. Apparently those present were unwilling to give an answer until they had consulted all who would be affected and the legate agreed to postpone the debate until the Council of London in July. Here the clerks agreed to contribute to the subsidy, but they expressed certain reservations about this latest papal demand. They pointed out that they had granted Gregory a tenth in 1229 on the condition that it would not be taken as a precedent for future exactions; and they questioned the wisdom of impoverishing the kingdom when it was beset by enemies and so many nobles were absent in the Holy Land.[127] The most formidable set of objections to the subsidy were, however, put forward by the rectors of Berkshire. Like the clerks assembled in London, they reminded the legate of the previous levy and complained that, although the pope and the emperor had reached an agreement none of its proceeds had been returned. But they then proceeded to question the papacy's right to tax the English church. The rectors pointed out that each church had its own independent patrimony and these could not be held liable to taxation because the physical security of Rome was threatened by the emperor.[128] At the same time they expressed some doubts about the use of the crusade against fellow Christians, but their significance should not be exaggerated. The rectors' opposition stemmed

[127] Matthew Paris, *CM* iv. 9–11, 35–8.

[128] Ibid. 38–43. According to the annalist of Burton, the same objections were advanced by the rectors of England in 1244 when Innocent IV requested a subsidy for the second crusade against Frederick II. See *Annales de Burtoneia, Annales monastici,* i. 265–6.

from their increasing resentment of papal demands; there is no obvious correlation between the force of criticism and the direction of the crusade. After the Council of London, Cardinal Otto negotiated separate agreements with the various ecclesiastical bodies[129] and, although some arrears were still due in 1244, most seem to have paid their contribution.[130] The subsidy was also collected in Scotland and Ireland and significantly the only chronicler to complain about its severity was Matthew Paris.[131]

In 1244, Innocent IV requested another aid for a second crusade against Frederick. This latest papal imposition aroused opposition from the English king and the baronage as well as the clergy. The pope's proposal was first discussed at a clerical assembly in the autumn, but, as in 1240, those present asked the nuncio Master Martin for permission to postpone their answer until they had consulted the Archbishop of Canterbury and the Bishops of Lincoln and Durham.[132] The situation was further complicated by Henry III's request for a royal aid. When the clergy met again in February 1245, they were still uncertain about their reply and they decided to appeal directly to the general council then assembled at Lyons.[133] The clerks' protests against the subsidy and the various other financial expedients adopted by Master Martin[134] were reinforced by an embassy from the king and the barons.[135] Even so Innocent refused to grant any major concessions. When the English envoys reported the pope's decision to the council assembled at London in March 1246, it was decided to make further representations.[136] Before these latest messengers could begin their journey, however, the situation had changed dramatically. In the interim, the Bishops of Lichfield, Lincoln, London, Norwich, Winchester, and Worcester had secretly undertaken to collect the subsidy at

[129] Matthew Paris, *CM* iv. 43; *Annales de Dunstaplia*, 154.
[130] *Annales de Dunstaplia*, 166; Lunt, op. cit. 199-204.
[131] Matthew Paris, *CM* iv. 55, 137; D. M. Williamson, 'The Legate Otto in Scotland and Ireland, 1237-41', *Scottish Historical Review*, xxviii (1949), 23.
[132] *Annales de Dunstaplia*, 166-7; Matthew Paris, *CM* iv. 374-5.
[133] Matthew Paris, *CM*, iv. 370, 375-6.
[134] See ibid. 285, 376, 391, 402, 416.
[135] Ibid. 419; *Close Rolls of the Reign of Henry III, 1242-7* (London, 1916), 355-7.
[136] Matthew Paris, *CM* iv. 378-9, 526-7, 554.

a reduced rate of six thousand marks; in his chronicle Matthew Paris quoted the Bishop of Norwich's letter ordering the monastery of St Albans to pay its assessment.[137] When Henry III heard of the bishops' insubordination, he forbade clerks to contribute and renewed his order to apprehend anyone bearing papal letters at their port of entry.[138] In his anger, the king paid no heed to the protests voiced by Bishop Grosseteste of Lincoln, and, when the second set of envoys returned from Lyons and reported that Innocent would still not give way, decreed that no more money should be sent from England to Rome. Such an extreme position could not, however, be maintained for long and, under the threat of a papal interdict, Henry accepted Bishop Grosseteste's advice and revoked his prohibition.[139] The six bishops then collected their six thousand marks and in other dioceses the subsidy seems to have been levied in the form of an income-tax of a twentieth.[140] Matthew Paris described Henry's final submission as a defeat for the English church and he lamented:

Thus the whole effort of the magnates and the bishops came to nothing and the hope of liberating the kingdom and the English church faded miserably away, not without bitter grief in many hearts, and the longings of Roman avarice were satisfied with impunity with regard to the said contribution.[141]

One reason for English resistance to the subsidies of 1239 and 1244 may have been clerical criticism of the use of the crusade against fellow Christians.[142] But above all it seems to have been a reaction to the cumulative burden imposed upon the church by frequent papal demands. In this context it is hardly surprising that there was also opposition to the taxes authorized by the First Council of Lyons in 1245— namely a triennial twentieth for the crusade in the Holy Land and a subsidy for the Latin Empire.[143] The English

---

[137] Ibid. 527–9, 554.

[138] Ibid. 510, 558. See also *Close Rolls*, 259.

[139] Robert Grosseteste, Bishop of Lincoln, *Epistolae*, ed. Luard (London, 1861), 338–42; Matthew Paris, *CM* iv. 560–1.

[140] Gervase of Canterbury, ii. 202.

[141] Matthew Paris, *CM* iv. 561.

[142] See below, p. 179.

[143] *COD* 295, 299.

envoys who had gone to Lyons to protest about the subsidy of 1244 used the opportunity to beg for relief from the latest exactions. But Innocent remained determined not to make any concessions,[144] and he appointed the papal chaplain Marinus to act as his collector in England.[145] There is no reference to the twentieth in the papal registers and it has been suggested that, having initially prevented its collection, Henry III persuaded the pope to convert it into a tenth for his proposed crusade.[146] Serious objections, however, were raised against the subsidy for the Latin Empire, which took the form of a moiety of the revenues of non-residential clerks. According to Matthew Paris, the clergy, assembled at the Council of London in December 1246, argued that the levy would injure the well-being of the church and they described a situation in which non-resident canons would no longer be able to afford to pay for a substitute or attend to the necessary repairs. Moreover, rectors would have to give up their hospitality and monks dependent upon the income from these benefices might be forced to beg.[147] The clergy and people of the province of Canterbury also sent letters to the pope and cardinals describing the impoverished state of the church and the heavy burden imposed by recent demands.[148] Once again Innocent seems to have ignored all their appeals[149] and in the end they were ordered to contribute. A few, however, must have remained obdurate, for some arrears were still due in 1262.[150]

In France criticism was directed at the tenth which Innocent had conceded to Louis IX for his crusade.[151] It was originally intended to be levied for three years, but in 1251 the regent Queen Blanche obtained permission to extend this to a five-

[144] Matthew Paris, *CM* iv. 473, 521-2.
[145] Ibid. 691-2.
[146] See Lunt, op. cit. 254.
[147] Matthew Paris, *CM* iv. 580-5. The annalist of Burton (278-85) attributed these pleas to a royal assembly which probably took place in February 1247.
[148] Matthew Paris, *CM* iv. 595-7.
[149] See *Foedera, conventiones, litterae et cuiuscumque generis acta publica inter reges Angliae et alios quos vis imperatores, reges, pontifices, principes vel communitates*, ed. T. Rymer *et al.*, i (Facsimile edn., Farnborough, 1967), (1). 155; Lunt, op. cit. 253.
[150] See Urban IV, i. no. 132.
[151] Innocent IV, no. 2053.

year period,[152] and it has been calculated that the proceeds amounted to £950,000 tournois, approximately two-thirds of the total cost of the expedition.[153] Fairly complete accounts of the ecclesiastical contributions towards the tenth have survived and the frequent references to unpaid assessments suggest considerable clerical resistance.[154] The same impression is conveyed by a form letter inventoried in the royal archives, 'ut persone ecclesiastice compellantur solvere decimam pro subsidio Terre Sancte'.[155] Indeed the Southern French bishops, led by the Archbishop of Narbonne, sought to escape payment altogether, on the grounds that they had been absent from the assembly which granted the tenth. At first Innocent supported their case, but in the end they were ordered to contribute and, whilst certain bishops had to be reminded to pay in 1248, according to a fragmentary royal account, the tenth had been levied in all the major Southern sees by 1250.[156] Only the diocese of Maguelone (Montpellier) seems to have been successful in claiming relief, probably on the grounds of hardship and poverty.[157]

The harshness of the levy also aroused opposition from the French nobility. The Duke of Lorraine and Brabant protested to Innocent about the weight of taxation upon his lands;[158] and this latest papal imposition may have been one of the factors which prompted a number of barons to form a league condemning the new customs of the church.[159] Both Louis IX and Innocent IV were accused of avarice. According to John of Joinville, before the crusade the king had never demanded money in such a way as to cause complaint, but

[152] Id. nos. 4928, 5154-5.

[153] J. R. Strayer, 'The Crusades of Louis IX', *History of the Crusades*, ii. 491.

[154] 'Triennis et Biennis Decima', RHGF xxi. 533-40; Jordan, op. cit. 82.

[155] 'Formulaires de lettres du XIIᵉ et du XIIIᵉ siècles', *Notices et extraits des manuscrits de la Bibliothèque nationale*, xxxv (1896), 795, item 6.

[156] Innocent IV, nos. 2492, 2980, 3055; HGL viii. col. 1222.

[157] *Bullaire de l'église de Maguelone*, ed. J. Rouquette and A. Villemagne (Paris and Montpellier, 1911-14), ii. 284-5, 294-5. The royal account of 1250 referred to the 'decima deposita' at all the major sees in Languedoc, but Jordan, op. cit. 81 n. 114, suggests that the papal letter exempting Maguelone might not have been received when deposits of the tenth were demanded.

[158] Innocent IV, no. 2033.

[159] Matthew Paris, *CM* iv. 590-2. For the history of this league, see Jordan, op. cit. 20-5.

at Acre many murmured that he had spent none of his own
wealth on the expedition, relying instead upon the contributions of the clergy.[160] Matthew Paris drew a connection
between Louis's rapacity and the fate of his army, and
held this up as a warning and example to Henry III. In order
to underline his point, Matthew told the story of a poor-
clerk who had apparently been reduced to beggary by a papal
tax-collector.[161]

The atmosphere of suspicion and hostility created by
repeated papal demands is further illustrated by the reaction
to the triennial tenth which Innocent granted to King Henry
III of England for his crusade in 1250.[162] As a safeguard the
pope stipulated that collection was to begin in 1254, two
years before Henry's proposed departure.[163] Even so the
clergy were reluctant to give their approval to the levy;
according to Matthew Paris, it was believed that the king was
using the crusade merely as a pretext to procure money from
his subjects.[164] Henry first broached the subject of the
tenth at a convocation of the province of Canterbury at
Reading in 1251.[165] As with earlier demands, the clergy
postponed their decision until they had consulted all those
who would be affected, and the situation was further complicated by the pope's request that the tax should be collected from 1253, rather than the following year as originally
planned. After a series of meetings the clerks agreed to
contribute to the levy,[166] but their acceptance was hedged
with conditions and a few continued to oppose the grant.[167]
In 1254 the Bishops of Norwich and Chichester and the
Abbot of Westminster were given formal commissions to
collect the tenth; however, their assessment seems to have
dissatisfied both Henry III and Pope Alexander IV, and in
the autumn of 1255 a new collector, the papal nuncio

---

[160] John of Joinville, 38-9, 151.
[161] Matthew Paris, *CM* v. 170-2. See also Vaughan, 146-7.
[162] *Foedera*, i (1), 159.   [163] Ibid. 161, 167, 183.
[164] Matthew Paris, *CM* v. 102, 282.
[165] *Annales de Theokesberia, Annales monastici*, i. 139-40.
[166] Matthew Paris, *CM* v. 324-33, 359-60; *Royal and Other Historical Letters
Illustrative of the Reign of Henry III*, ed. W. W. Shirley (London, 1862-6), ii.
94-5.
[167] For further details, see Lunt, *The Valuation of Norwich* (Oxford, 1926),
55-64.

Rostand, arrived in England.[168] He immediately ordered a second valuation to be made, and this time the proposals included a number of novel financial expedients. For this reason they were rejected by the magnates assembled at the Council of Westminster, and the clergy were granted permission to postpone their decision until the next meeting of convocation in January 1256.[169]

By the time the clerks reassembled they had additional and more pressing reasons for opposing the levy. After Frederick II's death in 1250, the papacy had continued its campaign against his heirs and, following a series of abortive negotiations with Richard, Earl of Cornwall, and Charles of Anjou, in March 1254 Innocent IV persuaded Henry III to accept the Sicilian throne on behalf of his son Edmund.[170] The pope urged the English king to launch an expedition against the Staufen ruler Manfred,[171] but at the same time he was reluctant to divert any resources from the East. This situation changed when Innocent died in December 1254. His successor Alexander IV immediately began preparations for a Sicilian crusade; in order to finance this project he authorized the transfer of the proceeds of the tenth from the Holy Land, decreed that the levy should be collected for a further two years,[172] and required repayment of the expenses which he had already incurred. In the face of these pressing demands Henry was forced to agree to a plan whereby the Bishop of Hereford negotiated loans with Italian merchants on behalf of certain monasteries, using the proceeds of the tenth as security.[173] This policy soon wreaked havoc in the English church. Matthew Paris's own house fell seriously into debt and was placed under an interdict;[174] and the experience of St Albans was shared by many other religious foundations. In his summary of the year 1255, Matthew commented that these exactions, emanating from the 'sulphurous fountain of

[168] Matthew Paris, *CM* vi. 296-7; Lunt, *Financial Relations*, 259, 261-2.
[169] Matthew Paris, *CM* v. 519-21, 524-7, 532; *Annales de Burtoneia*, 336, 360.
[170] *Annales de Burtoneia*, 339-40; *Layettes*, iii. 4020; *Foedera*, i (1). 182.
[171] *Foedera*, i (1). 183.
[172] *Annales de Burtoneia*, 351; Matthew Paris, *CM* v. 520.
[173] See Lunt, *Financial Relations*, 266-9, 271-2.
[174] Matthew Paris, *CM* v. 522; vi. 350, 382.

Rome', had diminished the people's respect for the papacy, and lamented that, whereas in the past ecclesiastics had taxed the laity, now the church was forced to contribute herself.[175] Similar objections were raised by the annalist of Burton, who recalled the burden imposed by earlier papal demands and declared that Rostand's oppressive measures had aroused a 'resounding murmur' and a 'tumult of tears', amongst the clergy.[176]

It was against this hostile background that Convocation met in January 1256. After consultation the clerks decided to list their grievances in a series of *cahiers* and to send them directly to the pope. Only the *cahiers* compiled by the proctors of the archdeaconry of Lincoln and the diocese of Lichfield have survived, but they provide valuable evidence of the range of objections advanced by the English clergy. Like their predecessors, the proctors complained of the harshness and frequency of papal exactions which had impoverished the church, and they refused to contribute to the tenth on the grounds that its original purpose had been changed. Yet another delegation was sent to Rome,[177] but, although Alexander made a few concessions and forbade Rostand to implement his new assessment, he continued his efforts to raise the tenth itself.[178]

In the face of these difficulties, early in 1256 Henry asked the pope for additional financial aid and permission to postpone his departure for Sicily. After much discussion, Alexander agreed to a postponement until May 1257, and, in order to ensure that the campaign against the Staufen was adequately financed, he authorized a series of new taxes upon the English church.[179] Not surprisingly these proposals met with serious resistance.[180] The clergy eventually decided to make a composition, on condition that the king undertook to remedy certain abuses. It proved impossible, however, to agree upon the details of this scheme; in the face of determined clerical opposition, Henry appealed to the pope

[175] Ibid. v. 524, 535–6.
[176] *Annales de Burtoneia*, 360, 364–7.
[177] Ibid. 360–3; Matthew Paris, *CM* v. 539–40.
[178] See Lunt, *Financial Relations*, 271–3.
[179] *Foedera*, i (2). 15; *Annales de Burtoneia*, 390; Matthew Paris, *CM* v. 623.
[180] *Annales de Burtoneia*, 390–1; Matthew Paris, *CM* vi. 353–65.

to release him from his debt.[181] The most that Alexander was prepared to concede was another delay in the payment of the tenth, and in return for this he insisted that the Bishops of Bath, Rochester, and Ely should repay a loan of 5,500 marks.[182] The pope's determination to collect the tax, coupled with Henry's increasingly critical financial position, helped to spark off a baronial revolt.[183] At first the reforming barons agreed to grant an aid towards the cost of the king's Sicilian project. But when their envoys returned from Rome with the news that Alexander refused to make any concessions, the baronial council prohibited any further payments to the curia. The pope soon realized that his expedition against the Staufen was unlikely to receive any more support from England and in December 1258 he withdrew his offer of the Sicilian throne.[184] As soon as Henry had regained power he appealed against this decision, but it was confirmed by Urban IV in 1263.[185] In his list of grievances the king complained that the barons had not proceeded with the business in Sicily as they had promised and pointed out that their neglect had left him seriously in debt;[186] but his pleas were not heeded. The clerical assembly at Merton refused to reinstate the tenth and later efforts on behalf of the papacy to collect the tax seem to have met with little success.[187] The clerks' only concession was to levy a thirtieth to repay the debts of the Bishops of Bath and Wells, Rochester, and Ely.[188] The lingering resentment of the papal exactions was highlighted by a list of grievances which the barons compiled in 1264. This covered a wide variety of subjects, including opposition to the use of the crusade against the Staufen.[189] But its authors were

---

[181] Matthew Paris, *CM* v. 637–8; *Foedera*, i (2). 29–30.

[182] Alexander IV, *Registres*, ed. C. Bourel de la Roncière *et al.* (Paris, 1902–31), no. 2379; Lunt, *Financial Relations*, 275–80.

[183] R. F. Treharne, *The Baronial Plan of Reform, 1258–65* (Manchester, 1932), 60.

[184] Matthew Paris, *CM* vi. 410–16.

[185] *Foedera*, i (2). 80–1.

[186] *Documents of the Baronial Plan of Reform and Rebellion, 1258–67*, sel. Treharne, ed. I. J. Sanders (Oxford, 1973), 212, 230–6.

[187] Urban IV, i, no. 132; Clement, IV, no. 765.

[188] Matthew Paris, *Flores Historiarum*, ed. Luard (London, 1890), ii. 433–4.

[189] See below, p. 183.

particularly concerned to point out the suffering endured by the church as a result of repeated papal demands for the king's abortive Sicilian scheme:

And to the greater confusion of the kingdom, a tenth of all ecclesiastical revenues was granted to him (Henry III) for five years, for their [the Sicilians'] overthrow, while churches by payment of these tenths . . . were impoverished, many thousands of marks having been collected in spoils of this kind, with enormous harm to the churches and the whole community, only to be thrown away in vain.[190]

The cumulative effect of papal taxation also seems to be the most likely explanation for clerical resistance to the subsidy which Urban IV requested in 1262, to finance an expedition to restore the deposed Emperor Baldwin of Constantinople to his throne.[191] According to Matthew Paris, the English clergy, assembled at the Council of Westminster in May 1263, rejected this latest papal imposition on the grounds of poverty.[192] A similar case was put forward by the French prelates' spokesman, the Archbishop of Tours, at the Council of Paris:

(He) pointed out the burdens with which the church of Gaul had long been oppressed, because of the subsidies which had been levied at the pope's request for the recovery of the Holy Land . . . And because of certain other special subsidies which it had paid to the pope, together with those for the land of Constantinople, with the common consent of all, he replied that at present we are not able to help that land.[193]

The pope remonstrated with the French clergy but does not appear to have attempted to make contribution compulsory.[194] There is no evidence that the subsidy was collected in either England or France.

The situation was exacerbated in 1263 when Urban IV authorized a new clerical income tax of a hundredth, to be levied for five years to finance the defence of the Holy Land.[195] It seems unlikely that this tax was ever collected in England, for in 1264 the barons forbade the clergy to send any money out of the realm without their approval.[196] It also

---

[190] *Documents of the Baronial Plan*, 278.
[191] Urban IV, ii. no. 131.
[192] Matthew Paris, *Flores historiarum*, ii. 478-9.
[193] Odo Rigaud, 440.
[194] Urban IV, i. no. 187.   [195] Ibid. ii. no. 468.
[196] *Calendar of Patent Rolls, 1258-66* (London, 1910), 413.

aroused further resistance in France. According to Archbishop Odo of Rouen, the bishops' proctors rejected the
pope's appeal for aid on the grounds that there were no signs
of preparations for an expedition to the East and the Muslims
and Christians had declared a truce. But once again their
main objection seems to have been the impoverishment of the
church:

because for a long time, or for many years, this land has been burdened
and oppressed by heavy subsidies for the Holy Land; so much so in fact
that because of the aforementioned subsidies they, their subjects, and
the churches are still under many obligations of debt.[197]

In spite of their pleas, the French prelates were eventually
persuaded to contribute towards the hundredth,[198] which was
also levied in Germany, Hungary, Sweden, and Portugal.[199]
Nevertheless there must have been some resistance in these
countries, for a few remittances were still outstanding in
1274.[200]

In addition to this general levy, in 1263 Urban IV requested
a triennial tenth from the clergy of the kingdom of France,
the county of Provence, and the ecclesiastical provinces
of Lyons, Besançon, Vienne, Embrun, and Tarentaise, to
finance Charles of Anjou's Sicilian expedition.[201] The pope
sought to reconcile the hard-pressed prelates to this latest
imposition by highlighting the benefits that would accrue
from the conquest of Sicily.[202] Once again his arguments
do not seem to have reassured the clergy and there were
complaints about the harshness of the levy. The papal legate
Cardinal Simon of Brie aroused particular hostility because
he based his assessment upon the reports of his agents rather
than on the testimony of the local clergy and the chronicler
of Limoges commented that, although Simon was a French-
man by birth, he had soon picked up the Roman custom of

---

[197] Odo Rigaud, 441-2.
[198] *Sacrorum conciliorum collectio*, xxiii. col. 1111.
[199] *Diplomatarium Suecanum* i. 413; *Thesaurus novus anecdotorum*, ed.
E. Martène and U. Durand, (Facsimile edn., Farnborough, 1968-9), ii. col. 6;
Vetera monumenta historica Hungariam sacram illustrantia, ed. A. Theiner
(Rome, 1859-60), i. no. 462; *Layettes*, iv. nos. 4773, 4776.
[200] Gregory X, *Registres*, ed. J. Guiraud (Paris, 1892-1906), no. 569.
[201] Urban IV, ii, no. 272.   [202] *Thesaurus*, ii, col. 58.

'gnawing at purses'.[203] A number of clerks were excommunicated for non-payment[204] or accused of giving fraudulent assessments,[205] and, although Urban's successor appealed to the French king and prelates to expedite the collection of the tax,[206] some arrears were still due in 1266.[207] Indeed, in certain cases the pope was forced to admit that churches were unable to pay because of lack of funds.[208] The representatives of the province of Lyons objected that the combination of the hundredth and the tenth had placed an intolerable burden upon the church.[209] But the most detailed criticism of the tax is to be found in a letter written by the cathedral chapter of Rheims. Whilst they accepted that the French church should be obedient to Rome in matters of faith, they stressed that their adherence to the pope should not be used as an excuse to reduce them to servitude. The chapter pointed out that ecclesiastical wealth was intended for alms and the repair of buildings, not to finance wars; although clerks might occasionally grant an aid for the defence of the church, they should be careful lest this became a custom. They concluded their letter with an exhortation to the prelates not to contribute even under the threat of excommunication.[210] Faced with such vociferous clerical opposition, it is hardly surprising that Clement IV rejected Charles of Anjou's request to levy the tenth for a fourth year,[211] and in a letter dated 1265 complained of the numerous obstacles which hindered the collection of papal revenues in Europe:

look around you at the regions of the world in turmoil and you will be able to discern the reasons for our poverty. England resists us, Germany scarcely obeys us, France sighs and complains, Spain is not sufficient for her own needs, Italy does not help but demands help, and where

[203] *Maius chronicon Lemovicense*, 770.
[204] *Thesaurus*, ii, cols. 138-9, 151, 242-5.
[205] Clement IV, nos. 180, 217; Odo Rigaud, 570.
[206] *Thesaurus*, ii, col. 245.
[207] Clement IV, no. 765.
[208] *Thesaurus*, ii, col. 355.
[209] Ibid. cols. 157-60. See also Andrew of Hungary, *Descriptio victoriae a Karolo Provinciae comite reportatae*, MGH SS xxvi. 563.
[210] *Archives législatives de la ville de Reims; Coutumes*, ed. Varin (Paris, 1840-52) i. 448-60.
[211] Clement IV, no. 1374.

can the Roman pontiff, if he fears God and has respect for men, find help in soldiers or money for himself and others?[212]

It is against this background that one should view the protests about the clerical tenth which Clement granted Louis IX for his Tunisian crusade. According to one contemporary chronicler, the chapters of Rheims, Rouen, and Sens declared that they would rather suffer excommunication than contribute, and reminded the pope that so many French prelates had been excommunicated for non-payment of taxes that the church resembled the Hebrews, who were powerless to resist their enemies (Josh. 7: 13-14)[213] Clement ignored the clerks' pleas to cancel the levy, but he granted a special exemption to the province of Auch, on the grounds that it had already contributed towards the Sicilian projects of both Henry III and Charles of Anjou.[214]

Criticism of repeated papal demands can also be found in the memoirs submitted to the Second Council of Lyons. Humbert of Romans maintained that many clerks had been disillusioned by papal avarice,[215] and Gilbert of Tournai commented that the Christians would never be victorious over the Muslims if they financed their expeditions 'from the labours of the poor, or the spoliation of the church'.[216] Not surprisingly there was considerable resistance to the tenth authorized by Gregory X for his crusade, but consideration of this lies outside our period.[217]

An obvious manifestation of clerical and lay resentment of papal exactions was the hostility shown towards papal envoys, particularly in England, from the time of the first clerical income-tax in 1199. As a precaution, the papal collector Master Philip had obtained a royal letter of recommendation to the prelates, but this did not shield him from bitter criticism.[218] Gerald of Wales complained that Philip

---

[212] *Thesaurus*, ii. col. 174. See also ibid. col. 355.

[213] Clement IV, no. 595; *Chronicon Normanniae*, extr. RHGF xxiii. 219-20.

[214] Clement IV, no. 508.

[215] Humbert of Romans, *Opus tripartitum*, 198.

[216] Gilbert of Tournai, *Collectio*, 39. Stroick, 434-5, draws parallels between this and Peter of Blois's letter to the Bishop of Orléans complaining about the Saladin tithe. See Peter of Blois, *Opera*, i. 346-50.

[217] See Throop, 74, 237-40; Gregory X, nos. 571, 541; *COD* 310.

[218] For further details about Philip, see Cheney, *Master Philip*, 342-50.

had wheedled large sums of money out of the English church with the acquiescence of Archbishop Hubert Walter;[219] and Ralph of Diceto, who may have confused the fortieth with other payments made to the nuncio, expressed concern that the money collected for the Holy Land would fall into the hands of the avaricious Romans.[220] These or similar complaints must have reached the ears of Innocent III, for in 1202 he instituted an enquiry into the amounts which Philip had collected. The pope wrote to Hubert Walter of rumours that his emissary 'was reputed to have received, and also exacted from many individuals, many things which redound not to our honour, but to our shame', he begged the archbishop to search out the truth lest the honour of the papacy were damaged by Philip's insolence.[221] Hubert Walter's reply has not survived, but he must have undertaken an investigation, for we have a list of the amounts rendered by religious houses in the diocese of York and a note from the Abbot of Whitby giving details of the envoy's visit. According to this, Philip decided not to burden the abbey with his presence and merely requisitioned a packhorse as its contribution.[222] Even so, if other monasteries were assessed on this scale, according to their income, a substantial total would have been collected.[223] Philip's visit certainly seems to have made an unfavourable impression upon the chroniclers. When John of Salerno, a papal legate, passed through England on his way to Scotland in 1201, Roger of Howden commented, 'he ate no meat, he drank neither wine nor cider, nor any inebriating liquor, but he thirsted for silver and gold'.[224]

As we have seen, the rigour of Stephen of Anagni's administration aroused bitter resentment,[225] but the legate himself does not seem to have been the object of any personal

---

[219] Gerald of Wales, *De iure et de statu Menevensis ecclesiae, Opera*, iii. 178–9. Gerald claimed that Hubert did this in order to win favour at the curia and defeat him in the dispute over the bishopric of St David's.

[220] Ralph of Diceto, ii. 169.

[221] Innocent III, *Selected Letters Concerning England*, ed. Cheney and W. H. Semple (London, 1953), 46–7.

[222] *HMC Report on Various Collections*, 216.

[223] See Cheney, *Innocent III and England*, 244.

[224] Roger of Howden, *Chronica*, 175. See also *Chronicle of Melrose*, ed. A. O. and M. O. Anderson (Facsimile edn., London, 1936), 51, 215.

[225] See above, pp. 131–2.

criticism. The same cannot be said of his successor Cardinal Otto. He may have visited England as a papal collector in 1225,[226] and when he returned as legate in 1237, with a commission to levy a variety of impositions, including the later subsidies for the Latin Empire and the crusade against Frederick II, anti-papal feeling turned to violence. From the beginning Otto appears to have had some fears for his safety, and when he attended the Council of London in November 1237 he asked Henry III to place a concealed guard of armed men in St Paul's. The most serious incident, however, took place during his visit to Osney in the following spring. When the Cardinal arrived at the abbey his Italian servants were attacked by a group of Oxford clerks and in the course of the fray his cook was killed. Otto himself took refuge in the church tower, and when the riot was over fled to seek the protection of the king at Abingdon.[227] According to Matthew Paris, the clerks continued to hunt for the cardinal, shouting, 'where is that usurer, that simoniac, that plunderer of revenues, and that thirster for money, who perverts the king and subverts the kingdom to enrich foreigners with its booty?'[228] But his description of the scene may have been coloured by resentment of Otto's treatment of Archbishop Edmund of Canterbury, who was the subject of one of Matthew's hagiological works.[229] Significantly, the legal sources present a very different picture of the English reaction to the legate. They show that Otto was often called upon to confirm privileges and issue indulgences and suggest that many clerks were anxious to have their cases heard by a papal representative well versed in canon law.[230] Indeed according to the annalist of Tewkesbury, even the Oxford clerks responsible for the riot at Osney had originally intended to lay petitions before the cardinal.[231]

The papal subsidy of 1244 was collected by a cameral

[226] See Williamson, 'Some Aspects of the Legation of Cardinal Otto in England, 1237-41', *EHR* lxiv (1949), 161; Lunt, *Financial Relations*, 611.

[227] Matthew Paris, *CM* iii. 416, 418, 481-3; *Annales de Burtoneia*, 253; *Annales de Dunstaplia*, 147; *Annales de Theokesberia*, 107; *Annales de Oseneia*, *Annales monastici*, iv. 84-6.

[228] Matthew Paris, *CM* iii. 483.

[229] See Vaughan, 166-7, 179.

[230] Williamson, 'Some Aspects of the Legation of Cardinal Otto', 145-74.

[231] *Annales de Theokesberia*, 107.

clerk, Master Martin. Although Martin was only described as a nuncio, Matthew Paris claimed that he had greater powers than previous legates and declared that only his reverence for the holy church made him refrain from dwelling upon his rapacity.[232] Matthew's description of the widespread opposition to the nuncio's demands is highly suspect, for a long passage is taken from Roger Wendover's account of Master Otto's exactions in 1226.[233] But there is other, more reliable evidence of baronial and royal hostility towards Martin. For example, in 1244 Henry III appealed to the nuncio to moderate his demands, emphasizing the bitter resentment which his behaviour had aroused amongst the baronage; in the following year the barons sent their own deputation to Rome to register their protest.[234] According to Matthew Paris, the matter was eventually settled by some knights who had assembled at Luton and Dunstable for a tournament. They selected a representative who travelled to London and ordered the nuncio to leave the kingdom. Henry III undertook to see that Martin was safely escorted to Dover, but he was said to have commented; 'May the Devil take you to hell and through it.'[235] Many of the details about the tournament seem to have been embellishments added by Matthew, for the annalist of Dunstable, who must have had access to local information merely recorded that the king gave Martin licence to depart.[236] However there appears to be some truth in the story that it was the barons who finally forced Henry to expel the nuncio.[237] The attack upon a papal agent in Pinchbeck, Lincs. may also be regarded as a reflection of popular lay resentment of repeated papal demands. Bishop Grosseteste received a formal complaint from the nuncio about this assault, but, although he agreed that the perpetrators of the outrage should be punished with excommunication, he urged that, for the honour of the papacy, even the appearance of wrong should be absent from its envoys' actions.[238]

[232] Matthew Paris, *CM* iv. 368, 416.
[233] Roger Wendover, ii. 296-7; Matthew Paris, *CM* iii. 102-3; iv. 374-5.
[234] *Close Rolls*, 259, 357.
[235] Matthew Paris, *CM* iv. 420-1.
[236] *Annales de Dunstaplia*, 167. See also Lunt, *Financial Relations*, 211-12.
[237] See *Close Rolls*, 259, 357.
[238] Robert Grosseteste, 315-17.

The exactions of the papal chaplain Rostand figured prominently in the list of grievances sent to Alexander IV by the proctors of the archdeaconry of Lincoln in 1255,[239] and, following further protests by the English clergy and laity, when he returned to Rome in July 1257 he was shorn of some of his powers.[240] The collector Lawrence of Sumercote must also have encountered considerable resistance, for in 1256 he declared that he would rather go to prison than return to Ireland to collect the tenth for Henry III.[241]

[239] *Annales de Burtoneia*, 361.
[240] Matthew Paris, *CM* v. 647, 666, 672-3.
[241] *Royal and Other Historical Letters*, ii. 117-19.

CHAPTER V

Redemption of vows

MOST contemporaries seem to have accepted the principle behind the policy of vow-redemption, namely that whilst all should contribute towards the cost of the crusade, only those capable of fighting or playing a useful role in the Holy Land should actually undertake the expedition.[1] But there was bitter criticism of those who were thought to have abused the system for their own financial advantage, particularly the papacy and its agents, the Franciscans and Dominicans.

The most outspoken of these critics was Matthew Paris. He accused the papacy of using vow-redemptions as a source of revenue and pointed out that through this policy it had forfeited the affection of the English clergy and people. Matthew remarked that it seemed absurd for the Roman curia to attempt to deprive God's simple people of their substance by such 'mousetraps' (*muscipula*) and to reinforce his argument he quoted from the death-bed speech of Bishop Grosseteste of Lincoln, who apparently complained that the pope sold crosses as the Jews had once sold sheep and doves in the Temple (John 2: 14-15). Matthew was often guilty of misrepresentation, putting his own views into the mouths of his characters to increase the dramatic effect, but on this occasion he seems to have had a reliable source, Grosseteste's friend and physician, the Dominican John of St Giles.[2]

The full force of Matthew's criticism was, however, reserved for the papacy's agents, the friars. Matthew believed that the ultimate authority lay in the Rule of St Benedict and he was critical of the way of life adopted by the new orders.[3] He protested that the friars' lives violated the ideal of stability and accused them of abandoning their early precepts of

---

[1] See Riley-Smith, *What were the Crusades?*, 46-7.

[2] Matthew Paris, *CM* iv. 9; v. 188-9, 400-1, 405.

[3] Ibid. v. 529; Gransden, 372.

simplicity and poverty.[4] Above all, Matthew resented their role as collectors of papal revenues: obventions, legacies, taxes, and vow-redemptions.[5] He labelled the Franciscans 'fishers of money not men' and complained that they gave the cross indiscriminately—to the poor, the sick, the old, and women—and then almost immediately absolved those who had taken it from their vows, sending the proceeds to the pope's favourite, Richard, Earl of Cornwall.[6] In 1249 the Bishop of Tortosa had arrived in England with news of the latest Muslim victories and the problems encountered by Louis IX's crusade. His visit prompted Matthew to launch another attack upon the friars:

At this time the Franciscans and Dominicans diligently busied themselves with their now lucrative preaching and, working hard in this business of the crusade, to the extent of making themselves hoarse with shouting and preaching, they gave the cross to people of every age, sex, and condition, including invalids. But on the following day, or even immediately afterwards, receiving back the cross for whatever price, they absolved those who had taken it from their vow of pilgrimage and collected the money into the treasury of some powerful person. To simple people this seemed unseemly and ridiculous and the devotion of many was cooled, for it [the cross] was being sold like sheep for their fleeces and out of this no small scandal arose.

Matthew, however, was sometimes carried away by his prejudices and towards the end of his life, perhaps impelled by a fear of divine judgement, he recognized the need to tone down some of his more violent attacks upon the Franciscans and Dominicans. Between 1256 and 1259, he wrote a second version of the passage cited above and pasted it over the first account. In this he gave a very different picture of events, praising the opportunities offered by the system of vow redemptions and its exponents, the friars:

At this time the Franciscans and Dominicans, as well as others expert and learned in the art of preaching, busied themselves with their sermons and, sowing useful seed in the Lord's field, they produced a variety of fruit. And in order that Christ's faithful should not be

---

[4] Matthew Paris, *CM* iv. 279–80; v. 194–5.

[5] Ibid. iv. 280, 604–5, 635; v. 194. For the friars' role as papal collectors, see Moorman, 300–1.

[6] Matthew Paris, *CM* iv. 133–4, 635.

deprived of the reward of the indulgence which they had promised to those who took the cross for the crusade, they courteously received a redemption according to the means of each so that, with the help of God's great munificence, a ready will might be reckoned (as good as) the deed. For it was considered that women, children, and invalids, as well as the poor and unarmed, would be of little use against the armed multitude of infidels.[7]

Matthew's denunciations of the friars were particularly outspoken; but similar complaints about the behaviour of papal agents can be found in the works of other contemporaries. In a exhortation to take the cross dated c.1262, the satirical French poet Rutebeuf accused the Franciscans of keeping for themselves the money donated for the Holy Land and protested: 'the cross is preached in such a way that one might think that paradise was being sold and delivered by the pope.'[8] And Gilbert of Tournai, himself an experienced crusade-preacher and the author of a number of crusade sermons,[9] described the resentment caused by the wanton absolution of vows. Gilbert denounced those who regarded this as an opportunity to extort money from the old and the weak, lamenting:

This scandal has redounded upon the preaching [of the crusade] so that if they [the clergy] again preach the indulgences of the cross it is uncertain what they will accomplish, but it is certain that they shall sustain various insults.[10]

Linked with these accusations was a charge that the papacy had redeemed the vows of able-bodied crusaders and thus deprived the East of much needed resources. In a poem written shortly after the loss of Damietta in 1221, the Northern French trouvère Huon de St Quentin denounced the clergy as traitors who had taken the part of Ganelon against the Lord's Roland, and he warned Rome that it had erred grievously in taking away the cross from those who had borne it for God:

[7] Id. *Historia Anglorum*, ed. F. Madden (London, 1866-9), iii. 51-2 n. 3. For Matthew's policy of emendation, see Vaughan, 121-4; Gransden, 370.

[8] Rutebeuf, 'La complainte de Constantinople', *Onze Poèmes concernant la croisade*, ed. J. Bastin and E. Faral (Paris, 1946), 31-2, 39.

[9] See Gilbert of Tournai, *Sermones ad omnes status de novo correcti et emendati* (Lyons, 1511), fols. 132^r-7^r.

[10] Id. *Collectio*, 40.

Our shepherd does not look after his flock when he sells it to a wolf for money . . . What will become of the wealth which he has villainously acquired through the false levies upon crusaders? . . . He has taken from Acre and Bethlehem that which had been promised to God.

Huon blamed clerical avarice for the delays in sending help to Egypt and the ultimate failure of the Fifth Crusade.[11]

This theme of criticism was taken up again at the time of Louis IX's first crusade. Matthew Paris complained that the pope had persuaded the crusaders who had been left behind at Aigues Mortes to redeem their vows in return for a large sum of money, and held Innocent responsible for the Count of Poitiers's unsuccessful attempt to launch an expedition to relieve Louis in the East: as soon as men had taken the cross they were apparently absolved from their vows.[12] Admittedly Matthew may have been guilty of exaggeration when he described the Count's eagerness to return to Egypt.[13] But other contemporaries also denounced the widespread redemption of vows. In his lament upon the disaster at Mansurah, the troubadour Austorc d'Aurillac commented:

St Peter held the right way, but the pope now deviates. He and the perfidious clergy whom he holds in his power wish evil upon many for the sake of money.[14]

In a similar way the Templar Ricaut Bonomel, writing after the fall of Arsuf and Caesarea to the Mamelukes in 1265, attributed the shortage of manpower in the East to papal avarice,[15] and this charge was repeated after Louis IX's death at Tunis by the troubadour Raimon Gaucelm de Béziers, who lamented:

I will tell you how those who once distributed the cross behave: for a sum of money they permit most to rid themselves of it.[16]

[11] 'Jerusalem se plaint et le pais', Chansons de croisade, 148-9; 'Rome, Jerusalem se plaint', La Langue, cols. 373-80.
[12] Matthew Paris, CM v. 24-5, 188.
[13] See Purcell, 77; Jordan, Louis IX, 112-13.
[14] Austorc d'Aurillac, '(Ai!) Dieus! per qu'as fa(ch)a tan gran ma(lez)a', st. vi, in 'Le troubadour Austorc d'Aurillac et son sirventes sur la septième croisade', ed. Jeanroy, Mélanges Chabaneau, Romanische Forschungen, xxiii (1907), 83.
[15] 'Ir e dolors s'es e mon cors asseza', Poesie provenzali, ii. 222-4.
[16] 'Ab grans trebalhs et ab grans marrimens', st. iv, in 'Les troubadours de Béziers', ed. G. Azais, Bulletin de la societé archéologique de Béziers, 2nd ser, i (1858), 191. See also Gilbert of Tournai, Collectio, 40.

The critics cited above, however, either came from areas bitterly hostile to the papacy such as Languedoc, or had personal reasons for attacking papal crusading policy;[17] in consequence their picture of events is somewhat distorted. There was obviously a danger of abuse. The prospect of rich financial rewards prompted impostors to tour the countryside persuading crusaders to redeem their vows for a large sum of money[18] and greed also corrupted a number of papal officials.[19] For practical reasons the question of the fitness of a crusader for his task was left to the discretion of the individual collector,[20] and some used their position as a source of revenue, redeeming the vows of able-bodied crusaders, as well as the poor, the old, and the weak. But the popes seem to have been as anxious as anyone to ensure that their agents did not exceed the terms of their commission and in the thirteenth century they made repeated attempts to deal with this problem. When Gregory IX heard in 1237 that some French crusaders had fled to the East out of fear that they would be forced to redeem their vows, he wrote immediately to his representatives, ordering them to see that this scandalous practice ceased.[21] Similar warnings were issued by Innocent IV at the time of Louis IX's first crusade. In a letter dated 1247, the pope ordered Walter Cantilupe, Bishop of Worcester, to make sure that able-bodied crusaders were not compelled to lay aside their crosses, and he instructed his legate, Odo of Châteauroux, to prevent the wanton absolution of vows in the border dioceses of Cambrai, Liège, Toul, Utrecht, Metz, and Verdun and the maritime districts such as Marseilles. The Bishops of Évreux and Senlis were given similar responsibilities for the whole of France.[22] Later popes exhibited an equal concern to prevent any abuse of the policy of vow-redemption. In 1263 Urban IV condemned the excesses of his collectors in Germany and Bohemia; two years later his successor Clement IV wrote to his legate in France, Archbishop Giles of Tyre, exhorting him to curb

---

[17] See above, pp. 8, 10, 13–14.
[18] *Diplomatarium Suecanum*, i. no. 263; Oliver of Paderborn, *Epistolae*, 316.
[19] See Odo Rigaud, 733.
[20] Gregory IX, no. 4635; Innocent IV, no. 2963.
[21] Gregory IX, nos. 3945, 4222.
[22] Innocent IV, nos. 2963, 3054, 3708, 3966.

the immoderate behaviour of his officials, lest this should create scandal.[23]

Another source of resentment was the exploitation of the system of vow-redemption by those who regretted having taken the cross and sought to escape their obligations without forfeiting the spiritual benefits which they conferred. The Cistercian Caesar of Heisterbach included two examples of this abuse and the subsequent fate of its perpetrators in his collection of *exempla* as a warning to the faithful. Caesar's first story concerned a usurer named Gottschalk:

When by Pope Innocent's commands the dispensators collected money for redemptions from the aged, the poor and the sick, this same usurer feigned poverty and gave one of the pope's agents the sum of five marks, to be released from his vows . . . The wretch then sat about in the taverns provoking God and mocking his pilgrims, in the following way: 'You fools will cross the seas and waste your substance and expose your lives to many dangers, while I shall sit at home with my wife and children, and get a similar reward to yours through the five marks with which I redeemed my cross.

Caesar commented that God soon intervened and punished the miser for his cunning. One night he was awakened by Satan and taken to hell on a coal-black horse, and he was warned that in three days he would take up his appointed place in the midst of its torments.[24] In his second example, Caesar described how, at the time of the Fifth Crusade, a peasant of the diocese of Cologne, who had feigned blindness in order to be released from his vow, was struck with real blindness as a punishment for his blasphemy.[25] Once again the papacy made every effort to see that those who had taken the cross and were capable of travelling to the Holy Land fulfilled their vows.

[23] Urban IV, i. no. 312; Clement IV, no. 1608.
[24] Caesar of Heisterbach, *Dialogus miraculorum*, i. 70-2.
[25] Id. 'Die Fragmente der Libri VIII miraculorum des Caesarius von Heisterbach', ed. A. Meister, *Römische Quartalschrift*, Supp. xiii (1901), 23-4.

CHAPTER VI

Crusading in Europe

BETWEEN 1095 and 1274 the papacy authorized crusades
against the Moors in Spain, pagans in north-eastern Europe,
heretics in Southern France and Germany, and schismatics
in Greece, and Christian lay powers in the West, as well as
the Muslims in the Holy Land, Egypt, and North Africa.

The extension of the status of a crusade to Spain dates
from Urban II's pontificate;[1] this privilege was renewed by
his successors at frequent intervals during the twelfth and
thirteenth centuries.[2] On these occasions participants seem
to have been awarded the same indulgence as crusaders in
the Near East, and the *Reconquista* appears to have been
regarded as part of a general campaign against the enemies
of the faith. The armies were mainly recruited from the
Spanish kingdoms, but in 1211 Innocent III issued a general
appeal to the faithful to unite against the Moors.[3] According
to the troubadour Gavaudan,[4] English, French, and German
knights took the cross; but they were not prepared to fight
a lengthy campaign and most soon turned back.[5]

At the same time, the Christians in north-eastern Europe
were engaged in a continuous struggle with their pagan

[1] 'Papsturkunden in Spanien, Vorarbeiten zur Hispania Pontificia: (i)
Katalonien (ii) Urkunden und Regesten', ed. Kehr, *Abhandlungen der Gesellschaft
zu Göttingen, Philologisch-historische Klasse*, xviii (1926), 287–8.

[2] Paschal II, *Opera*, PL clxiii, cols. 64–5, 407; *Regesta Pontificum Romanorum*,
comp. Jaffé, no. 6485; Calixtus II, *Bullaire*, ed. U. Robert (Paris, 1891), ii. 266–7;
Eugenius III, *Opera*, cols. 1345–7, 1539; 'Papsturkunden in Spanien: Katalonien',
346–7; 'Papsturkunden in Spanien: Navarra und Aragon (i)', ed. Kehr, *Abhandlungen der Gesellschaft der Wissenschaften zu Göttingen*, xxii (1928), 272–3;
Innocent III, PL ccxvi, col. 380; Honorius III, no. 5665; Gregory IX, nos. 268,
518, 3483; Innocent IV, no. 1758; Clement IV, nos. 15–17.

[3] Innocent III, PL ccxvi, col. 699.

[4] Gavaudan, 'Senhor per los nostres peccatz', in 'Poésies du troubadour
Gavaudan', ed. Jeanroy, *Romania*, xxxix (1905), 535. For the dating of this
poem, see Gaztambide, 115.

[5] *Primera Crónica General de España que mandó componer Alfonso el Sabio*,
ed. R. Menéndez Pidal (Madrid, 1955), ii. 696; A. Mackay, *Spain in the Middle
Ages: From Frontier to Empire, 1000–1500* (London, 1977), 33–4.

neighbours—the Wends, Livs, Estonians, and Prussians.[6] The first campaign to be awarded the status of a crusade was the German expedition against the Wends in 1147,[7] but this privilege was later extended to several of the wars in the Baltic.[8] Not all participants received the full crusading indulgence. For example, the members of the Livonian crusade of 1199 were granted the same indulgence as pilgrims to Rome.[9] Nevertheless, there seems to have been no doubt in their own minds that they were taking part in a true crusade. At the Fourth Lateran Council, Bishop Albert of Riga was said to have called Livonia the land of the Virgin Mary and to have argued that its conquest was as important as the recovery of Christ's patrimony in the East.[10] In his memoir submitted to the Second Council of Lyons, Bishop Bruno of Olmütz went much further: he advocated that Gregory X's proposed crusade should be diverted to north-eastern Europe, on the grounds that the pagans presented a much greater threat to Christendom than the Muslims.[11] This thesis was disputed by Humbert of Romans, who had hopes of converting the Prussians by preaching and teaching.[12] But the only real criticism of the use of the crusade in north-eastern Europe came from Roger Bacon, writing c. 1268. He maintained that the use of force had antagonized the pagans and made them embittered against the Christian faith. Even so, the main force of his argument was directed against the land-hungry Teutonic knights rather than against the crusaders themselves.[13]

Contemporaries may have accepted the use of the crusade against the Moors and the pagans in north-eastern Europe, but there was severe criticism of the papal campaigns against heretics, schismatics, and Christian lay powers.

[6] See E. Kennan, 'Innocent III, Gregory IX and Political Crusades: A Study in the Disintegration of Papal Power', in *Reform and Authority in the Medieval and Reformation Church*, ed. G. F. Lytle (Washington, DC, 1981), 17-19, 29-32.

[7] *Eugenius III, Opera*, cols. 1203-4.

[8] See *Diplomatarium Suecanum*, i, nos. 55, 298, 307; *Diplomatarium Norvegicum*, ed. C. A. Lange and C. R. Unger, i (Christiania, 1847), nos. 24, 27; *Regesta Diplomatica Historiae Danicae*, i (Copenhagen, 1847), nos. 826, 846.

[9] See *Diplomatarium Suecanum*, i. 114.

[10] Henry of Livonia, 126.

[11] Bruno of Olmütz, 20-2.

[12] Humbert of Romans, *Opus tripartitum*, 195.

[13] Roger Bacon, *Opus maius*, ed. J. H. Bridges (London, 1897-1900), iii. 121-2. See also Gilbert of Tournai, *Collectio*, 39.

It is important to establish the extent of this opposition and whether it reflected widespread popular resentment of the use of the crusade in Europe.

Crusades against heretics

In 1179 the Third Lateran Council granted a limited indulgence to all who fought against heretics,[14] and two years later a small expedition, under the command of the papal legate Cardinal Henry of Albano, was sent to the Languedoc. It succeeded in capturing the fortress of Lavaur,[15] but, although some prominent heretics were forced to recant, the Cathars continued to flourish; and in the early thirteenth century Innocent III appealed to the King of France for aid. Because of his continued conflict with England, Philip Augustus was not prepared to lead a crusade himself; but a number of his vassals took the cross in 1207-8 and were awarded the same indulgence as the crusaders in the Latin East.[16]

The Albigensian Crusade aroused vociferous protests from certain Provençal troubadours. But the extent of this opposition has been exaggerated, partly because of a misinterpretation of the life and work of the poet Perdigon.[17] According to the various versions of his *vida*, Perdigon was the son of a fisherman in the small town of Lesperon. His poetic talents brought him to the notice of the Dauphin of Auvergne, and as a reward for his services he was made a knight and given lands and revenues. Perdigon was apparently a fierce opponent of the Cathars and after the murder of the papal legate Peter of Castelnau he accompanied Bishop Fulk of Toulouse on a mission to Rome. The purpose of this embassy was to persuade the pope to organize a crusade against Count Raymond VI of Toulouse and other protectors of heretics. After his return Perdigon acted as a propagandist for the Albigensian Crusade; he composed songs exhorting men to take the cross and rejoiced that the French had defeated

[14] *COD* 224-5.

[15] Geoffrey of Vigeois, 448-9; *Chronicon Clarevallense*, col. 1250. See also M. Roquebert, *L'Epopée cathare*, Toulouse (1970-7), i. 88-92.

[16] Innocent III, *PL* ccxv, cols. 361-2, 526-8, 1155-6, 1246-7, 1469-70. See also Roquebert, i. 163-5, 204-5, 223-6, 230-1.

[17] See Throop, 36.

the Southern forces at the battle of Muret. Within a few years of this victory, however, the balance of power had shifted; Raymond VII gradually reconquered his father's lands and after the death of Simon of Montfort Perdigon was abandoned by his former patrons. The Dauphin of Auvergne took back his lands and honours and according to the author of the *vida*, in desperation Perdigon begged Lambert of Montélimar to find him a refuge amongst the Cistercians at Silvacana. His pleas were heeded and he spent the remaining years of his life in this abbey.[18] Using this *vida* as their source, literary scholars have argued that Perdigon's fellow troubadours formed an alliance to expel him from the Languedoc and historians have quoted this as an example of the widespread opposition to the Albigensian Crusade. But in fact, as Hoepffner has shown, there is no evidence that Perdigon was associated with the crusaders. Of the fourteen poems which have survived, only one line could be said to refer to the French crusade: an exhortation to the Kings of Aragon and Castile to unite against the 'renegatz',[19] and the meaning of this is far from clear. Perdigon's most recent editor, H. J. Chaytor, believed that the 'renegatz' referred to the Albigenses.[20] But other scholars have suggested that they were knights in the forces of King Sancho I of Portugal who were suspected of treachery on behalf of the Muslims.[21]

There is certainly no evidence that the troubadours formed a united and powerful body of opinion against the Albigensian Crusade. Even if one makes an allowance for poems which may have been lost, only a very small proportion of the poets writing in the Languedoc made any reference at all to the crusade.[22] The main theme of their poetry was love, and this was true even of troubadours like Guilhem de Durfort, Bernart Arnaut de Moncuc, and Hugh de Mataplana who

---

[18] *Biographies des troubadours*, 408–15.
[19] Perdigon, 'Entr'amor e pessamen', st. vi, *Les Chansons*, ed. H. J. Chaytor (Paris, 1926), 17.
[20] Ibid. pp. iv–v.
[21] See F. Diez, *Leben und Werke der Troubadours* (2nd edn., Leipzig, 1882), 440; E. Hoepffner, 'La Biographie de Perdigon', *Romania*, liii (1927), 350–1, 359–64; Gere, 'The Troubadours', 64–6.
[22] See Gere, 6–8, 61–2.

were personally involved in the fighting.[23] The poet Raimon de Miraval was a close friend of Raymond VI of Toulouse and probably accompanied him to Spain after his defeat at the battle of Muret in 1213. Yet, although his own castle had fallen to the crusaders in 1211, he made only a brief mention of the expedition. In a love song addressed to Count Raymond's wife Leonora, he appealed to her brother King Peter of Aragon to help him to recover his castle, for he wished to present it as a gift to his *domna*:

Song, go on my behalf and tell the king whom joy guides and clothes . . . that in him there is nothing awry . . . Provided that he recovers Montégut and returns to Carcassonne he will then be the emperor of fine reputation and the French will fear his shield over here and the Muslims likewise over there.

My lady, you have always helped me so much that it is for you that I still sing, even though I did not expect to compose a song about you until I had given back to you the fief of Miraval which I have lost.

But the king has promised me that I will recover it shortly and that my Audiart (Raymond VI) will recover Beaucaire. Then ladies and lovers will be able to return to the joy that they have lost.[24]

One later writer claimed that there was a link between this plea and the king's subsequent campaign, culminating in the battle of Muret; but this seems to be pure invention.[25]

Admittedly there were a few troubadours who criticized the crusaders, but at first even they seem to have been unaware of the significance of this latest incursion from the North. For example, the Dauphinois jongleur Guilhem Augier composed a *planh* or lament upon the death of Raimon Rogier of Trencavel in prison in Carcassonne in 1209, and accused the crusaders of his murder;[26] but his poem conveyed a sense of personal loss rather than opposition to the expedition

---

[23] 'Er can li rozier', in 'Three Troubadour Poems with Historical Overtones' ed. F. M. Chambers, *Speculum*, liv (1979), 46-51; Nelli, 151-2, 154-5; Hugh de Mataplana, 'Arondeta de ton chantar m'azir', ed. G. Bertoni, *Annales du Midi*, xxv (1913), 58-64 and Roquebert, ii. 170.

[24] Raimon de Miraval, 'Bel m'es q'ieu chant e coindei', in *Les Poésies du troubadour Raimon de Miraval*, ed. Topsfield (Paris, 1971), 305-6; P. Andraud, *La Vie et l'œuvre du troubadour Raimon de Miraval* (Paris, 1902), 24-5, 73-6, 152-4; Topsfield, 219, 236-7.

[25] *Biographies des troubadours*, 404-7.

[26] 'Quascus plor et planh son dampnatge', *Anthologie des troubadours*, 235-9. See also Innocent III, PL ccxvi, col. 739.

itself. And, although the troubadour Gavaudan denounced those who joined Bishop Fulk of Toulouse's militia and fought against Raymond VI at Lavaur, his main theme appears to have been betrayal for money and the righteous vengeance of a lord:

Let no one . . . imagine that he can have peace without difficulty when they struggle against such a mighty lord . . . Believe me if punishment comes late, it cannot fail to strike those whom God hates.[27]

The Languedoc was accustomed to invasion and the troubadours relished the pageantry of war.[28] And in the period before the battle of Muret and the Fourth Lateran Council, the crusade seems to have been regarded as some form of feudal or territorial dispute between, on the one hand, the King of France, supported by the church, and, on the other, the King of Aragon and the Count of Toulouse.[29] Troubadours could be found fighting on both sides, and their allegiance seems to have been determined by feudal and military considerations.[30] This view of the expedition was reflected in their poetry. An anonymous partisan of the Count of Toulouse reminded King Peter of Aragon that, although he had won a great victory over the Almohads at the battle of Las Navas de Tolosa, he still had obligations to his vassals in the Languedoc:

Go Hugonet, without delay to the noble King of Aragon and sing him this new *sirventes*. Tell him that he has waited too long, that people are saying he has failed. For they say here that for a long time the French have occupied at liberty his defenceless lands.

I should be glad . . . to see our men engage the French, in order to learn who shall have the prize of chivalry. Since right is on our side, I think that they must lose.[31]

And, according to the continuator of *La Chanson de la croisade albigeoise*, when the king addressed his soldiers before the battle of Muret he gave the following reason for going to war:

[27] Gavaudan, 'A la pus langa nuech de l'an', ed. cit. 504–6. For a discussion of this poem, see Gere, 'The Troubadours', 29–30.
[28] See 'Three Troubadour Poems', 44–6.
[29] See *HGL* viii. 612–19.   [30] Gere, 'The Troubadours', 67–86.
[31] 'Vai Hugonet, ses bitensa', *Anthologie*, 240–3. See also Peire Cardenal, 'Per fols tenc Polhes e Lombartz', ed. cit. 104–9.

The clerks and the French wish to deprive the count, my brother-in-law, of his inheritance and chase him from his lands, though no one can accuse him of error or wrongdoing.[32]

After Peter's death and the defeat of the Southern forces, the troubadour Guilhem Anelier prayed that Christ would grant the young King James strength to defeat his foes, and he lamented:

The church was greatly lacking in wisdom when it wished to establish the French here where they have no right to be.[33]

- The situation changed after the humiliating settlement imposed upon the Count of Toulouse and his young son Raymond VII by the Fourth Lateran Council. Writing in the spring of 1216, the Tarascon knights Tomier and Palazi denounced the shameful peace and exhorted men to follow the example of Avignon, which had declared against the French. In his bull *Quia maior*, Innocent III had revoked the crusading indulgence for all except the inhabitants of the Languedoc,[34] giving priority to the Fifth Crusade; the poets reminded those who continued to fight in Southern France of their obligations in the Holy Land:[35]

He who abandons the Holy Sepulchre does not have a sincere faith in God. The clergy and the French do little about the shame inflicted upon the Lord, but God will be avenged upon those whose rapacity has cut the paths and closed the ways that lead to Acre and Syria.[36]

Two other troubadours exhorted Raymond VI to resist the French.[37] But it was still only a very small group of poets

[32] *La Chanson de la croisade albigeoise*, ii. 2. See also ibid. 290. The same argument was put forward by an Aragonese chronicler, *Gesta veterum comitum Barcinonensium*, ed. P. de Marca in *Marca Hispanica* (Paris, 1688), col. 554.

[33] Guilhem Anelier, 'Ara farai, no.m puesc tenir', *Der Troubadour Guilhem Anelier von Toulouse, vier provenzalische Gedichte*, ed. M. Gisi (Solothurn, 1877), 26–30.   [34] Tangl, 94.

[35] For similar criticism, see Pons de Capdouilh, 'So c'om plus vol e plus e voluntos', stt. v, vi, in *Leben und Werke des Trobadors Ponz de Capduoil*, ed. M. von Napolski (Halle, 1879), 67–9; C. Fabre, 'Le Troubadour Pons de Chapteuil, quelques remarques sur sa vie et sur l'esprit de ses poèmes', *Mémoires et procès-verbaux de la société agricole et scientifique de la Haute-Loire*, xiv (1905-6), 39–42. See also Pons de Capdouilh, 'En honor del pair'en cui es', 89–91.

[36] 'Si col flacs molins torneja', in 'Un sirventes en faveur de Raimon VII (1216)', ed. Jeanroy, *Bausteine zur romanischen Philologie: Festgabe für A. Mussafia* (Halle, 1905), 629–40. For the counts' enthusiastic welcome in the Languedoc after their return from Rome, see *La chanson de la croisade*, ii. 90.

[37] See Montan Sartre, 'Coms de Tolsan', in 'Poésies inédites des troubadours

who actually condemned the use of the crusade against the Albigenses. According to the anonymous continuator of the *Chanson*, when Innocent III accused the Count of Foix of heresy and murder, the latter replied:

no pilgrim engaged in a holy journey instituted by God has been maltreated or robbed, killed by me, or attacked on his way by any of my men. But as for those brigands, traitors, and perjurers who bearing the cross have come to ruin me, those who have been captured have had their eyes put out . . . I rejoice over those I have killed and massacred and regret those that have escaped and fled.[38]

Writing some time after 1216, Guilhem Figueira denounced the false preaching of the church,[39] and the troubadour Peire Cardenal, a fierce critic of the clergy and an ardent supporter of Raymond VI, lamented that falsehood and wrong had now triumphed over truth and right.[40]

The leader of the Southern revolt was the young Count Raymond VII;[41] his first major success was the capture of the stronghold of Beaucaire after a prolonged siege in 1217. In a *sirventes* celebrating this triumph, the troubadour Guilhem Rainol d'Apt exhorted the Catalans and Aragonese to avenge the death of King Peter and to join forces with Languedoc against the French and the clergy:

If he [Simon of Montfort] should want to gather in his taxes, I would advise him not to return to Beaucaire . . .

Let us defend our plains and marshes lest they be lost through indifference. When the French come back to us unarmed then we shall know their secret designs. God and right have overturned their schemes despite those who accepted the peace.[42]

Like Tomier and Palazi, Guilhem Rainol reminded the faithful of their duties in the Holy Land and urged them to hasten

du Périgord', ed. C. Chabaneau, *Revue des langues romanes*, 3rd ser. xxx (1885), 157-8. Gui de Cavaillon, 'Senher coms, saber volria', in *Le Parnasse occitanien ou Choix des poésies originales des troubadours tirées des manuscrits nationaux*, ed. M. de Rochegude (Toulouse, 1819), 271.

[38] *La Chanson de la croisade*, ii. 52.
[39] Guilhem Figueira, 'Nom laissarai per paor', ed. cit. 45-6.
[40] Peire Cardenal, 'Falsedatz et desmesura', ed. cit. 78-83.
[41] See Guilhem Adémar, 'Mout chantera de joi', stt. vii, viii, *Poésies du troubadour Guilhem Adémar*, ed. K. Almquist (Uppsala, 1951), 146-8.
[42] 'A tornar m'er enquer al premier us', *Anthologie*, 244-8.

to avenge the Muslim victories in the East.[43] The anonymous continuator of the *Chanson* went much further and declared that the use of the crusade in the Languedoc was against God's will. He regarded the fog, which enabled Raymond to enter Toulouse without being seen, as a sign of divine favour; and commented that the stone which killed Simon of Montfort hit him 'just where it was necessary'. The fact that the church mourned Simon as a saint and martyr seemed to him to be a further indication that the 'traditional' concept of the crusade had been perverted:

the epitaph relates . . . that he is a saint and martyr . . . destined to rise again . . . to wear a heavenly crown and sit in the heavenly kingdom. And I have heard it said that it may well be so; if by killing men, by shedding blood . . . by following evil counsels . . . by seizing lands . . . a man can defeat Jesus Christ in this world, then he should wear a crown and shine in heaven.[44]

No poems have survived from the period between 1219 and 1225, when Raymond VII reconquered the South from Simon's heir Amaury of Montfort. The resumption of the crusade in 1226, however, aroused further criticism from the same small group of troubadours. In a *sirventes*, probably written whilst Louis VIII was marching on Avignon, Tomier and Palazi denounced 'those who come under the false pretext of a crusade', and they reassured those who resisted the king that God fought on their behalf: '[the French] will soon have to flee without even lighting their campfires'. Although the indulgence had been restored to the campaign in the Languedoc in 1218,[45] the poets still protested that the papal legate Cardinal Romanus paid no heed to the fate of Damietta, and they reminded those who joined the French expedition of their duties in the East:

Those who bear the cross against us have deprived the sepulchre of help and assistance and that is ungodliness. The false fools will ill enjoy the silver—*argenza*—thus acquired.[46]

[43] 'Auzir cugei lo chant', *Gedichte der Troubadours*, ed. C. A. F. Mahn (Berlin, 1856–73), ii. 9–10.

[44] *La Chanson de la croisade*, ii. 274–6, 308; iii. 206, 228.

[45] Honorius III, no. 1578.

[46] 'De chantar farai', *Poesie provenzali*, ii. 54–7. The poets intended to make a pun, for *argenza* was also the name of the district around Beaucaire. See ibid. 56, n. 46.

The most outspoken critic was again Guilhem Figueira. He attributed the failure of the Fifth Crusade to papal avarice and urged Rome to devote its energies to the campaign against the Muslims rather than fight the Christian inhabitants of the Languedoc. Guilhem predicted that if Raymond VII lived two years more, France would grieve for the papacy's trickery and he lamented:

Rome, truly I know without doubt that with the trickery of false pardons you delivered up to torment, far from paradise, the French baronage. Rome, you have killed the good King Louis, for your false preaching drew him out of France.

. . . Rome, may God give me no share in the pardon or in the pilgrimage which you make for Avignon.[47]

When the troubadour Fulk de Romans returned to the Languedoc from Italy in 1226, he condemned this use of the crusade and commented: 'I would have liked to go on the first crusade but nearly all I see of this one displeases me'.[48]

A settlement was eventually reached in 1229 between Raymond VII, the papacy, and the King of France, but the harshness of its terms provoked further complaints from certain troubadours;[49] and several poets composed *sirventes* expressing support for the Southern rebellion in 1242.[50]

The Albigensian Crusade also aroused criticism from the small group of Northern French trouvères who had blamed papal intervention, and particularly the interference of the legate Cardinal Pelagius, for the failure of the Fifth Crusade.[51] Like some of the troubadours, they argued that the campaign in the Languedoc was not a true crusade and protested that valuable resources were being diverted from the East. Writing shortly after the surrender of Damietta, Huon de Saint Quentin lamented:

[47] Guilhem Figueira, 'D'un sirventes far', stt. vi, vii, x, xii, xxii. See also Peire Cardenal, 'Ben volgra si Dieus o volgues', ed. cit. 62-6.

[48] Fulk de Romans, 'Quan cug chantar', ed. cit. 59.

[49] See Bernart de La Barta, 'Foilla ni flors', 'Three Troubadour poems', 52-4; Guilhem de Montanhagol, 'Del tot vey remaner valor', *Le Troubadour Guilhem de Montanhagol*, ed. J. Coulet (Toulouse, 1898), 87-9.

[50] See Jeanroy, 'Le soulèvement de 1242 dans la poésie des troubadours', *Annales du Midi*, xvi (1904), 311-30.

[51] See above, pp. 10, 34-5.

The river (Jordan), the sepulchre, the cross cry out with one voice that Rome plays with false dice. It appeared well in Albi and showed that our law is far worse than it used to be.[52]

And an anonymous poet maintained that Amaury of Montfort's failure to retain his father's conquests was an indication that the French expedition was against God's will.[53] The most detailed attack upon the use of the crusade against heretics came, however, from the pen of Guillaume le Clerc. In his poem *Le Besant de Dieu*, he described the state of discord in the world and criticized the papacy for sending the French to attack the inhabitants of the South:

When one of her sons has done wrong, but is willing to make reparation, Rome ought not, it seems to me, to send her eldest son to destroy him. It would be far better for her to summon him and talk gently with him and admonish him than to order that his lands be laid waste. When the French attack the people of Toulouse, whom they regard as heretics, and the Roman legate leads and guides them, that I think is not right at all.

Guillaume declared that those who perished in support of unjust demands upon another people were guilty of mortal sin; and he lamented that Louis VIII had been driven to his death by this preaching: the king had sought to drive out the people of Provence, but, when he seemed to be victorious, all hope failed him and his empire was reduced to a mere seven feet of earth. Guillaume stressed that it was more important to fight the Muslims than the Albigenses, and exhorted Christians to concentrate their energies upon the recapture of the Holy Sepulchre. There is no evidence, however, that these outspoken views attracted widespread support: *Le Besant de Dieu* has survived in only one manuscript and it is not quoted by any other contemporary poet.[54]

This 'diversion' of the crusade was also denounced by the English chronicler Roger Wendover, who seems to have regarded the inhabitants of the Languedoc as fellow victims of papal aggrandisement. Roger condemned the papal legate Romanus for his refusal to accept Raymond VII's submission at the Council of Bourges in 1225, and claimed that most

[52] 'Rome, Jherusalem se plaint', *La Langue*, col. 375.
[53] 'Bien mostre Dieus apertement', *Chansons satiriques*, 10.
[54] Guillaume le Clerc, ll. 159-74, 829-46, 2387-99, 2470-87; ed. cit. 70.

crusaders had taken the cross out of fear of the Cardinal and Louis VIII, rather than from any sense of justice. Indeed he described the French campaign as 'bellum injustum' and commented that the heavy casualties during the siege of Avignon were a divine judgement, for the predominant motive in the army was greed.[55]

In his study of opposition to the Albigensian Crusade, Throop suggested that the objections raised by Roger and the trouvères reflected a much larger body of opinion;[56] but there is no evidence to support this conclusion. As we have seen, both the St Albans chroniclers and the Northern French poets were determined opponents of the papacy, and cannot be said to represent public opinion. Indeed, far from its arousing widespread resentment, there are indications that the expedition against the heretics in the Languedoc received considerable support and was regarded as part of a general campaign against the enemies of the faith. Chroniclers in Belgium and Germany recorded that men flocked to take the cross[57] and according to William of Tuleda, the author of the first part of *La Chanson de la croisade albigeoise*, the crusading army included contingents from Bavaria, Saxony, Frisia, Anjou, Normandy, Brittany, Poitou, Gascony, Provence, and Lombardy.[58] One of the most prominent crusaders was Duke Leopold VI of Austria and Styria, who fought in Spain and the Languedoc in 1212 and then took part in the Fifth Crusade.[59] Guilhem Figueira's savage denunciation of papal crusading policy was challenged by another troubadour, Gormonda de Montpellier, who declared that heretics were a greater threat to the church than the Muslims in the East.[60]

[55] Roger Wendover, ii. 305-6, 314-15. See also Matthew Paris, *CM* ii. 110, 118; *Annales de Dunstaplia*, 101.

[56] Throop, 44.

[57] *Annales Parchenses*, MGH SS xvi. 606; *Annales Floreffienses*, ibid. 626; *Annales Sancti Jacobi Leodiensis*, ibid. 663, 665; *Annales Stadenses*, 355; *Chronica regia Coloniensis*, 230-1, 233.

[58] *La Chanson de la croisade albigeoise*, i. 112, 132-4, 248. See also Peter of Vaux de Cernay, i. 176-7; ii. 7, 9.

[59] *Annales Marbacenses*, 172. For Leopold's varied crusading career, see Riley-Smith, *The Crusades*, 19-20.

[60] 'Greu m'es a durar', in *Poesie provenzali*, ii. 108. See also Lanfranc Cigala, 'Si mos chans fois de ioi ne de solatz', ed. Bertoni, *I trovatori d'Italia* (Modena, 1915), 352.

Between 1232 and 1234 Gregory IX authorized a crusade against another group of heretics in the diocese of Bremen, known as the Stedingers, who had been a source of anxiety to the church since the late twelfth century.[61] Once again participants received the same indulgence as crusaders in the Holy Land and according to the chroniclers men flocked to take the cross in Germany and the Low Countries. Amongst those who took part were the Landgrave of Thuringia, the Duke of Brabant, and the Counts of Holland and Cleves.[62] The only area where the preachers encountered resistance was Groningen, where the local population had good reason to oppose the papal campaign, having recently experienced the so-called 'crusade' launched by Bishop Wilbrand of Utrecht.[63]

Crusades against schismatic Greeks

There is some dispute whether Pope Paschal II was deceived about the goal of Bohemond of Antioch's crusade of 1107-8: whether it was preached in terms of an expedition to Jerusalem or as a campaign against the Byzantine Empire.[64] But, after the failure of Bohemond's attack upon Durazzo and the humiliating settlement imposed by the Emperor Alexius, the chronicler Orderic Vitalis complained that the crusade had been misused:

by the just providence of God the attempt of men greedy to seize the property of their neighbours was brought to nothing, so that the proud

---

[61] MGH Epistolae saeculi XIII, i. 393-4, 436-7; *Regesta Pontificum Romanorum*, comp. Potthast, no. 9076. See also H. Lea, *A History of the Inquisition in the Middle Ages* (New York, 1906), iii. 182-9; Kennan, 'Innocent III, Gregory IX', 25-8.

[62] MGH Epistolae saeculi XIII, i. 466-7; *Annales Stadenses*, 361; *Chronica Bremensis*, ed. H. Meibom, in *Scriptores Germanici Rerum Germanicarum* (Helmstedt, 1688), ii. 58-9; *Chronicon Rastedense*, ibid. 101.

[63] *Corpus documentorum Inquisitionis haereticae pravitatis Neerlandicae*, ed. P. Fredericq (Ghent 1899-1903), i, cols. 102-3; Kennan, 'Innocent III, Gregory IX', 26-9.

[64] See J. G. Rowe, 'Paschal II, Bohemond of Antioch and the Byzantine Empire', *Bulletin of the John Rylands Library*, xlix (1966-7), 176-202; R. B. Yewdale, *Bohemond I, Prince of Antioch* (Princeton 1924), 107-12; M. W. Baldwin, 'The Papacy and the Levant during the Twelfth Century', *Bulletin of the Polish Institute of Arts and Sciences in America*, iii (1945), 284-8; Hehl, 14-16.

army of ambitious men secured none of those things which they had vainly imagined to be within their grasp.[65]

This criticism, however, was directed against the leaders of the expedition, rather than papal crusading policy itself.

The same seems to have been true of most opposition to the Fourth Crusade. The original goal of this expedition was probably Egypt, whose conquest had come to be regarded as an essential preliminary to a successful campaign in the Holy Land.[66] And the crusaders' decision to divert their forces to Zara and then Constantinople not only aroused the wrath of Innocent III, but also created considerable opposition within the crusading army itself. Our chief sources for this are the chronicles of Geoffrey of Villehardouin and Robert of Clari—the former one of the leaders of the crusade, the latter a poor Picard knight. But the monk Gunther of Pairis and the anonymous author of the *Devastatio Constantinopolitana* also provide valuable evidence of dissension in the crusading camp.

According to Robert of Clari, the common people knew nothing of the Venetian proposal to attack Zara.[67] However rumours probably circulated in the army and, even at this early stage, there is some evidence of disaffection.[68] The prolonged delay at Venice had exhausted the resources of some of the poorer crusaders, forcing them to return home; but others chose to leave the host because they were unwilling to incur the risk of excommunication by attacking the lands of a fellow Christian and crusader, King Emery of Hungary. They either returned home or headed for the Apulian ports and set sail for Syria. On their journey they apparently encountered some Germans and others who were marching to join the army at Venice, who, when they learned of the change of plan, turned back as well.[69] A number of more prominent crusaders also expressed their reservations about the proposed diversion to Zara. According to

[65] Orderic Vitalis, iii. 182.
[66] See Geoffrey of Villehardouin, i. 30; Robert of Clari, 7; Gunther of Pairis, 70-2 and Queller, *The Fourth Crusade*, 13-15.
[67] Robert of Clari, 12.
[68] See Geoffrey of Villehardouin, i. 66.
[69] *Devastatio Constantinopolitana*, 10; Gunther of Pairis, 71-2.

Gunther of Pairis, Abbot Martin begged the papal legate
Peter Capuano to release him from his crusading vow and to
permit him to return to the tranquillity of the cloister,
because he feared that the Venetian plan would delay the
crusade and result in the deaths of fellow Christians. Similar
concerns may have prompted Bishop Conrad of Halberstadt
to ask leave to return to his diocese. Both these requests
were refused by the legate, who argued that Innocent III
preferred to overlook the proposed wrong in order to maintain the unity of the army.[70]

After the crusaders had set up their camp before the walls
of Zara, the opposition party within the army was led by
Abbot Guy of Vaux de Cernay, Simon of Montfort, and
Enguerrand of Boves. It seems likely that Abbot Guy had
received Innocent III's letter condemning the attack upon
fellow Christians[71] and he forbade the crusaders, in the
pope's name, to continue the siege. This intervention achieved
nothing, and in the end the abbot and his followers registered
their disapproval by camping away from the main body of
the army.[72] When Innocent III heard the news of the capture
of Zara, he immediately excommunicated the crusaders
and wrote a letter to King Philip of France and King John
of England complaining that this attack had emboldened
the Muslims to take the offensive against the Christians
in the Latin East;[73] but the pope later remitted his sentence
upon the Franks.[74] On the whole it seems to have been
accepted that the diversion had been forced upon the army
by its inability to pay its debts to the Venetians, and at this
stage it still seemed likely that the crusaders would resume
the campaign against the Muslims in the East. According to
Gunther of Pairis, although they went about the siege of
Zara with heavy hearts, they considered it less objectionable

[70] Gunther of Pairis, 72–3; Anonymous of Halberstadt, 12.
[71] See R. H. Schmandt, 'The Fourth Crusade and the Just War Theory',
Catholic Historical Review, lxi (1975), 205 n. 38; Queller, *The Fourth Crusade*,
186 n. 78.
[72] Geoffrey of Villehardouin, i. 84. Peter of Vaux de Cernay (i. 108-10) and
Robert of Clari (14) claim that the dissenters abandoned the host at this point
and went to the court of the King of Hungary, but their chronology seems to be
muddled. See Queller, op. cit. 188 n. 22.
[73] Innocent III, PL ccxv, cols. 1178–9 and *Selected Letters*, 58.
[74] Geoffrey of Villehardouin, i. 108.

to fight against a Christian city than to abandon their crusading vow.[75]

The proposal to divert the crusade to Constantinople, however, created serious disaffection in the host, for it aroused fears that the army would never reach the Holy Land. Boniface of Montferrat may have had preliminary discussions with Philip of Swabia in the autumn of 1202, but according to Villehardouin, the first that the other leaders of the crusading host heard of the scheme to restore the deposed emperor Isaac Angelus and his son Alexius to the Byzantine throne was when an embassy arrived at Venice.[76] Envoys were sent to discuss these proposals with Philip and, whilst the army was wintering at Zara, they returned with generous offers of men and supplies for the campaign against the Muslims. The supporters of the Byzantine scheme within the crusading camp argued that it offered the best chance of winning back the 'land oversea', but this argument was dismissed by the critics, who reminded the crusaders that their main duty was to fulfil their vows to go to Jerusalem. At this point Abbot Guy and Simon of Montfort finally decided to leave the host and make their own way to the East and several other nobles followed their example.[77] According to Geoffrey of Villehardouin, only twelve signed the agreement with the Byzantines on behalf of the French.[78] Many more of the lower ranks seem to have deserted and five hundred were drowned when one overloaded ship sank.[79] The decision to go to Constantinople also appears to have been responsible for another major defection from the army. The Flemish fleet, commanded by John of Nesles, Governor of Bruges, and Count Baldwin's son, Thierry, probably received news of the change of plan at Marseilles, where it had wintered, having been delayed by summer storms. Although there is no record of their reaction, opposition to the Byzantine scheme seems the

[75] Gunther of Pairis, 72, 74.

[76] For the controversy about Boniface's role, see Queller, op. cit. 30-5.

[77] Geoffrey of Villehardouin, i. 90-8, 102.

[78] Id. i. 98-100. A letter from Count Hugh of St Pol to Duke Henry of Brabant cited twenty signatories. See *Chronica regia Coloniensis*, 203; Queller, op. cit. 194 n. 121.

[79] Geoffrey of Villehardouin, i. 100-2, 110-12.

most likely explanation for their decision to sail directly to Syria.[80]

The most serious challenge to the Byzantine plan, however, occurred after Prince Alexius had joined the crusaders at Corfu. According to Robert of Clari, the critics in the host protested, 'what shall we do in Constantinople? We have our pilgrimage to make and also our plan of going to Babylon [Cairo] or Alexandria'. The advocates of the diversion countered that the crusaders did not have sufficient resources to mount a successful campaign against the Muslims, but this argument failed to convince their opponents. They decided to get in touch with Walter of Brienne and to ask him to send ships to ferry them across to Brindisi on the mainland, whence they would travel to the East. The leaders of the army soon realized the extent of the resistance and Geoffrey of Villehardouin described the dramatic scene in which they appealed to the 'would-be deserters' not to abandon the host. In the end the dissenters were persuaded to stay on the condition that after Michaelmas they would have the right to demand ships at a fortnight's notice to go to Syria.[81] They recalled this agreement after Alexius had been restored to his throne; but in response to the leaders' pleas they consented to postpone their departure again, until his position was more secure.[82] They remained determined to go to the Holy Land, however, and they can probably be identified with the group who expressed doubts about the justice of their cause after the failure of the first assault on Constantinople and who, according to Geoffrey of Villehardouin, wished to see the army disbanded. In the end they were persuaded to stay until the city was captured.[83]

After the establishment of the Latin Empire of Constantinople, Baldwin of Flanders reiterated his intention of going to the East.[84] But before he could do so he had to deal with the threat of invasion and various internal problems.

[80] Id. i. 50-2, 102-4; ii. 28-30; Queller, T. K. Compton, and D. A. Campbell, 'The Fourth Crusade: The Neglected Majority', *Speculum*, xlix (1974), 454-8.

[81] Robert of Clari, 31-2; Geoffrey of Villehardouin, i. 114-20.

[82] Geoffrey of Villehardouin, i. 196-202.

[83] Robert of Clari, 71-2; Geoffrey of Villehardouin, ii. 40-2.

[84] Arnold of Lübeck, 230.

These delays aroused the criticism of the troubadour Raimbaut de Vaqueiras, a member of Boniface of Montferrat's entourage. In the early summer of 1204, Raimbaut reminded the emperor of the original purpose of the crusade and urged him to hasten to the Holy Land:

For he and we alike bear guilt for the burning of churches and palaces, wherein I see both clerks and laymen sin; and if he (Baldwin) does not succour the Holy Sepulchre and if the conquest does not advance, then our guilt before God will be greater still, for the pardon will turn to sin. But if he be liberal and brave, he will lend his battalions to Babylonia [Egypt] and Cairo with the greatest ease.

All his power and strength must he display to the Turks beyond Rouais [Edessa] for all the sultans . . . are hoping to wield lances . . . And Nevelon [Bishop of Soissons] will be denounced and the twelve electors will be blamed if the Sepulchre remains in captivity; and the doge will be accused of deception if he is minded to turn him aside from this succour.

It is significant that Raimbaut used the present tense, for it implied that the crusaders were still in a state of sin and would only be cleansed if they reconquered the Holy Sepulchre.[85]

As for Innocent III, he had opposed the crusaders' plan to attack the Greeks from the beginning. And, although he welcomed the prospect of the reunion of the Greek and Latin churches, he remained determined that the Christians in the Latin Kingdom should not be deprived of resources. In a letter dated 1205, he rebuked his legate Peter Capuano for authorizing crusaders to remain in the Latin Empire rather than fulfil their vows to go to Jerusalem:

because you . . . who ought to have encouraged others to aid the Holy Land . . . sailed on your own initiative to Greece, taking in your footsteps not only the pilgrims but even the natives of that unfortunate land . . . It was your duty to attend to the business of your legation and to give careful thought not to the capture of the Empire of Constantinople, but rather to the defence of what is left of the Holy Land and, if the Lord so wills, the restoration of what has been lost . . .

How can we call upon the other Western peoples for aid to the Holy Land . . . when the crusaders having given up the proposed pilgrimage

[85] Raimbaut de Vaqueiras, 'Conseil don a l'emperador', *Poems*, ed. J. Linskill (The Hague, 1964), 22-35.

return absolved to their homes; when those who plundered the afore-said empire turn back and return with their spoils, free of guilt.[86]

All the critics cited above directed their attacks against the crusaders themselves. Two vernacular poets, however, held the papacy itself responsible for the diversion of aid from the Latin Kingdom. In his satirical treatise *La Bible*, com-posed *c.*1206, the Cluniac monk Guiot de Provins blamed papal avarice for the use of the crusade against the Greeks,[87] and the same accusation was made by Guilhem Figueira in his famous poem 'D'un sirventes far':

Treacherous Rome, avarice leads you astray, so that you shear too much wool from your sheep. May the Holy Spirit who takes on human flesh hear my prayer and break your beak. Rome, you will never have a truce with me because you are false and treacherous with us and the Greeks.

Rome, you do little harm to the Saracens, but you massacre Greeks and Latins. In hellfire and perdition you have your home, Rome . . . [88]

But both were determined opponents of the papacy and there is no evidence that they represented a large body of opinion.

In fact it was only in 1236, as a result of appeals from the Latin Empire, that the papacy actually launched a crusade with the avowed intention of attacking the Greeks.[89] Gregory IX justified his action on the grounds that they were schis-matics,[90] and the security of Constantinople was essential to the success of future campaigns in the Holy Land;[91] he urged crusaders who had undertaken to go to Jerusalem to commute their vows to the Greek expedition.[92] Not surprisingly the leaders of the Eastern crusade, Richard of Cornwall and Philip of Dreux, were reluctant to do

---

[86] Innocent III, PL ccxv, cols. 107, 260-2, 700-2.

[87] Guiot de Provins, 'La Bible', ll. 776-82.

[88] Guilhem Figueira, 'D'un sirventes far', stt. iii, vii, ed. cit. 36-7.

[89] See R. Spence, 'Gregory IX's attempted expeditions to the Latin Empire of Constantinople: The Crusade for the Union of the Latin and Greek Churches', *Journal of Medieval History*, v (1979), 163-76.

[90] Gregory IX, nos. 4154-5.

[91] Ibid. no. 4605. See also Innocent III, PL ccxv, col. 455; Honorius III, no. 5186.

[92] Gregory IX, nos. 3395, 4219, 4608, 4741, 4983; *Annales Erphordenses*, MGH SS xvi. 33.

this,[93] and Theobald of Champagne exhorted men to hasten to avenge the Muslim victories in Syria.[94] But significantly the only evidence of criticism of the use of the crusade against the Greeks is to be found in Matthew Paris. According to the *Chronica maiora*, when the English nobles met at Northampton in November 1239 they swore to go to the Holy Land without delay and to avoid shedding Christian blood in Greece and Italy.[95] The English clergy also appear to have rejected Gregory's request for a thirtieth to finance the expedition to Constantinople.[96] As we have seen, however, this should be attributed to their resentment of papal taxation rather than any reservations about the direction of the crusade.

Crusades against Christian lay powers

The first 'political' crusade seems to have been Innocent II's expedition against Roger II of Sicily and the antipope Anacletus II.[97] Although in 1135 the Council of Pisa awarded participants the same indulgence as crusaders in the East,[98] there is no evidence of criticism of this use of the crusade. The same is true of the crusade which Innocent III proclaimed in 1199 against Markward of Anweiler, the imperial lieutenant in Southern Italy. Those who took the cross were offered the same indulgence as the members of the Fourth Crusade,[99] and it seems to have been accepted as a necessary preliminary to the campaign in the East.[100]

There was an outspoken and hostile reaction to the papacy's use of the crusade against Frederick II and his heirs. But once again the extent and significance of this opposition has

[93] See S. Painter, 'The Crusade of Theobald of Champagne and Richard of Cornwall', *History of the Crusades*, ii. 466-8, 482.

[94] 'Au tans plein de felonie', *Chansons de croisade*, 178-82.

[95] Matthew Paris, *CM* iii. 620.

[96] See Lunt, *Financial Relations*, 194-6.

[97] See Hehl, 38-45.

[98] 'Das Pisaner Konzil von 1135 in der Überlieferung des Pisaner Konzils von 1409', ed. D. Girgensohn, in *Festschrift für Hermann Heimpel* (Göttingen, 1971-2), ii. 1099-100.

[99] Innocent III, *PL* ccxiv, cols. 780-2. See also Kennan, 'Innocent III and the First Political Crusade: A Comment on the Limitations of Papal Power', *Traditio*, xxvii (1971), 231-49; Riley-Smith, *What were the Crusades?*, 27-8.

[100] See Geoffrey of Villehardouin, i. 34.

been exaggerated. Gregory IX excommunicated Frederick for the first time in 1227, justifying his action on the grounds that the emperor had failed to fulfil his crusading vow and was guilty of oppressing the church.[101] In 1229 the pope asked for military aid. Gregory made it clear that his promise of remission of sins was not equivalent to a full crusading indulgence.[102] Nevertheless his declaration of war against a Christian lay power aroused criticism from a number of contemporaries. These critics merit attention, for they advanced the same arguments as later opponents of the crusades against the Staufen: they condemned the use of force against fellow Christians, and protested that valuable resources were being diverted from the Holy Land.

The most forthright objections were raised by two Provençal troubadours writing in the Languedoc in the aftermath of the Albigensian Crusade. Peire Cardenal denounced John of Brienne's invasion of Southern Italy at the head of a papal force while the emperor was still in Jerusalem, and assured the Muslim leaders that the clergy would not seize their lands, for they were more interested in winning territory in Europe:

Kings and emperors, dukes, counts, nobles, and with them knights used to rule the world; today I see sovereignty held by the clergy by means of robbery, treachery, hypocrisy, violence, and preaching . . .

They are anxious to discover how they can make the world theirs and expel Lord Frederick from his home.[103]

As for Guilhem Figueira, he regarded the papal campaign against the emperor as a further indication of the corruption of Rome. He lamented that this policy had caused many to forfeit their chances of salvation and denied the validity of the indulgences issued for the war; 'where, Rome do you find that one should kill Christians?'[104]

Not surprisingly the papal campaign also aroused bitter opposition from certain quarters in Germany. One of Frederick's supporters, Abbot Burchard of Ursperg, accused the pope of authorizing attacks upon men who had taken the

[101] *HD* iii. 24-30.
[102] Gregory IX, nos. 350-2.
[103] Peire Cardenal, 'Clergue si fan pastor', stt. ii, v, ed. cit. 170, 174.
[104] Guilhem Figueira, 'D'un sirventes far', stt. viii, ix, xix, ed. cit. 38, 41.

cross for the Holy Land and complained that many Germans were thus prevented from fulfilling their vows.[105] Several vernacular poets also protested about the diversion of resources from the East. The moralist Freidank, who probably lived in the Staufen heartland in Germany, accompanied Frederick on his crusade to Jerusalem, and after his return composed a collection of *sprüche* entitled *Bescheidenheit*. This included a poem relating to the expedition in which Freidank observed that the emperor was beset on all sides, by Christians, heathen, and the clergy, and lamented that, because of the papal ban, little aid had been sent to the East:

> The cross was given that one might be redeemed from sin,
> Now that one is denied these by the ban
> How can one save one's soul?[106]

This theme was also taken up by the minnesinger Walther von der Vogelweide. Walther longed to go to the Holy Land himself and to win an eternal reward, and he complained that Frederick's excommunication had deprived many of such happiness.[107] Bruder Wernher, a poet at the court of Duke Frederick of Austria, also exhorted the pope to make peace and to allow the Germans to go to the Holy Sepulchre to expiate their sins.[108]

In England the main focus of opposition was the abbey of St Albans. The chroniclers Roger Wendover and Matthew Paris seem to have regarded Frederick as a fellow victim of papal avarice;[109] to underline this point, in his *Flores historiarum*, Roger included a letter addressed to the emperor by Count Thomas of Acerra, who had just returned to Southern Italy from Syria. This recorded the successes of John of Brienne's army; the author declared that Frederick's lay and ecclesiastical friends were astonished that the pope's conscience permitted him to make war upon Christians.[110] Matthew Paris used a similar device to express his opposition

[105] Burchard of Ursperg, 116.
[106] Freidank, 'Von Âkers', *Bescheidenheit*, ed. W. Grimm (Göttingen, 1834), 157, ll. 17-20; 159, ll. 15-18; 162, ll. 4-25.
[107] Walther von der Vogelweide, 'Owê war sint verswunden', ed. cit. 170.
[108] 'Gregorie, bâbest, geistlicher vater', *Minnesinger*, ii. 227.
[109] See Vaughan, 147-8; Plehn, 99-100.
[110] Roger Wendover, ii. 358-60.

to the papal campaign. In his *Chronica maiora* Matthew copied from Roger the text of a letter in which the emperor described the capture of Jerusalem. But when he transcribed it into his *Flores historiarum* he added a fictitious report of Frederick's troubles upon his return, stressing the harm wrought by papal interference:[111]

> because in this world bitter things are always mixed with sweet, when we were returning to our Empire . . . we crushed our enemies who were supported to our detriment by . . . the pope, our father. And had not this business recalled us in such great haste, the state of the church would by the grace of God have been consolidated and wonderfully exalted.[112]

Frederick was excommunicated again in 1239, and on this occasion Gregory ordered that a crusade should be preached against him in Lombardy and Germany. The pope justified his action on the grounds that the emperor was endangering the liberty of the church[113] and those who took the cross were granted the same indulgence as the members of Theobald of Champagne's expedition to the Holy Land. In fact Gregory authorized his legate in Hungary to commute vows for Jerusalem to the crusade against Frederick.[114]

Not surprisingly this 'diversion' of the crusade aroused protests from adherents of the emperor in Germany and Italy. At the Diet of Eger in Bohemia, the assembled princes and bishops refused the request of the papal legate, Albert of Beham, to break their oath of fealty to Frederick. Instead prominent ecclesiastics and nobles such as the Dukes of Brunswick and Saxony determined to seek a reconciliation between the two parties; in the spring of 1240, they sent the Master of the Teutonic Order, Conrad of Thuringia, to Rome with letters begging the pope to reach a settlement. On the whole the content of these appeals was the same: they described the discord in Germany and reminded Gregory that his strife with the emperor was damaging the church and preventing aid being sent to the East.[115] Indeed, such

---

[111] See Vaughan, 132.

[112] Roger Wendover, ii. 365-9; Matthew Paris, *CM* iii. 173-6, *Flores historiarum*, ii. 197-8.   [113] Gregory IX, nos. 5092-4.

[114] *Vetera monumenta historica Hungariam sacram illustrantia*, i. 178.

[115] *Annales Erphordenses*, 33; MGH Constitutiones, ed. L. Weiland *et al.* (Hanover, 1893-1906), ii. 225-32.

was the feeling of resentment amongst members of the imperial party that, when the legate left for Rome, the dean and chapter of Passau declared a counter-crusade against him.[116] The most notable Italian critic of papal policy was the Ghibelline, Brother Elias, Minister-General of the Franciscan Order from 1232 to 1239. He apparently accused Gregory of wrathfully attacking the rights of the empire and asserted that he had 'employed fraudulently the money collected for the Holy Land'.[117] As proof of his allegiance to Frederick, Elias promoted an abortive plot to hand over Assisi to the Ghibellines.[118]

The use of the crusade against a Christian lay power also aroused some opposition in England. According to Matthew Paris, the people were confused by the virulence of the pope's attacks upon the emperor; and the clergy assembled at the Council of London denounced the proposed expedition on the grounds that it would result in the spilling of Christian blood. Moreover, the rectors of Berkshire pointed out that the church's wealth was intended for charitable purposes, not to finance wars, particularly when they were directed against fellow Christians.[119] There is no evidence, however, that these critics represented a large body of opinion, and the main purpose of their arguments was to reinforce the clergy's opposition to papal taxation.[120]

Understandably, objections were also raised by those taking part in the crusade to the East. At the time Theobald of Champagne was preparing to go to the Holy Land; in a poem composed shortly before his departure from Lyons he urged men to hasten to the aid of Syria, lamenting:

In this time of felony, envy and treason, of injustice and misdeeds . . . I see excommunicated those who have most right on their side.[121]

---

[116] Albert of Beham, 'Die Aventinischen Excerpte aus den Acten des Albert von Beham', ed. C. Höfler, in *Albert von Beham und Regesten Pabst Innocenz IV* (Stuttgart, 1847), 17.

[117] Matthew Paris, *CM* iii. 628.

[118] See R. B. Brooke, *Early Franciscan Government* (Cambridge, 1959), 174–5.

[119] Matthew Paris, *CM* iii. 609; iv. 37, 40.

[120] See above, pp. 133–4.

[121] 'An tans plein de felonie', *Chansons de croisade*, 181–2.

According to Matthew Paris, members of Theobald's expedition had to be restrained from violence when the papal legate ordered them to postpone their departure for the East.[122]

At the Council of Lyons in 1245, Innocent IV proclaimed a second crusade against Frederick, and on this occasion participants were awarded the same indulgence as the members of Louis IX's expedition to Egypt.[123] Fears about the French reaction probably prompted the pope to advise his legate Odo of Châteauroux to keep the plans for the crusade against the emperor secret, and it was at Louis's request that Innocent ordered that preaching for the Holy Land in the imperial dioceses on the French border should not be impeded.[124] But, although the king made several attempts to restore peace to Europe before his departure,[125] there is no evidence that he actually objected to the use of the crusade against the Staufen: his main concern was that it should not divert resources from his own expedition.

The papal crusade, however, aroused opposition from the same quarters as the earlier campaigns against Frederick. In a *sirventes* written after the fall of Jerusalem to the Khwarizmian Turks in 1244, Guilhem Figueira exhorted the pope to settle his dispute with the emperor and to send aid to the Holy Land;[126] and another troubadour, Austorc d'Aurillac, blamed the disaster at Mansurah upon the false clergy and suggested that a counter-crusade should be launched against Rome.[127] According to Matthew Paris, the French complained that the blood wasted in Germany and Italy might have contributed to the recapture of the East.[128] Such was the resentment amongst the members of the Ghibelline party in Germany that anyone found wearing a cross in the town of Regensburg was condemned to death.[129]

At the same time the emperor issued his own propaganda

---

[122] Matthew Paris, *CM* iii. 614–15.

[123] MGH Epistolae saeculi XIII, ii. 151.   [124] Innocent IV, nos. 2935, 3384.

[125] See Alberic of Troisfontaines, *Chronica*, MGH SS xxiii 944; Matthew Paris, *CM* iv. 484, 523–4; Jordan, *Louis IX*, 26–30.

[126] Guilhem Figueira, 'Del preveire maior', ed. cit. 31. See also Lanfranc Cigala, 'Si mos chans fois de ioi ne de solatz', *I trovatori d'Italia*, 350–2.

[127] Austorc d'Aurillac, '(Ai!) Dieus! per qu'as fa(ch)a tan gran ma(lez)a', st. vi, ed. cit. 83.   [128] Matthew Paris, *CM* v. 172–3.

[129] *Annales ecclesiastici*, ed. O. Raynaldus *et al.* ii (Lucca, 1747), 398.

against the papacy. In this he exploited the arguments put forward by other critics; parallels have been drawn between some of Frederick's letters and Guilhem Figueira's poem 'D'un sirventes far'.[130] Like certain troubadours, the emperor complained about the diversion of resources from the East. He stressed his desire to go to the Holy Land, and protested that the pope's hostility had prevented him from renewing the campaign against the Muslims. Writing in the aftermath of the disaster of Mansurah, Frederick condemned the bloodshed in Germany and Italy, and like Matthew Paris held Innocent to blame for the failure of Louis IX's expedition.[131]

It has been suggested that the critics cited above reflected widespread public discontent about the papacy's use of the crusade against Christian lay powers.[132] But, as we have seen, their opposition was dictated by personal interests, or, in the case of the St Albans chroniclers and certain Provençal troubadours, coloured by prejudice against the papacy. At the same time, a number of other writers expressed their support for Rome. For example, the poet Uc de Saint Circ called upon the King of France to take up arms against Frederick, whom he denounced as a heretic;[133] and in his treatise *Morale scholarium* John of Garland exhorted the emperor to hasten to Jerusalem, and accused him of raging unjustly against the pope.[134]

After Frederick's death in 1250, Innocent IV declared a crusade in Germany against his son Conrad.[135] This aroused the same sort of criticism as earlier campaigns. The Provençal troubadour Boniface de Castellane accused the false clergy of seeking to disinherit Conrad in order to make gifts to their illegitimate children.[136] And, according to Matthew Paris,

---

[130] See *Poesie provenzali*, i. pp. liii–liv.

[131] *HD* iii. 72; v. 296; vi. 257, 351, 774.

[132] See Throop, 26–7, 57.

[133] Uc de Saint Circ, 'Un sirventes vuelh far en aquest son d'en Gui', *Poésies*, ed. Jeanroy and J. J. Salverda de Grave (Toulouse, 1913), 96.

[134] John of Garland, *Morale scholarium*, ed. L. J. Paetow (Berkeley, Calif., 1927), 171–2. See also ibid. 158, 165.

[135] Innocent IV, nos. 5031, 5032, 5036.

[136] Boniface de Castellane, ˙Era pueis yverns es el fil', in 'Bonifazio di Castellane', ed. A. Parducci, *Romania*, xlvi (1920), 496. Boniface took part in a revolt against Angevin rule in 1262. See ibid. 488–90.

there were protests from Louis IX's family about the diversion of resources from the king's expedition in the East. The Counts of Anjou and Poitiers were apparently angered by the pope's refusal to reach a settlement as a preliminary to sending aid to Louis and Queen Blanche ordered that anyone who took the cross against Frederick's heirs should have his lands confiscated. She was said to have remarked: 'let those who fight for the pope be sustained by the pope'; her example was followed by many French nobles. Matthew also expressed his own sympathy for Conrad's plight, and described how the pope's hostility had helped to bring about his early death.[137] Not surprisingly Innocent's campaign against the Staufen also aroused resentment within the empire itself; and when the canonist Hostiensis accompanied the papal legate to Germany in 1251, he encountered critics who declared that it was wrong to preach the cross against Christians.[138]

At the same time Innocent supported a rebellion against Conrad in Sicily. The pope offered the Sicilian throne in turn to Richard, Earl of Cornwall, and Charles of Anjou, but both refused and Staufen rule was eventually reasserted by Frederick's illegitimate son Manfred. After Conrad's sudden death in April 1254, Innocent tried to negotiate with Manfred, but their amity proved short-lived and in October Manfred rose in rebellion against the pope. Innocent's successor, Alexander IV, sought military aid from Henry III of England, who had accepted the Sicilian crown on behalf of his second son Edmund. Some years previously the king had taken the cross for the Holy Land, and now he agreed to divert his expedition to Sicily. This change of direction aroused bitter protests in England. The annalist of Burton called Henry's decision 'stupid and ill-considered' and ascribed it to 'wicked counsel'.[139] According to Matthew Paris, when the nuncio Rostand preached the cross against Manfred the English people marvelled at the mutability of preachers who promised the same reward for shedding Muslim and Christian blood.[140] In fact the king's Sicilian project seems

[137] Matthew Paris, *CM* v. 188, 260-1, 459-60.
[138] Hostiensis, col. 905; C. Lefebvre, 'Hostiensis', in R. Naz (ed.), *Dictionnaire de droit canonique*, v (Paris, 1953), cols. 1513-16.
[139] *Annales de Burtoneia*, 360.
[140] Matthew Paris, *CM* v. 521-2.

to have been one of the major causes of the baronial revolt; when the reforming barons drew up a list of grievances in 1264 they protested that Henry's crusading vow had been

unreasonably converted against all hope and expectation, from a crusade against the Saracens, who are the foes of Christ's cross, into an attack upon fellow subjects of the same Christian religion.[141]

As in 1240, however, the main cause of resentment in England was papal taxation and there is no evidence from other sources of widespread opposition to the use of the crusade against the Staufen.[142]

After the failure of Henry III's Sicilian project, Pope Urban formally offered the throne of Sicily to Charles of Anjou and this agreement was confirmed by his successor Clement IV in April 1265. In the intervening years Manfred had reconquered Southern Italy and negotiated a series of alliances with tyrants in the North, including Ezzelino of Romano; and Charles undertook to launch a crusade to protect the papacy from this renewed Staufen attack. The Angevin forces reached Rome in January 1266; Manfred was defeated and killed at the battle of Benevento late in February.

As before, the attitude adopted by chroniclers and poets towards the papal-Angevin campaign depended upon their location and circumstances. In Provence there were protests from two troubadours embittered by Charles of Anjou's rule. In a *pastorela* attributed to Paulet de Marseille and dated between April 1265 and February 1266, a shepherdess asked why Charles wished to disinherit Manfred, who had done him no harm. The poet replied that the Count of Anjou was spurred on by the clergy, but he predicted that if Manfred retained the adherence of his followers, the Angevin plan would come to nothing.[143] Another native of Marseilles, the poet Raimon de Tors, declared his firm support for the Staufen ruler of Sicily.[144] And in the course of their protest

---

[141] *Documents of the Baronial Plan*, 278.   [142] See above, p. 142.

[143] Paulet de Marseille, 'L'autrier m'anav'ab cor pensiu', 'Le troubadour Paulet de Marseille', stt. iii, iv, ed. E. Levy, *Revue des langues romanes*, xxi (1882), 281–2. For a discussion about the authorship of this poem, see ibid. 264–5.

[144] Raimon de Tors, 'Ar es ben dretz', in 'Raimon de Tors, trovatore marsigliese del secolo XIII', ed. Parducci, *Studi romanzi*, vii (1911), 34–5.

against papal taxation in 1263, the chapter of Rheims again emphasized Manfred's hereditary rights and the injustice of the papal attack.[145] In Northern Italy, such critics belonged to the Ghibelline party.[146] Writing after the Florentine defeat at the battle of Monteaperti in 1260, an anonymous poet denounced the false clergy who sought to destroy Manfred;[147] and Perceval Doria, the Staufen vicar of the March of Ancona and Romagna and the Duchy of Spoleto, paid tribute to the latter's bravery and generosity.[148] In a lament upon Manfred's death an anonymous Italian poet observed, in a manner reminiscent of critics of the Albigensian Crusade, that truth and right had been conquered by falsehood and wrong.[149] The papal Angevin expedition also aroused protests from adherents of the Staufen in the South. The Calabrian historian Saba Malaspina denounced the savage massacre of the German forces after the battle of Benevento,[150] and the Sicilian chronicler Bartholomew of Neocastro wrote of the church's campaign to disinherit Manfred.[151] A few chroniclers in Germany also expressed compassion for the fate of Frederick II's heirs, but most declared their support for the papacy. As for the minnesingers, their main concern seems to have been Rome's intervention in the dispute over the imperial election and it was only in this context that they criticized the diversion of resources from the East.[152]

It is hardly surprising that the papal campaign also aroused criticism from areas directly threatened by the Muslims, in other words Spain and the Holy Land. The Catalan chronicler Ramon Muntaner declared that the day of the pope's grant of Sicily to Charles had been.

---

[145] *Archives législatives*, i. 452-3.   [146] Merkel, 375-422.

[147] 'Ma voluntatz me mou guerr'e trebalh', *Poesie provenzali*, ii. 205-8. See also 'Quor qu'om trobes Florentis orgulhos', ibid. 225-6; Jeanroy, *La Poésie lyrique*, ii. 235-6.

[148] 'Felon cor ai et enic', *Poesie provenzali*, ii. 191-2. See also *I trovatori d'Italia*, 89-92.

[149] 'Totas honors e tug fan benestan', *Poesie provenzali*, ii. 234-7. See above, p. 163.

[150] Saba Malaspina, *Historia rerum Siciliarum*, RIS viii, cols. 827-8.

[151] Bartholomew of Neocastro, *Historia Sicula*, RIS xiii (3) (new edn., Bologna, 1912), 5-6.

[152] See Merkel, 326-65.

an accursed day for Christians, for by this grant all the lands of Outremer were lost and the kingdom of Anatolia fell to the Turks . . . (This grant) also brought about the death of many Christians, wherefore it may be said that that day was one of weeping and grief.[153]

These sentiments were reiterated by another Catalan historian, Bernat Desclot.[154] In a poem written after the fall of Arsuf and Caesarea, a Templar in the Latin Kingdom, Ricaut Bonomel, complained of the absence of aid from the West. In 1265 Clement IV had decreed that vows to the Holy Land might be commuted to the expedition against Manfred;[155] and it was probably this ruling which prompted Ricaut to lament:

the pope bestows indulgences generously to Charles and the French who go to fight against the Germans . . . whoever wishes can replace his pilgrimage with an expedition to Lombardy.

He exhorted the French to hasten to avenge Muslim victories and reminded them that Alexandria had done them more harm than Lombardy.[156] Archbishop Giles of Tyre, who headed a mission to the West appealing for aid for the Kingdom of Jerusalem, also protested about the diversion of resources from the East.[157]

For a short time after Manfred's death, Charles of Anjou was accepted as ruler in Sicily. In 1268, however, Conrad's son Conradin mounted an invasion of Italy to claim his inheritance. He was received with enthusiasm by many Italians, and his arrival in Sicily provoked a rebellion against Angevin rule. Clement IV immediately organized another crusade, and in August Charles of Anjou defeated Conradin's forces at the battle of Tagliacozzo. A few days afterwards Conradin was captured and sent to Naples for execution.

Once again there was criticism of the use of the crusade against the Staufen. Like his grandfather Frederick II, Conradin

---

[153] Ramon Muntaner, *Crònica* (Barcelona, 1927-51), i. 79.
[154] Bernat Desclot, *Crònica*, ed. M. Coll i Alentorn (Barcelona, 1949-51), ii. 162.
[155] *Regesta Pontificum Romanorum*, comp. Potthast, no. 19050.
[156] 'Ir'e dolors s'es a mon cor asseza', *Anthologie*, 296-300.
[157] 'Emprunts de Saint Louis en Palestine et en Afrique', ed. G. Servois, *Bibliothèque de l'école des chartes*, xix (1858), 288; E. Jordan, *Les Origines de la domination Angevine en Italie* (Paris, 1909), 386-7.

complained to the pope that Christ's cross was being turned against the faithful rather than the Muslims.[158] This theme was taken up by certain troubadours in the Languedoc and Northern Italy. In a lament upon the evils of his time Guilhem Fabre, a burgher of Narbonne, condemned the use of force against fellow Christians and pointed out that this strife was displeasing to God. He lamented that because of these quarrels in the West the Muslims held the Holy Land without any opposition, and exhorted the faithful to hasten to Christ's aid.[159] Calega Panza, a Genoese cloth-merchant with trading interests in the East, described the devastation wrought by the Angevin campaigns in Tuscany and Lombardy and protested that the Count treated Christians more cruelly than he did the Muslims: Charles had negotiated a truce with the Muslims of Lucera, but neither the Greeks nor the Latins could expect any aid from him. Calega criticized the church for its neglect of the Holy Land: 'you have made a truce with the Turks and Persians in order to kill here French and Germans', and he called upon Conradin to avenge these shameful deeds. Like the anonymous continuator of *La Chanson de la croisade albigeoise*,[160] he complained that this 'diversion' of the crusade was a perversion of Christian ideals:

He who wishes to kill or live by rapine can quickly and easily attain salvation. He has only to murder a hundred Christians and whoever should strive to kill a thousand would have a higher place in paradise. O false clergy, you have abandoned the (right) way, the precepts God made pure and holy and Moses who wrote the commandments.[161]

The Venetian merchant Bartolomeo Zorzi composed a lament upon the death of Conradin,[162] and, although the Provençal

---

[158] *Code Italiae Diplomaticus*, ed. J. C. Lünig (Frankfurt and Leipzig, 1725–35), ii. 939.

[159] 'Hon mays vey, pus truep sordeyor', 'Pus dels majors princeps auzem conten', in 'Deux troubadours narbonnais: Guilhem Fabre et Bertran Alanhan', ed. Anglade, *Bulletin de la commission archéologique de Narbonne*, viii (1905), 414–20.   [160] See above, p. 164.

[161] 'Ar es sazos c'om si deu alegrar', in 'Un sirventes contre Charles d'Anjou, 1268', ed. Jeanroy, *Annales du Midi*, xv (1903), 146–8. See also ibid. 149–62 and *I trovatori d'Italia*, 112–13.

[162] 'S'il monz fondes a maravilha gran', *Poesie provenzali*, ii. 260–2. See also *I trovatori d'Italia*, 114–18.

troubadour Austorc de Segret was saddened by the failure
of Louis IX's Tunisian expedition, he rejoiced at Charles's
discomfiture, for he claimed that no one had done Christianity so much harm.[163]

It has been suggested that these critics reflected a growing
resentment of the papacy's use of the crusade in Europe.[164]
But the facts do not support this conclusion: in spite of their
geographical spread, the writers cited above either were
'traditional' enemies of the papacy or had personal reasons
for opposing the diversion of resources from the East.
Admittedly they were more vociferous than the supporters
of the papal Angevin campaigns, but they cannot be said
to represent public opinion and their evidence should be
balanced against the picture of events given by the Guelf
chroniclers. They show that, far from condemning the papal
expeditions, many were anxious to take the cross against the
Staufen.[165] According to Salimbene and several other Italian
historians, Charles of Anjou's army included men from
traditional Guelf areas such as Mantua, Bologna, Ferrara,
Lombardy, and Tuscany[166] and the Tournai chronicler,
Gilles le Muisit, wrote that 'a multitude of nobles and common people' left Flanders to join the Count's forces.[167] Not
surprisingly Charles's campaigns also attracted recruits from
Provence and the kingdom of France.[168] Moreover, a number
of vernacular poets composed *sirventes* supporting the papal
Angevin cause. For example, the Provençal troubadour Peire
de Castelnau rejoiced that Charles had defeated Manfred at
the battle of Benevento[169] and, although Rutebeuf encouraged

---

[163] Austorc de Segret, '(No) sai quim so tan sui desconassens', in 'Le sirventes
d'Austorc de Segret', ed. Fabre, *Annales du Midi*, xxii (1910), 469-72. This
edition omits the important phrase, 'crestiandatz pres tan gran falhida', see
Jeanroy, *La Poésie lyrique*, ii. 236 n. 5.

[164] See Throop, 58-68.

[165] See Housley, *The Italian Crusades*, 156-62.

[166] Salimbene, *Chronica*, MGH SS xxxii. 435-6; *Annales Mantuani*, MGH SS
xix. 24; Saba Malaspina, col. 810; Giovanni Villani, *Cronica*, ed. F. Gherardi-
Dragomanni (Florence, 1845), i. 312. See also *Annales de Burtoneia*, 352; Andrew
of Hungary, 568.

[167] Gilles le Muisit, *Chronique*, ed. H. Lemaître (Paris, 1906), 7-8. See also
Le Garçon et l'aveugle, ed. M. Roques (Paris, 1911), 5, 8, 10-12.

[168] *Thesaurus*, ii. 153; *Annales Parmenses maiores*, MGH SS xix. 679; *Maius
chronicon Lemovicense*, 771.

[169] 'Hoimais nom cal far plus long atendenza', *Poesie provenzali*, ii. 230.

Christians to resume the struggle against the Muslims, he emphasized the danger posed by the enemies of the faith in the West and wrote two songs exhorting the faithful to join the crusade against the Staufen.[170] Large numbers of Italians also flocked to take the cross against Manfred's allies, Alberic and Ezzelino of Romano.[171]

Nor is there any sign that the 'diversion' of the crusade to Europe led to widespread disillusionment about the value of the indulgence or to a decline in the numbers taking the cross for the Holy Land, even in areas directly affected by papal preaching. It is significant that a number of the passengers on board the crusade ship *St Victor* in 1250 came from areas where papal agents had preached the cross against Frederick II.[172] Chroniclers described the expeditions against the Staufen in the same terms as the struggle against the Muslims, attributing victories to divine aid;[173] they seem to have been regarded as part of a general campaign against the enemies of the faith, with some crusaders fighting in the Holy Land and some in Europe. According to Pope Clement IV, many Christians planned to go to the East as soon as the conflict in Sicily had been settled;[174] a number of veterans of Louis IX's Egyptian crusade were to be found both in the Angevin forces at the battle of Benevento and later with the French army at the siege of Tunis. According to his epitaph, one French knight fought in Egypt, North Africa, Sicily, Calabria, the Abruzzi, and the Romagna.[175] Philip of Montfort, son of the Lord of Tyre, probably travelled to the East to seek aid for the Kingdom of Jerusalem, but in 1265 he was employed by Charles of Anjou in negotiations in Italy and, after the battle of Benevento, he

---

[170] Rutebeuf, 'La chanson de Pouille', 'Le dit de Pouille' ed. cit. 43-5.

[171] Housley, *Italian Crusades*, 126, 159-60, 168-9; Rolandinus of Padua, *Chronicon*, MGH SS xix. 107; Martino da Canale, *Cronaca veneta*, in *Archivio storico italiano*, viii (1845), 426-7, 436-9.

[172] Kedar, 'The Passenger List', 278-9.

[173] *Maius chronicon Lemovicense*, 771; *Annales Ianuenses*, MGH SS xviii. 255. See also Housley, *Italian Crusades*, 162-9.

[174] Clement IV, no. 838.

[175] 'Épitaphe de Jean d'Eppé', ed. V. le Clerc, *Histoire littéraire de la France*, xxiii (Paris, 1856), 483. See also 'Requête adressée au roi de France par un vétéran des armées de Saint Louis et de Charles d'Anjou', ed. Berger, *Études d'histoire du Moyen Âge dédiées à Gabriel Monod* (Paris, 1896), 343.

spent some time as a captain of troops defending the papal states before he returned to the East with the French king.[176]

[176] See Jordan, *Les Origines*, 403 n. 1.

CHAPTER VII

Scepticism and fundamental criticism

ALTHOUGH a number of the lesser nobility joined the forces of Peter the Hermit, there seems to have been some opposition to the First Crusade in Germany as a result of the bitterness aroused by the Investiture Contest.[1] But this attitude soon changed, and there was a sizeable contingent of Germans on the 1101 crusade.[2] In fact, with the exception of a small group of pacifists who will be discussed later, most criticism of the crusading movement itself seems to have stemmed from disillusionment after a defeat in battle or the failure of a campaign. This opposition took two forms: on the one hand there was scepticism about the advisability of crusading and a reluctance to take the cross; on the other there was fundamental criticism of the actual concept of the crusade.

The first sign of disillusionment is to be found after the unexpected defeat of the forces of Emicho of Leiningen at the siege of Wieselberg. Chroniclers offered a variety of explanations for this disaster;[3] but, according to Ekkehard of Aura, these did not satisfy some of the more simple brethren, who dismissed the whole expedition as 'vain and frivolous'.[4] The most serious reaction, however, occurred after the major reversal of Christian fortunes at Damascus on the Second Crusade. Several chroniclers lamented that the expedition, which had aroused such expectations, had achieved nothing;[5] and there seems to have been a general

[1] Ekkehard of Aura, *Hierosolymita*, 17–18; Green, 301–3.
[2] Green, 303–4.   [3] See above, pp. 000–0.
[4] Ekkehard of Aura, *Hierosolymita*, 21.
[5] *Cronica Sancti Petri Erfordensis*, ed. O. Holder-Egger, *Monumenta Erphesfurtensia* (Hanover, 1899), 176; *Chronicon Mauriniacense*, 88; *Gesta abbatum Sancti Bertini Sithiensium: continuatio*, 664; Robert of Torigni, 154; *Annales Sancti Jacobi Leodiensis*, 641.

atmosphere of bewilderment and despondency.[6] This was manifested in various ways. First, because of his advocacy of the crusade, St Bernard received much personal criticism,[7] and one chronicler went so far as to question the divine inspiration of his preaching.[8] Secondly, there was a poor response to Abbot Suger's efforts to launch a new crusade.[9] In May 1150, Louis VII summoned French nobles and ecclesiastics to an assembly at Chartres in order to discuss plans for another expedition to the East. But according to St Bernard, the barons were reluctant to take the cross;[10] the proposed meeting at Compiègne in July never took place. It is interesting that two chroniclers attributed the lack of enthusiasm for the new crusade to opposition from the Cistercians,[11] who appear to have suffered as a result of their involvement in the previous expedition;[12] and when Suger died in 1151, no one took up his initiative.[13] The abbot's plans also aroused criticism from other quarters. According to his biographer, Wulfric of Haselbury reminded Alured of Lincoln of the fate of the Second Crusade and advised him that the new expedition would come to nothing.[14]

[6] See Otto of Freising, *Gesta Friderici*, 91; Bernard, *De consideratione, Opera*, iii. 410-14; *Lamentum lacrymabile*, PL clv, cols. 1095-8.

[7] *Vita Sancti Bernardi* and *Vita secunda Sancti Bernardi*, cols. 308-9, 516; William of St Denis, *Dialogus*, 86; Nivard, *Ysengrimus*, ed. E. Voigt (Halle, 1884), 265.   [8] *Annales Brunwilarenses*, MGH SS xvi. 727.

[9] See E. Vacandard, *Vie de Saint Bernard* (Paris, 1895), ii. 424-33.

[10] Bernard, *Opera*, viii. 163-5, 318.

[11] *Continuatio Premonstratensis*, MGH SS vi. 455; *Chronicon Turonense*, RHGF xii. 474.

[12] Several historians have argued that the decline in the number of new foundations and the value of donations to the Cistercian Order after 1147 can be attributed to disillusionment after the failure of the Second Crusade. See P. I. Pfeiffer, 'Die Cistercienser und der zweite Kreuzzug: Die Cistercienser und der unglückliche Ausgang des II. Kreuzzuges', *Cistercienser-Chronik*, xlviii (1935), 145; F. Winter, *Die Cistercienser des nord-östlichen Deutschlands* (Gotha, 1868-71), ii. 56; R. Fossier, 'L'essor économique de Clairvaux', in *Bernard de Clairvaux* (Paris, 1953), 105-7. But this seems to be an exaggeration. 1147 was a peak year (*Originum Cisterciensium tomus I*, ed. P. L. Janauschek (Vienna, 1877), 291-5) and although the reverse at Damascus played its part, there were several other reasons for the drop in the number of foundations. For example, in 1152 the Chapter-General (*Statuta*, i. 45) placed a restriction upon the number of new houses and there was also a decline after the death of St Bernard in 1153. See Constable, 'The Second Crusade', 276 n. 324; Schmugge, 'Zistercienser, Kreuzzug und Heidenkreig', *Die Zistercienser: Ordensleben zwischen Ideal und Wirklichkeit* (Cologne, 1980) 61-2.

[13] William of St Denis, 'Vie de Suger', 399-401.

[14] John of Ford, 112. See also H. Mayr-Harting, 'Functions of a Twelfth

A note of caution was also sounded by the Latin poet Nivard, a clerk from Lille in Flanders. There is some dispute about the date of his satirical animal poem *Ysengrimus*, but it seems most probable that it was written in 1151 or 1152 and that its reference to the disastrous outcome of the Second Crusade was intended to dissuade Count Thierry of Flanders from returning to the Holy Land.[15]

Pope Eugenius III called the Second Crusade 'the most severe injury of the Christian name which the church of God has suffered in our time',[16] and fears of a similar catastrophe seem to have made the papacy cautious about supporting future expeditions. For example, Eugenius appears to have had doubts about the wisdom of Abbot Suger's plans[17] and when his successor Hadrian IV learned that Louis VII was anxious to mount a campaign against the Moors in Spain in 1159, he counselled him to take care, recalling the criticism aroused by the failure of his previous undertaking:

on that occasion, when Conrad . . . and you . . . undertook the journey to Jerusalem with little caution you did not receive the expected result and hoped for reward . . . how great a disaster and loss resulted therefrom to the church of God and almost all the Christian people. And the Holy Roman church because she had given you advice and support in this matter was not a little weakened by this; and everyone cried out against her in great indignation saying that she had been the author of so great a peril.[18]

In the 1160s and 1170s the Latin Kingdom of Jerusalem sent a series of appeals for aid to the West, but, although Philip of Flanders led a minor crusade in 1177, no major expedition was sent to the Holy Land.[19]

This situation changed after the battle of Hattin in 1187. Even so the minnesinger Albrecht von Johansdorf recorded that some crusade preachers had encountered opposition from sceptics:

Century Recluse', *History*, lx (1975), 346: Constable, 'A Lost Crusading Sermon', 54-5.

[15] Nivard, pp. cxii–xviii, 391-2, 399, 404-5; L. Willems, *Étude sur l'Ysengrimus* (Ghent, 1895), 21, 128. For another interpretation of this work, see F. J. and E. Sypher, *Ysengrimus by Magister Nivardus* (New York, 1980), p. xxiv.

[16] Eugenius III, *Opera*, col. 1414. See also ibid. col. 1396.

[17] See Vacandard, ii. 428-30.

[18] Hadrian IV, *Opera*, PL clxxxviii, cols. 1615-17.   [19] See Smail, 7-19.

Those who leave this country tell us . . . that Jerusalem, the pure city and the country have never been in greater need of help. This appeal is greeted with derision by the simple ones. They all say, 'if Our Lord was offended, he could avenge himself without all these soldiers having to cross the sea'.[20]

The limited achievements of the Third Crusade aroused further complaints directed against God. In a *tenso* composed after Richard I's release from captivity in 1194, the Monk of Montaudan accused God of not caring whether the Muslims were victorious and declared that 'he is a fool who follows you into battle'.[21] And in his lament upon the English king's sudden death, before he had fulfilled his vow to return to the Holy Land, Gaucelm Faidit suggested that the Lord willed that the Muslims should triumph.[22]

Similar accusations were made in the thirteenth century. At the time of the Fourth Lateran Council, Thomasin von Zirclaira recorded doubts about the crusading movement[23] and the minnesinger Neidhart, a member of Leopold of Austria's contingent, described the sufferings of the army besieging Damietta and ridiculed those who did not take the first opportunity to return home.[24] Writing after the collapse of the Fifth Crusade, the chronicler Richard of San Germano asked Christ why he permitted his enemies to defeat the faithful;[25] and the reversal of Christian fortunes seems to have led to a reluctance to take the cross, particularly in Germany.[26] Further doubts were voiced at the time of Frederick II's expedition to the Holy Land[27] and in the aftermath of Louis IX's defeat and capture in Egypt. According to the Italian chronicler Salimbene, when news reached the West of the disaster at Mansurah, the friars who had

---

[20] 'Die hinnen varn', *MF* 185. See also Heinrich von Rugge, 'Ein tumber man iu hât', *MF* 196.

[21] 'L'autrier fui en paradis', *Les Poésies du Moine de Montaudan*, ed. M. J. Routledge (Montpellier, 1977), 105–6.

[22] Gaucelm Faidit, 'Fortz chausa est que tot lo major dan', st. v, ed. cit. 417.

[23] Thomasin von Zirclaira, ll. 11499–506; Rocher, 711–12.

[24] Neidhart, 'Ez gruonet wol diu heide', stt. i, viii, *Die Lieder*, ed. E. Wiessner (Tübingen, 1955), 24–5.   [25] Richard of San Germano, 341–2.

[26] See Hoogeweg, 'Die Kreuzpredigt des Jahres 1224 in Deutschland mit besonderer Rücksicht auf die Erzdiöcese Köln', *Deutsche Zeitschrift für Geschichtswissenschaft*, iv (1890), 72–3.

[27] Walther von der Vogelweide, 'Der anegenge nie gewan', ed. cit. 112; Freidank, *Bescheidenheit*, 155, ll. 13–15.

preached the cross were publicly insulted and the people protested that Muhammad was more powerful than Christ.[28] Matthew Paris recorded that in France many Christians began to blaspheme, expressing amazement that God had abandoned those who fought on his behalf; he claimed that the inhabitants of several Italian cities were in danger of apostasy.[29] The troubadour Austorc d'Aurillac contrasted the expectations of the crusaders with the disastrous outcome of the expedition and lamented:

Ah! God, why did you bring this misfortune upon our French king . . . when you permitted him to suffer such shame; he who has striven to serve you with all his power.

. . . It is with good reason that we cease to believe in God and worship Muhammad . . . because God and the blessed Mary desire that we be conquered against all justice and that the evil ones shall receive all the honour.[30]

These complaints were repeated in the 1260s against the background of the Muslims' continued success. In a poem composed after the fall of Arsuf in 1265, the Templar Ricaut Bonomel protested that God slept whilst Muhammad fought on behalf of the Mameluke Sultan Baibars;[31] and in Rutebeuf's mock disputation, written just after Louis IX had taken the cross for a second time, in March 1267, the *descroizié* declared that he preferred to remain in France, for he had observed that previous crusaders had suffered in vain.[32] There were renewed protests after the failure of Louis IX's Tunisian expedition.[33] Like other troubadours Austorc de Segret lamented the king's death and the heavy French casualties; but he went on to question whether it was God or the Devil who had led the army astray and permitted Christians to be killed whilst the Muslims triumphed.[34] The poet Daspols

[28] Salimbene, 444-5.

[29] Matthew Paris, *CM* v. 108-9, 169-70.

[30] Austorc d'Aurillac, '(Ai!) Dieus per qu'as fa(ch)a', stt. i, iii, ed. cit. 82-4.

[31] 'Ir'e dolors s'es e mon cors asseza', *Poesie provenzali*, ii. 222-4.

[32] Rutebeuf, 'La desputizons dou croisié et dou descroizié', ed. cit. 84-94.

[33] See Olivier le Templier, 'Estat aurai lonc temps en pessamen', in Lewent, 119-20; Raimon Gaucelm de Béziers, 'Ab gran trebalhs', stt. i, ii, in 'Les troubadours de Béziers', 190-1.

[34] Austorc de Segret, '(No) sai qui.m so, tan suy (des)conoyssens', st. i, ed. cit. 469-70.

declared that Louis would have defeated the Muslims had he lived and, in a debate said to have taken place in Paradise, he replied to complaints that the faithful made no attempt to recover the Holy Land. Daspols asked the Lord why he permitted his enemies to be victorious, and suggested that if he showed the Muslims the error of their ways there would be no need for Christians to shed blood in the East.[35]

The main evidence of disillusionment after Louis's death at Tunis is, however, to be found in the memoir which Humbert of Romans submitted to the Second Council of Lyons. In this Humbert listed the various groups of critics, including those who were bewildered by the heavy Christian casualties, who questioned the advisability of future crusades, and who pointed out that the Christians fought at a disadvantage because they were on unfamiliar territory. Humbert noted that some believed that the continued failure of the expeditions was a sign that they were against God's will:

For how could the Lord have allowed Saladin to retake from us almost . . . all the land which had been won with so much Christian blood and toil, and the Emperor Frederick to perish in shallow water as he hastened to bring aid, and King Louis . . . to be captured in Egypt with his brothers and almost all the French nobility. And when he had started out again on this undertaking, to die with his son when he reached Tunis . . . and so great an army to have achieved nothing and countless other such events, if this kind of proceeding had been pleasing to him.[36]

But it should be remembered that the purpose of his treatise was to warn Gregory X of any possible sources of opposition to his crusade; and there is no indication that any of these groups of critics represented a large body of opinion.

Evidence of scepticism can also be found in an undated *exemplum* included in the *Speculum Laicorum*, a collection of tales compiled by an English clerk some time after Henry III's death. A friar was apparently preaching the crusade in the vicinity of Cambridge when he was interrupted by a mason who had been to the Holy Land and who tried to

---

[35] 'Fortz tristors es e salvaj'a retraire', and 'Seinhos aujos, c'aves saber e sens', in 'Les derniers troubadours de la Provence', ed. Meyer, *Bibliothèque de l'École des chartes*, xxx (1869), 285-9.

[36] Humbert of Romans, 'Opus tripartitum', 191-4, 197, 203.

discourage members of the audience from taking the cross. That night the detractor received a warning vision, but he paid no heed to it, and soon afterwards, when he was working, he fell from a great height and bit through his tongue.[37] A more frivolous attack upon the crusading movement is to be found in a manuscript in the British Museum which contains a number of Latin theological works and may have been connected with St Peter's abbey at Gloucester. It takes the form of some lines of Latin poetry written in a thirteenth-century hand. The first three stanzas are a conventional exhortation to take the cross; then there is a complete volte-face: the potential crusader is warned against preachers whose Ciceronian eloquence might deceive him into becoming a 'prisoner of the cross' and the author stresses the perils by land and sea that will face the recruit. This dramatic contrast suggests that, although there is no break in the manuscript, these are really two separate poems; and the fact that the sceptical and satirical verses are in the same metrical form as the preceding stanzas implies that they were intended to be a parody of the crusading exhortation.[38]

It has been argued that these expressions of doubt and despair became more frequent in the thirteenth century, in particular after the failure of Louis IX's two expeditions.[39] But in fact there is no evidence that the sense of disillusionment was any greater in the 1250s and 1270s than it had been in the aftermath of the Second Crusade. On the contrary, the reaction to these latest reversals in Christian fortunes may have been less severe. Admittedly after the catastrophe at Mansurah certain writers accused God of deserting his people and expressed doubts about the advisability of crusading. But as we have seen these attacks represented the 'standard' response to a defeat, and this type of criticism can be traced from the beginning of the crusading movement. There was certainly no lull in crusading activity to match the relative quiet of the years between 1149 and 1187. Although they lamented the severe loss of life, the

[37] *Speculum Laicorum*, ed. J. T. Welter (Paris, 1914), 34–5. See also Humbert of Romans, *De praedicatione sancte crucis*, ch. xxi; *Opus tripartitum*, 191, 199.
[38] 'A Strange Crusader's Song', ed. H. Pflaum, *Speculum*, x (1935), 337–9; *Catalogue of Western Manuscripts*, i. 217.
[39] Throop, 180; Prawer, ii. 385–7; Stickel, 204–11.

poets called upon the faithful to resume the struggle against the Muslims. In the 1260s the Northern French poet Rutebeuf composed a series of crusading exhortations,[40] and the Provençal troubadour Gauceran de Saint-Didier reminded the Kings of England, France, Aragon, and Castile of their duty to avenge the loss of the Holy Land.[41] The poet Guilhem de Murs addressed a similar personal appeal to King James of Aragon.[42] Further doubts about the wisdom of launching a crusade were expressed after the collapse of Louis IX's Tunisian expedition. But, although several poets composed laments upon the king's death, at the same time they exhorted the faithful, particularly Western rulers, to hasten to Syria.[43] The most suitable leaders for this enterprise were thought to be the King of Aragon and Edward I of England, who was already in the Holy Land; in the early 1270s the troubadours Peire Cardenal and Olivier le Templier urged these princes to avenge the Christian defeats.[44]

In the mid thirteenth century, the crusade still retained its popular appeal. For example, over 75 per cent of the passengers on board the crusade ship *St Victor* in 1250 were commoners,[45] and in his mock disputation Rutebeuf's *descroizié* recalled the vast numbers of ordinary people who had travelled to the Holy Land.[46] As late as 1267 the Patriarch of Jerusalem appealed to the Master of the Temple in France to persuade the lay and ecclesiastical authorities to prevent the poor, the old and the weak from

[40] Rutebeuf, 'La complainte d'Outremer', 'La complainte du comte Eudes de Nevers' and 'La voie de Tunis', ed. cit. 52–83.

[41] 'El temps quan vey cazer fuelhas et flors', in *Choix des poésies originales des troubadours*, ed. M. Raynouard (Paris, 1816–21), iv. 133–5. For the authorship of this poem, see Jeanroy, *La Poésie lyrique*, i. 370, 382.

[42] 'D'un sirventes far me sis dieus guitz', *Choix des poésies*, v. 203. For the dating of this poem, see 'Les derniers troubadours', 290.

[43] See Fulk de Lunel, 'Al bon rey qu'es reys de pretz car', st. vi, *Choix des poésies*, iv. 240–1; Raimon Gaucelm de Béziers, 'Ab gran trebalhs', 'Les troubadours de Béziers , 190–2.

[44] Olivier le Templier, 'Estat aurai lonc temps', in Lewent, 120–1; Peire Cardenal, 'Totz lo mons es vestitz et abrazatz', in 'Un sirventes de Cardinal, encore inédit en partie (1271-2)', ed. Fabre, *A Miscellany of Studies in Romance Languages and Literatures Presented to L. E. Kastner* (Cambridge, 1932), 218, 225–43.   [45] Kedar, 'The Passenger List', 271.

[46] Rutebeuf, 'La desputizons', ed. cit. 92.

taking the cross, for they always proved a burden to the army.[47]

Some of the most fundamental criticism of the crusading movement can also be traced to the aftermath of the Second Crusade. It has been suggested that the reverse at Damascus encouraged St Bernard to predict the imminent arrival of the Antichrist[48] and two contemporaries claimed that the expedition itself was the work of the Devil. Virtually nothing is known about one of these, the annalist of Würzburg, but he was probably a clerk or monk in the city, and seems to have witnessed the massacres of the Jews at the beginning of the crusade. He also obtained information about the army's difficulties in Asia Minor from crusaders who had just been released from Turkish captivity.[49] Like other chroniclers, the annalist criticized the behaviour of the crusading host and commented upon the variety of motives which had led men to take the cross, lamenting that few had been driven by love of the divine majesty. But, whereas other contemporaries saw the expedition as an opportunity for salvation, his startling suggestion was that the crusade itself was a revolt inspired by the Devil against God's righteous punishment of the world:

God allowed the Western church on account of its sins to be cast down. Thereupon there arose certain pseudo-prophets, sons of Belial and witnesses of Antichrist, who seduced Christians with empty words. Through preaching they compelled all sorts of men to set out against the Saracens in order to liberate Jerusalem . . . they were so influential that the inhabitants of nearly every region by common vows offered themselves up for common destruction.[50]

The annalist's main source for this was the Book of Revelation. In it the dragon Satan conferred his power upon the beast from the sea, who reigned over every race, people, language, and nation; and this authority was subsequently transferred to the beast from the land, who persuaded men to adore his master through deceptive prodigies (Rev. 13).

[47] 'Emprunts de Saint Louis', 290-3.
[48] See McGinn, 'St Bernard and Eschatology', in *Studies presented to J. Leclercq*, Cistercian Studies series, XXIII, (Washington DC, 1973), 170-1, 181-4; Bernard, *Vita S. Malachiae, Opera*, iii. 307.
[49] See *Annales Herbipolenses*, 5.
[50] Ibid. 3.

In this context the annalist of Würzburg denounced the preachers of the cross as false prophets and slaves of the Devil, and he complained that they deceived men into taking the cross, to the peril of their bodies and souls.

The other severe critic of the crusade in the mid twelfth century was Gerhoh of Reichersberg. Born between 1093 and 1094, Gerhoh was educated at the schools in Freising, Mosburg, and Hildesheim; he then taught for a time at Augsburg. But his undisguised support for Pope Calixtus II, rather than the Emperor Henry V, brought him into conflict with the bishop of that city and in 1120 or 1121 he found it expedient to retire to a community of canons at Rottenbuch. Gerhoh remained there until the settlement of the Investiture Contest at the synod of Worms in 1122. In 1126 the Bishop of Regensburg appointed him parish priest of Cham, and six years later he was elected provost of the Augustinian house of Reichersberg in the diocese of Passau.[51] Gerhoh seems to have been on excellent terms with Eugenius III,[52] and probably had access to some first-hand information about the Second Crusade, for a number of local lords, with whom he must have been acquainted, including the Bishops of Freising and Passau and Duke Henry of Bavaria, took part in the expedition.[53] There are references to the crusade in two of his major works, the *Commentarius in Psalmos* and *De investigatione Antichristi*.

In his commentary upon Ps. 33, written in 1146 or 1147, Gerhoh described the achievements of the First Crusade;[54] in a passage composed in the following year, before news reached the West of the reverse at Damascus,[55] he praised the knights who had gone to avenge the loss of Edessa. Gerhoh identified all heretics as the precursors of Antichrist on earth, and he maintained that this latest expedition against the enemies of Christ's sepulchre, the Muslims,

---

[51] See D. van den Eynde, *L'Œuvre littéraire de Géroch de Reichersberg* (Rome, 1957), 3-10.

[52] See Eugenius III, *Opera*, col. 1139.

[53] P. Classen, *Gerhoch von Reichersberg* (Wiesbaden, 1960), 132-3.

[54] Gerhoh of Reichersberg, *Commentarius*, 429-31. For the dating of this chapter, see Classen, 413; van den Eynde, 308-11.

[55] See Classen, 413; van den Eynde, 311-12.

was a sign of the beginning of the end of chaos and the emergence of a new spirit of piety.[56]

Gerhoh's attitude towards the Second Crusade had changed dramatically by the time he wrote the final version of the *De investigatione Antichristi*, between 1160 and 1162.[57] In this work he identified the three main evils of his time as the disputes between the empire and the papacy, the schism between Victor IV and Alexander III, and the failure of the crusade; and suggested that there was a connection between these disasters and the presence of the Antichrist. Like other chroniclers, Gerhoh attributed the sufferings of the crusaders in Asia Minor to Greek treachery,[58] but he emphasized that the main guilt for the failure of the siege of Damascus and the crusade as a whole lay with the inhabitants of the Kingdom of Jerusalem. A number of contemporaries had accused the Syrian barons of accepting bribes from the Muslim governor of Damascus to make sure that the siege was unsuccessful,[59] but Gerhoh went much further: he suggested that avarice was the motive for the Syrian Franks' initial appeal for aid from the West and lamented that their desire to amass silver and gold had ultimately led to heavy Christian casualties. According to Gerhoh, during the siege of Damascus the inhabitants of Jerusalem did not wish for peace with the Muslims, but 'almost solely the acceptance of money, whether from the offerings of pilgrims or from the redemption of the besieged'; he commented that the Lord had punished them in kind, for most of the coins which they received were copper not gold. Gerhoh then proceeded to cite several examples of avarice at work in the church, and portrayed greed as one of the beasts of the Apocalypse which had fled from Rome to Jerusalem and then back again. But, although he was highly critical of the Syrian Franks, Gerhoh still believed that some of the blame for the failure of the expedition lay with the crusaders themselves. He lamented that because the Christians had deviated from the

---

[56] Gerhoh of Reichersberg, *Commentarius*, 435–7. See also Gerhoh's sermon preached on Christmas Day 1147. Classen, 132 n. 19.

[57] For the dating of this work, see van den Eynde, 121–4, 131–8; Classen, 421–4.

[58] See Odo of Deuil, 82, 90. See also above, p. 77.

[59] See Robert of Torigni, 154; *Chronica regia Coloniensis*, 84.

right way, God willed that those who took the cross should be deceived by preachers and false miracles and perish miserably in the East; and he described the marvellous portents which had presaged the disastrous outcome of the expedition.[60]

Gerhoh also played a part in the compilation of the annals of his house.[61] But, whilst they derive much of their information about the Second Crusade from the *De investigatione Antichristi* and are critical of the Syrian Franks' avarice, they do not draw the same extreme conclusions about the presence of the Antichrist. In fact the annals adopt the traditional formula *peccatis exigentibus hominum* to explain the failure of the expedition.[62]

Another challenge to the crusading movement came from Joachim of Fiore and his followers, the Joachites. Joachim was born in Southern Italy in *c.*1135 and was probably the son of a notary. In 1156 or 1157 he made a pilgrimage to the Holy Land; according to his biographer, he experienced a conversion during an outbreak of plague and returned to the West determined to devote his life to God. In *c.*1159 Joachim entered the Cistercian Order, probably at Sambuciana, and eighteen years later he was elected Abbot of Corazzo. By 1188 or 1189, however, he had become disillusioned with the Cistercian way of life and, influenced by the Calabrian tradition, he left the cloister and founded a community of hermits at Fiore. This attracted royal patronage and developed into the Florensian Order, whose Rule was approved by Celestine III in 1196.[63]

Joachim owed his reputation, however, to his revolutionary interpretation of history, the result of prolonged contemplation of the Scriptures. He saw the past as a series of complex patterns of twos, threes, fives, sevens, and twelves; but his grand design was the doctrine of the three *status*: the ages of the Father, Son, and Holy Ghost; periods of chastisement, action, and contemplation. He drew parallels between events in the Old and New Testaments and predicted the glories of the forthcoming third age. Joachim interpreted the

---

[60] Gerhoh of Reichersberg, *De investigatione Antichristi*, 377–84.

[61] See Classen, 435; van den Eynde, 10.

[62] *Annales Reicherspergenses*, MGH SS xvii. 461–4.

[63] Bloomfield, 'Joachim of Flora: A Critical Survey of his Canon, Teachings, Sources, Biography and Influence', *Traditio*, xiii (1957), 291–4.

seven seals of the Book of Revelation (Rev. 5:1) as seven periods
of persecution and maintained that the tribulations suffered by
the Hebrews foreshadowed wars in the era after Christ. In this
context he discussed the crusading movement and the rise of
Saladin and used the beast of the Apocalypse, a red dragon
with seven heads, as a symbol to illustrate his argument.[64]

Joachim made his most famous pronouncement on the
subject of the crusades shortly after Christmas 1190, when
he appeared before Richard I at Messina. At the time the
English king was on his way to take part in the siege of
Acre, and Joachim's prophecies about the success of the
Third Crusade were recorded by the chronicler Roger of
Howden. According to his account in the *Gesta*, Joachim
identified the seven heads of the beast of the Apocalypse as
the seven persecutors of the church—Herod, Nero, Constan-
tius, Muhammad, Melsemutus, Saladin, and Antichrist—and
he predicted that Saladin would soon be defeated and the Holy
Land restored to the faithful, assuring Richard I that the
Lord had reserved this magnificent victory for his army.[65]
In fact the Muslim leader died of natural causes in 1193, and
in the *Chronica* Roger of Howden gave a slightly different
version of events. Joachim now predicted that Jerusalem
would return to the Christian fold seven years after its fall,
that is in 1194. In the light of this prophecy Richard was
made to ask whether his expedition was premature. Joachim
replied that the presence of the king's army was essential for
the final victory over the Muslims.[66]

Joachim also expressed a variety of views about the future
success of the crusading movement in his own works. Unfortunately little is known about their date of composition,
except that they were presented to the pope for his approval
in 1200;[67] but some indication of their sequence may be

[64] Reeves and B. Hirsch-Reich, 'The Seven Seals in the Writings of Joachim
of Fiore', *Recherches de théologie ancienne et médiévale*, xxi (1954) 214-26;
Reeves, *Joachim of Fiore and the Prophetic Future* (London, 1976), 2-22.

[65] Roger of Howden, *Gesta*, ii. 150-3. For the authenticity of this account,
see E. Jamison, 'The Sicilian Norman Kingdom in the Mind of Anglo-Norman
Contemporaries', *Proceedings of the British Academy*, xxiv (1938), 263-6; Reeves
and Hirsch-Reich, *The Figurae of Joachim of Fiore* (Oxford, 1972), 86-8.

[66] Roger of Howden, *Chronica*, iii. 75-8.

[67] See E. R. Daniel, 'Joachim of Flora and the Joachite Tradition of Apocalyptic Conversion in the Later Middle Ages' (unpubl. thesis, Virginia, 1966), 29-30.

given by their different predictions about the crusades.[68] In the *Liber Figurarum*, which was written either by Joachim or by a member of his circle,[69] it was prophesied that the dragon's sixth head, Saladin, would be defeated by the Christians and brought almost to destruction, but like the beast of the Apocalypse (Rev. 13: 3):

after a few years its wound will be healed and the king who is over it, whether it be Saladin, if he is still alive, or another in his place, will gather together a much larger army than before and will wage a general war against God's elect.[70]

In the *Liber introductorius*, however, Joachim made no mention of an Islamic defeat: Saladin was both the beast's sixth head and Daniel's eleventh or little horn (Dan. 7: 8). Joachim declared that the Muslim leader had grown strong as a punishment for the sins of the Christians, and predicted that either he or his successor would humiliate three kings.[71] The main reason for this change in attitude seems to have been Joachim's disillusionment as a result of the heavy casualties suffered by Frederick I's expedition and the limited achievements of the Third Crusade as a whole. And by the same time he wrote the *Expositio in Apocalypsim* he had come to question the advisability of launching another expedition against the Muslims. In this work Joachim described the successes of the First Crusade and other Christian victories over the Turks and Moors, but concluded that the full force of Islam was still to be felt. He argued that during the period of the Christian successes the beast had been wounded almost unto death, but it would soon recover and wage war against the faithful.[72] In 1195 Joachim had met a man who, whilst he was a prisoner at Alexandria, had been told of a Muslim alliance

---

[68] Id. 'Apocalyptic Conversion: The Joachite Alternative to the Crusades', *Traditio*, xxvi (1969), 133-5.

[69] Reeves and Hirsch-Reich, *The Figurae*, 97-8.

[70] Joachim of Fiore, *Liber Figurarum (Il Libro delle Figure)*, ed. L. Tondelli, Reeves and Hirsch-Reich (Turin, 1953), Pl. xiv; Reeves and Hirsch-Reich, *The Figurae*, 146-50.

[71] Joachim of Fiore, *Liber introductorius in Apocalypsim*, fol. 10[r-v], prefacing *Expositio Apocalypsim* (Venice, 1527). See also id. 'De vita Sancti Benedicti et de officio divino secundum eius doctrinam', ed. C. Baraut, *Analecta Sacra Tarraconensia*, xxiv (1951), 52-3.

[72] Id. *Expositio*, fols. 164[v]-5[v].

with the Patarene heretics, and he interpreted this as a sign of the dreaded union of the beast from the sea with the beast from the land (Rev. 13: 12) and as an indication that the sixth seal was about to be opened, heralding a further period of persecution. (Rev. 6: 12–17) According to the Apocalypse, when the sixth angel poured his phial upon the River Euphrates, the barrier protecting the Empire against the heathen would collapse (Rev. 16: 12), and they would flood across and wreak vengeance upon the faithful. It seemed to Joachim that this disaster was foreshadowed by the death of Frederick I in Asia Minor and the subsequent destruction of his army.[73] In the *Liber Figurarum* and the *Liber introductorius* Joachim had given hints of a future when the Christians would triumph over the Muslims by preaching, not fighting;[74] in the *Expositio* he underlined this theme, emphasizing that the crusaders would never be victorious by force of arms. According to Joachim's plan of history the third age or *status* would begin between 1200 and 1260; and he prophesied that a race of *viri spirituales* would emerge and convert the Jews and Gentiles and gather them peacefully into Christ's fold.[75]

Joachim himself never actually attacked the concept of the crusade. But after his death in *c*.1202 his ideas spread rapidly to Northern Europe,[76] and his prophecy that the Muslims would be converted by peaceful means in the new age was taken up and developed by his followers, the Joachites. For our purposes their most important work was the commentary on Jeremiah, *Super Hieremiam*, composed between 1243 and 1248.[77] There is some dispute about whether its author was a member of a Joachite circle in Calabria or a Spiritual Franciscan,[78] but it seems to have been a popular treatise. Within a few years it was cited by the

[73] Joachim of Fiore, *Expositio*, fols. 133ʳ-4ᵛ.

[74] Id. *Liber Figurarum*, Pls. xiv, xxii; *Liber introductorius*, fol. 8ᵛ.

[75] Id. *Expositio*, fols. 164, 197. See also 'De vita Sancti Benedicti', 82, 84–5.

[76] Bloomfield and Reeves, 'The Penetration of Joachism', 772–93.

[77] See Reeves, *The Influence of Prophecy in the Later Middle Ages: A Study in Joachimism* (Oxford, 1969), 518.

[78] Id. 'The Abbot Joachim's Disciples and the Cistercian Order', *Sophia*, xix (1951), 367; Bloomfield, 'Recent scholarship on Joachim of Fiore and his influence', in A. Williams, (ed.), *Prophecy and Millenarianism: Essays in honour of M. Reeves* (London, 1980), 25.

chroniclers Alexander of Bremen and Albert of Stade,[79] and it was also quoted by Salimbene, who regarded it as Joachim's own work and held it in the highest respect.[80]

Salimbene had first learned of Joachim's teaching from an abbot of the Florensian Order, who had taken refuge from the Emperor Frederick II in the Franciscan convent at Pisa, and in the early 1240s he heard the Joachite Hugh of Digne preach at Lucca and Tarascon. Hugh seems to have made a great impression, for in 1247 Salimbene decided to abandon his studies in Paris and travel to Hyères to listen to his discourses.[81] On his journey there he met the friars Bartholomeo Guiscolo and Gerardino of Borgo San Donnino, who apparently showed him a copy of the *Super Hieremiam*. At the time Louis IX was preparing to go on crusade and, according to Salimbene, the friars mocked and derided, saying that he would fare ill if he went. They pointed to a passage in the treatise which prophesied that 'the King of France shall be captured and the French defeated and many shall be carried off by the plague'.[82] And when Gerardino accompanied the Franciscan Minister-General, John of Parma, to Constantinople in 1250, he was said to have predicted the exact time of Louis's capture.[83]

Unfortunately Salimbene gave no precise reference to the text and it is therefore impossible to determine the source of the friars' prophecy. But there is no doubt that the author of the *Super Hieremiam* condemned further attempts to launch a crusade. Indeed he claimed that this was against God's commands, for the Lord wished the pope to look after the souls of the faithful and to defend his own Jerusalem, the church, from its real enemy, Frederick II. The anonymous author pointed out, moreover, that another crusade could

---

[79] Alexander of Bremen, *Expositio in Apocalypsim*, ed. A. Wachtel, Die Deutschen Geschichtsquellen des Mittelalters, 500–1500, II (Weimar, 1955), 437, 493; *Annales Stadenses*, 372.

[80] For Salimbene's knowledge of Joachim's works, see D. E. West, 'The Education of Fra Salimbene of Parma: The Joachite Influence', in *Prophecy and Millenarianism*, 204–5.

[81] Ibid. 200–1.

[82] Salimbene, 236–7.

[83] Angelo of Clareno, *Historia septem tribulationum ordinis minorum*, ed. F. Ehrle, *Archiv für Literatur und Kirchen-Geschichte des Mittelalters*, ii (1886), 268–9. See also Daniel, 'Joachim of Flora', 159 n. 110.

actually be harmful to the church, for, by sending Christians to the barbarous nations 'under the appearance of salvation and the cross', the prelates altered the balance of power and consequently weakened the barrier which protected Christendom from the heathen.[84] He clearly referred to a third age in which a race of *viri spirituales* would emerge and convert the *gentes incredulas*;[85] and this concept is also to be found in other Joachite treatises, such as the *Super Esaiam* and the associated collection of figures known as *Praemissiones*[86], which were composed between 1260 and 1267,[87] and an anonymous Ghibelline prophecy dated 1268.[88]

In addition Salimbene claimed to have been shown a verse prophecy which had been sent to certain cardinals and to a Dominican provincial chapter before the election of Gregory X in 1271; and he included one version of it, together with his own commentary, in his chronicle. According to Salimbene's interpretation, Gregory's early death was a result of his repeated attempts to launch another expedition against the Muslims; he pointed out that the crusade was against God's plan for the future, for the year 1260 had passed. Henceforward those outside the church would be converted by peaceful means.[89]

The extent to which the concept of apocalyptic conversion had developed by the mid thirteenth century should not, however, be exaggerated;[90] and it is important to establish whether this criticism of the crusades was confined to the Joachites' small circle of adherents or influenced a wider body of opinion. As we have seen, by 1250 the treatise *Super Hieremiam* was well known in Germany and Italy and by the late thirteenth century manuscripts of this work were to be found in libraries throughout Europe. The same

[84] Pseudo-Joachim, *Super Hieremiam Prophetam* (Venice, 1525) fols. 45^V-6^V.

[85] Ibid. fols. 2^V, 50^V, 57^r-8^r.

[86] Pseudo-Joachim, *Praemissiones* and *Super Esaiam Prophetam* (Venice, 1517), fol. 56^V.

[87] For the authorship of these works, see Reeves, 'Abbot Joachim's disciples', 367 and *Influence of Prophecy*, 521.

[88] Reeves, *Influence of Prophecy*, 312.

[89] Salimbene, 492-5.

[90] See Reeves, 'History and Prophecy in Medieval Thought', *Medievalia et Humanistica*, n. s. v (1974), 63-4.

was true of the *Super Esaiam* and *Praemissiones*.[91] Marginal notes attest to the enthusiasm with which these works were read, but it seems that the audience were principally interested in their theological content and theories of biblical exegesis.[92] There is no evidence that the Joachites' criticism of the crusading movement attracted much support. Like Gerhoh of Reichersberg and the annalist of Würzburg, they were isolated individuals and thousands continued to take the cross.

Admittedly in the 1260s there is some evidence of criticism of the crusades on the grounds that they hindered the conversion of the Muslims, but historians have tended to overstate its importance.[93] The Franciscan Roger Bacon may have been influenced by Joachite ideas of apocalyptic conversion,[94] and in his *Opus maius* he placed great emphasis on the knowledge of languages as an aid to missions. He exhorted Christians to follow the example of the early church, which had converted the Gentiles by preaching alone, and in the aftermath of Louis IX's defeat at Mansurah, he questioned the value of further crusades:

if the Christians are victorious, no one stays behind to defend the conquests. Nor are unbelievers converted in this way, but killed and sent to hell. Those who survive the wars together with their children are more and more embittered against the Christian faith because of these wars and are indefinitely alienated from Christ and inflamed to do all the harm possible to Christians.[95]

But, if one examines Roger's other works, it is not always clear that he advocated preaching and teaching rather than the use of force. For example, in the *Opus tertium* and the *Compendium studii philosophiae*, dated 1267 or 1268, while he looked forward to the adoption of the Christian faith by the Tartars and the return of the Greeks to the fold, he expected the Muslims to be destroyed.[96] In what may have

---

[91] Reeves, *Influence of Prophecy*, 56, 518-19, 521-2.
[92] Ibid. 39.
[93] See Throop, 132-40; Prawer, ii. 389-90; Stickel, 234-41.
[94] See S. C. Easton, *Roger Bacon and his Search for a Universal Science* (Oxford, 1952), 134-40; Daniel, 'Joachim of Flora', 162-9.
[95] Roger Bacon, *Opus maius*, iii. 120-2.
[96] Id. *Opus tertium* and *Compendium studii philosophiae*, *Opera hactenus inedita*, ed. Brewer (London, 1859), 86, 402-3. See also Reeves, 'History and Prophecy', 64.

been a direct reference to Roger Bacon, Humbert of Romans recorded that some people,

> are asking what is the use of this attack upon the Saracens? For they are not roused to conversion by it, but rather are provoked against the Christian faith. When we are victorious and have killed them, moreover, we send them to hell, which seems to be against the law of charity. Also when we gain their lands we do not occupy them as colonists, because our countrymen do not want to stay in these regions, and so there seems to be no spiritual, corporeal, or temporal benefits from this sort of fighting.[97]

But once again he gave no indication of the extent of this opposition. As Minister-General of the Dominican Order, Humbert had some knowledge of missionary work and, although he was optimistic about the peaceful conversion of the pagans in north-eastern Europe, he stressed that only force would succeed against the Muslims. Humbert repeated the classic defence of the crusading movement and pointed out that this was the only way of preventing the spread of Islam.[98]

At the same time, in the penultimate sentence of his treatise submitted to the Second Council of Lyons, the Dominican William of Tripoli dismissed the need to use force:

> solely by the word of God, without philosophical argument, without military weapons, they [the Muslims] will seek like simple sheep the baptism of Christ and will enter into the flock of God.

William quoted prophecies which showed that the time was right for the conversion of the Muslims.[99] But there is no evidence that he criticized the crusade as such.[100] The main theme of his work was the similarities between Islam and Christianity.

As early as the twelfth century there also seem to have been some pacifists who objected in principle to the use of force against the Muslims, but they do not appear to have

[97] Humbert of Romans, *Opus tripartitum*, 196.
[98] Ibid. 94–5; R. P. Mortier, *Histoire des maîtres généraux de l'ordre des frères prêcheurs* (Paris, 1903–9), i. 518–32. See also Fidenzio of Padua, 23.
[99] William of Tripoli, 597–8.
[100] See Throop, 120, 122.

been numerous and their arguments have survived only because they were recorded by preachers and apologists of the crusade.[101] For example, in a letter probably written between 1128 and 1136, Hugh of St Victor sought to answer criticism of the recently founded Order of the Temple. Hugh reassured the knights of the justice of their profession:

(for) we have heard that some of you have been troubled by foolish men, claiming that the profession to which you have devoted your lives: bearing arms against the enemies of the faith and peace, in the defence of Christians, that your profession, I say, is illicit or pernicious, in other words that it constitutes a sin,

and emphasized that they contended for justice against iniquity. He warned that it was the Devil who exhorted men to be humble and to lay down their arms, and pointed out that Christ himself had struggled on earth against sinners, because this was the only way to achieve real peace. Hugh concluded that even if the knights received little earthly praise, they would be rewarded amply elsewhere.[102]

St Bernard's apologia *De laude novae militiae*, written at the request of the founder of the Order of the Temple, Hugh of Payns, also seems to have been intended as a reply to some pacifist criticism of the Templars and the crusading movement as a whole. In it he stressed that, if there had been any other way of preventing the Muslims from oppressing the faithful, it would have been employed; as it was, it was better to kill them than to risk the spread of their iniquity. St Bernard drew a contrast between the secular knight, who fought from worldly motives, and the *miles Christi*, who only

---

[101] See Haines, 385-6.

[102] 'Un document sur les débuts des Templiers', ed. Leclercq, *Revue d'histoire ecclésiastique*, lxx (1957), 86-9. Leclercq argues that, although the letter was attributed to Hugh of St Victor in the manuscript, there are no stylistic parallels with his other works; he suggests that it was probably written by Hugh of Payns. C. Sclafert, however, ('Lettre inédite de Hugues de Saint-Victor aux chevaliers du Temple', *Revue d'Ascétique et de mystique*, xxxiv (1958), 275-99), maintains convincingly that the author was Hugh of St Victor. He points out that the style resembles that which he used on less formal occasions and there is no reason why the subject should not have interested him, particularly since St Bernard was so closely involved. More recently M. L. Bulst-Thiele, ('Sacrae Domus Militiae Templi Hierosolymitani Magistri', *Abhandlungen der Akademie der Wissenschaften in Göttingen, philologisch-historische Klasse*, lxxxvi (1974), 23 n. 19) has reaffirmed that Hugh of St Victor was the author of this letter. She argues that it could not have been written by a layman such as Hugh of Payns.

took up arms to defend the faithful. He emphasized that it was not a crime to slay a Muslim: on the contrary a knight who died in such a battle was worthy to be classed as a martyr.[103]

The most detailed justification of the use of force, however, is to be found in Gratian's discussion of the just war in Causa XXIII of the *Decretum*. Although Gratian did not refer to the crusade as such, it clearly formed the background to his inquiry,[104] and he listed the various arguments advanced by pacifists before proceeding to refute them point by point. According to Gratian, the main authorities for pacifism were Christ's injunction to his followers to be patient and to turn the other cheek (Matt. 5: 39/Luke 6: 29); St Paul's warning that God had reserved vengeance for himself (Rom. 12: 19); and Christ's admonition to Peter that 'All who take the sword shall perish by the sword' (Matt. 26: 52). In reply Gratian quoted various other biblical texts and passages from the early fathers which stated that war waged for a just cause was neither sinful nor against God's commands, and emphasized that those who fought with just authority defended the peace of the church and were therefore not guilty of homicide.[105]

Causa XXIII came to be regarded as the classic defence of Christian warfare, and as early as the 1150s or 1160s it was used to counter criticisms of the crusading movement. As we have seen, the failure of the Second Crusade led to serious doubts about the advisability of further expeditions against the Muslims. Concern about this seems to have prompted the Patriarch of Jerusalem to ask Peter of Troyes for some reassurance that it was permissible for Christians to make war upon the Muslims and to put them to death. Peter's reply took the form of a canonical quaestio: he quoted the various authorities for the just war cited by Gratian, and concluded that those who fought against the enemies of the church served God and did not commit homicide.[106] Peter of Blois must also have encountered some pacifists when he was

---

[103] Bernard, *De laude novae militiae, Opera*, iii. 213–17.

[104] See Hehl, 80–9.

[105] Gratian, *Decretum, C.* XXIII, q. 1.

[106] Leclercq, 'Gratien, Pierre de Troyes et la seconde croisade', *Studia Gratiana*, ii (1954), 589–93.

preaching the Third Crusade, for in his exhortation to take
the cross he considered it necessary to remind men that they
would not incur penalties for murder by fighting against the
Muslims. Peter admitted that in certain circumstances the
Lord abhorred bloodshed, but he stressed that God deemed
it a meritorious act to attack those who blasphemed Christ
and polluted his sanctuary.[107]

In his treatise *De re militari*, Ralph Niger advocated a policy
of moderation towards the Muslims, on the grounds that
'they are men of the same nature as we' and he quoted one
of the main pacifist texts, Ezek. 33: 11,

As I live, saith the Lord God, I desire not the death of the wicked,
but that the wicked should turn from his ways and live.

But if this passage is placed in context, it becomes obvious
that Ralph was merely repeating the established canonical
ruling that men should not be compelled to renounce their
faith,[108] and there is no evidence that he opposed the crusade
on pacifist grounds. Indeed, far from objecting to the use of
force, Ralph argued that in certain circumstances it was right
to wage war; and he clearly had a detailed knowledge of
military equipment and its uses, perhaps acquired during his
sojourn at the Young King's court.[109]

In his sermons to the Military Orders, delivered in the early
thirteenth century, James of Vitry replied to further pacifist
criticism of the crusades. James denounced those 'who
falsely assert that you are not allowed to take up the physical
sword or fight bodily against the church's enemies' and
pointed out that, if the Christians had not resisted their foes
in the past, the Saracens and heretics would have destroyed
the whole church. He attributed such arguments to the
machinations of the Devil and, following Gratian, cited
authorities which proved that it was right to repel violence
and avenge injuries. Like Hugh of St Victor and St Bernard,
James stressed that the knights of the Military Orders had
been given the material sword in order to protect the church,

---

[107] Peter of Blois, Ep. 237, *Opera*, ii. 229-30.
[108] Ralph Niger, *DRM* 196.
[109] Flahiff, 'Ralph Niger: An Introduction', 108 and 'Deus non vult', 167. See
also W. L. Warren, *Henry II* (London, 1973), 580-4.

and denied that they were motivated by love of vain praise, greed, or cruelty. In fact he declared that it was the duty of all Christians to protect their homeland from the attacks of barbarians.[110]

Humbert of Romans also referred to critics who argued that it was wrong for Christians to initiate wars through which blood might be shed. He cited the main authorities for pacifism—the patient suffering of Christ and the example of the early Christian martyrs—and countered that God had given men earthly powers in order that they might defend the church against its enemies. Humbert stressed that Christians were bound to protect themselves from their worst foe, the Muslims, and observed that Christ's injunction to Peter to sheathe his sword (Matt. 26: 52) was intended for that occasion only and was not applicable to the laity.[111]

Apart from these anonymous criticisms, the only other pacifist objections to the crusades were advanced by the Cathars and Waldensians. Few treatises composed by the heretics themselves have survived, but the main tenets of their doctrines can be gathered from the records of the Inquisition and the works of Christian polemicists.

The Cathars believed that, after Satan's fall from heaven, man's soul was trapped in a body of corrupt and perishable flesh. It could only be released if he received the *consolamentum* and became one of the elect, a *perfectus*, and if an ordinary believer died without having taken the sacrament, his soul was condemned to a further period of wandering on earth. For this reason the Cathars denounced capital punishment and war and forbade the *perfecti* to take part in anything which involved bloodshed. In most cases this prohibition of homicide was described in general terms,[112] but there are a few examples of Cathar criticism of the crusades.

One of these is to be found in an anonymous heretical treatise, written in Provençal sometime between 1210 and 1240. This took the form of a discussion of the powers of the Cathar church and a defence of its moral standards;

[110] James of Vitry, *Sermones vulgares*, ed. J. B. Pitra, *Analecta novissima* (Paris, 1885-8), ii. 405, 414, 419-20.

[111] Humbert of Romans, *Opus tripartitum*, 191-2.

[112] See Rainier of Sacconi, *Summa de Catharis*, ed. A. Dondaine, in *Liber de duobus principiis* (Rome, 1939), 65.

in this context the anonymous author quoted Christ's admonition that 'if thou wilt enter into life, thou shalt do no murder' (Matt. 19: 17-18). He then proceeded to cite other authorities which enjoined the faithful to bear suffering patiently, in particular the example of the early Christians, and accused the Roman church of ignoring Christ's teaching:

for it is not persecuted for the goodness or justice which is in it, but on the contrary it persecutes and kills all who refuse to condone its sins and its actions . . . it is feared by kings and emperors and other barons. Nor is it like a sheep among wolves, but rather like wolves among sheep or goats, for it endeavours to rule over pagans and Jews and Gentiles. And above all does it persecute and kill the Holy Church of Christ [the Cathars].

It is not clear whether the last sentence was intended as a criticism of the Albigensian Crusade or the judicial killing of the Cathars; but the author's reference to the pagans suggests that he was opposed to all aspects of the crusading movement.[113]

The reports of inquisitorial proceedings tended to follow a set pattern of question and answer, concentrating upon points of doctrine. But fortunately on one occasion it was considered relevant to record the heretic's attitude towards the crusade. In Lent 1247, Peter Garcias, a citizen of Toulouse, discussed his Cathar beliefs with his relative Friar William Garcias in the city's Franciscan convent. He spoke frankly, for he believed that this was a private conversation, but Friar William was aware that their discussion was being overheard by several other brothers who were concealed in the common-room. The depositions of these witnesses were heard by the inquisitors, Bernard of Caux and John of Saint-Pierre, between August and December 1247, and in the following February Peter was condemned and excommunicated as a contumacious heretic, his property being confiscated. According to the testimony of Friar William Cogot, Peter denounced the preachers of the cross as murderers and Friar Deodat of Rodez noted that, whilst he did not damn the Franciscans along with other ecclesiastical bodies, he

---

[113] 'Un recueil cathare: le manuscrit A6: 10 de la "collection vaudoise" de Dublin', ed. T. Venckeleer, *Revue belge de philologie et d'histoire*, xxxviii (1960), 823, 828-9.

stated that the Order was worthless because it preached the crusade. Peter apparently believed that

God desired no justice which would condemn anyone to death. On this point he vituperated a certain friar, a preacher of the crusade, who at Auvillars gave the cross to about seven hundred persons, saying that it was not a good deed for crusaders to march against Frederick II, or against the Saracens, or against any castle like Montségur when it opposed the church, or against any place where death could occur.[114]

The Cathars' opposition to the crusades was also recorded by the polemicist Moneta of Cremona, a Dominican professor at the University of Bologna, who composed a treatise entitled *Summa adversus Catharos et Waldenses* between 1241 and 1244.[115] His description of the doctrine of absolute and mitigated dualism concluded with a justification of Christian warfare which is particularly valuable for our purposes, for, in listing the main authorities for the prohibition of homicide, Moneta underlined that he had put down only those arguments which he had heard from the lips of heretics or read in their writings. Amongst other sources, the Cathars apparently recalled the patience of Christ and his apostles in the face of their detractors. They pointed out that the Lord had commanded Peter to sheathe his sword (Matt. 26: 52) and urged his followers to pray for their persecutors (Matt. 5: 44); they condemned the church on the grounds that it preached and issued indulgences for the crusade in the Holy Land. To reinforce their argument, they quoted 1 Cor. 10: 32, 'Be without offence to the Jews and to the Gentiles (*gentes*) and to the church of God'; in this context *gentes* referred to the Muslims rather than the Greeks. In his defence Moneta countered that when the secular ruler took up his sword, he was acting as God's minister, and he repeated that the crusades were just wars waged in defence of the church in order to recover lost territory. He reminded the heretics that St Paul himself had been guarded by soldiers when there was a danger of a Jewish ambush (Acts 23: 17–32) and concluded that, if the safety of the church's

---

[114] *Documents pour servir à l'histoire de l'Inquisition dans le Languedoc*, ed. C. Douais (Paris, 1900), ii. 94, 97, 99–100, 104, 113-14.

[115] For the dating of this work, see W. L. Wakefield and A. P. Evans, *Heresies of the High Middle Ages* (New York, 1969), 307, 744 n. 1.

lands was at stake, she might also seek aid from secular rulers. Moneta added that Christians employed force only because the Muslims persisted in their violence.[116]

A prohibition of homicide was also one of the main tenets of the Waldensian heresy,[117] and there is some evidence of Waldensian opposition to the crusades. Writing before 1212, Ebrard of Béthune observed that the heretics denounced those who fought against the infidels as murderers[118] and Stephen of Bourbon, who derived his information about the Waldenses from his own experience as Inquisitor, commented:

(they) say that all judges commit a sin in pronouncing the death penalty and they regard as murderers and damned souls those who preach war against the Saracens and Albigenses and other men, except for wars against the infernal Saracens and Albigenses, whom they call demons.[119]

Stephen was the only contemporary to note this distinction between the ordinary and infernal Saracens and unfortunately he did not explain its significance. In his treatise compiled between 1260 and 1266[120] the so-called Anonymous of Passau added that the heretics condemned those who used the sword to force others to accept their faith;[121] it has been suggested that this was a reference to Waldensian criticism of the crusades against the pagans in north-eastern

---

[116] Moneta of Cremona, *Adversos Catharos et Waldenses*, ed. T. A. Ricchinius (Rome, 1743), pp. xxiii, 2, 513-32.

[117] See Alan of Lille, *Contra haereticos*, PL ccx, col. 394; Peter of Vaux de Cernay, i. 18-19; iii. 7; *Manifestatio haeresis Albigensium et Lugdunensium*, ed. Dondaine, *Archivum Fratrum Praedicatorum*, xxix (1959), 271. For further details, see P. Biller, 'Medieval Waldensian Abhorrence of Killing pre-c.1400', *Studies in Church History*, xx (1983), 129-46.

[118] Ebrard of Béthune, *Liber Antihaeresis*, in *Maxima Bibliotheca Veterum Patrum*, ed. M. de la Bigne, xxv (Lyons, 1677), 1556-8.

[119] Stephen of Bourbon, *Anécdotes historiques, légendes et apologues*, ed. Lecoy de la Marche (Paris, 1877), 296.

[120] See M. A. E. Nickson, 'A Critical Edition of the Treatise on Heresy Ascribed to Pseudo-Reinerius with an Historical Introduction' (unpubl. thesis, London, 1962), pp. xlvii-viii; A. Patschovsky, *Der Passauer Anonymus: Ein Sammelwerk über Ketzer, Juden, Antichrist aus der Mitte des 13. Jahrhunderts*, MGH Schriften, XXII (Stuttgart, 1968), 2.

[121] W. Preger, 'Beiträge zur Geschichte der Waldesier im Mittelalter', *Abhandlungen der Bayerischen Akademie der Wissenschaften, philosophisch-historische Klasse*, xiii (1) (1877), 245.

Europe.[122] The heretics may also have raised objections to the use of the crusade against the Staufen. A revised version of the Anonymous's treatise, written sometime after 1270 and known as Pseudo-Reinerius, declared that the Waldenses condemned the pope and other ecclesiastics as murderers because of the wars they waged;[123] it seems likely that this was an implied criticism of the papal expeditions in Germany, Northern Italy, and Sicily.[124] Biller argues that the Waldensian abhorrence of killing was widely known in the thirteenth century,[125] but, although they may have attempted to discourage some crusaders from going to the Holy Land and were scornful of the value of the crusading indulgence,[126] there is no evidence that the Waldenses' opposition to the use of force against the Muslims, pagans, or Christian lay powers influenced a large body of opinion. The same applies to the Cathars, whose prohibition of homicide was confined to the small circle of the elect or *perfecti*.

---

[122] Biller, 135.   [123] Nickson, 29.
[124] See G. Leff, *Heresy in the Later Middle Ages* (Manchester, 1967), ii. 459.
[125] Biller, 141–5.
[126] Nickson, 36, 41; Preger, 245. See also Humbert of Romans, *Opus tripartitum*, 191.

Conclusion

IN the Central Middle Ages most critics were concerned with abuses or with particular aspects of the crusading movement, rather than with the concept itself. Their primary aim was to make suggestions for improvements which they believed would contribute towards the success of future campaigns.

Particularly after the disastrous experience of the Second Crusade, both lay and ecclesiastical authorities were anxious that expeditions should be militarily effective and not burdened by large numbers of non-combatants; the poor, the old, and the weak were discouraged from taking the cross. It was recognized that some monks and clerks were needed as spiritual counsellors to the army, but they were reminded that they had other duties and obligations. And it was feared that the presence of women would compromise the moral standing of the host. Another source of anxiety and criticism was non-fulfilment of vows: in this period the papacy made repeated attempts to ensure that all those who were qualified to take the cross went to the Holy Land; and the vacillations of prominent crusaders such as Richard I and Philip Augustus aroused a storm of protest from crusading apologists and Latin and vernacular poets. In fact, the pressure of public opinion seems to have forced the kings to leave for the East. There was similar criticism of Frederick II's slowness to fulfil his vow, but, because of the changed situation in the Latin Kingdom, this does not seem to have been as widespread or to have had the same impact.

The historiographical tradition which attributed defeats to a divine judgement upon human sinfulness had its origins in the Old Testament, but it was exploited by apologists of the crusades because it provided the most satisfactory explanation for a reverse in a war supposedly willed by God; and chroniclers in the thirteenth century used the formula *peccatis exigentibus hominum* in the same way as historians of the First Crusade. From the beginning the clergy exhorted

the crusaders to seek God's forgiveness by means of a penitential ritual, and by the late twelfth century the success
of the crusade became associated with the reform of the
church as a whole. This explanation for a defeat was originally
intended to counter criticism of crusading, but its very
success seems to have made it in turn a stimulus to criticism
of the crusaders. Chroniclers and poets depicted the ideal
crusader as one who possessed 'right intention'; a connection
was drawn between the army's conduct and a defeat and
chroniclers pointed out the lessons to be drawn from
previous expeditions. The most common accusations levelled
against the crusaders were that they were guilty of pride,
avarice, sexual incontinence and extravagance in dress and
demeanour; the repetition of these criticisms implies that the
chroniclers were searching for an explanation for the series
of Christian defeats.

In the years before 1274 there is also evidence of increasing resentment of royal and papal demands for taxation for
the crusades in Europe and the Near East. Apart from the
Spanish clergy and certain religious orders who claimed
exemption, the main reason for both clerical and lay opposition seems to have been the harshness and frequency of these
levies, coupled with the fear that consent would establish
a dangerous precedent for the future and there were pleas
for reform and moderation. On the whole, the French
opponents of royal taxation seem to have been more successful than their English counterparts. In the face of their
vociferous opposition, Philip Augustus was forced to issue
an ordinance of abolition for the Saladin tithe, whereas
Henry II ignored the English protests and the tithe laid the
foundations of a system of national taxation. The thirteenth
century witnessed the beginning of papal taxation. Not surprisingly prelates throughout Europe resented the burden
imposed upon the church and complained of impoverishment. But the focus of opposition seems to have been England,
which bore the brunt of papal demands. Admittedly our
picture of events is somewhat coloured by the prejudice
of Matthew Paris, but there are other signs of the growing
hostility towards papal impositions, particularly amongst
the barons, and one manifestation of this was the attacks

upon papal envoys. At the same time, some contemporaries accused the papacy of using the system of vow-redemption as a source of revenue and attributed the shortage of man-power in the Near East to papal avarice; but these critics had personal reasons for opposing papal crusading policy and cannot be said to reflect public opinion. In the thir-teenth century the popes appear to have been as anxious as anyone to ensure that their agents did not exceed the terms of their commission.

In this period the crusades against the Moors in Spain and pagans in north-eastern Europe seem to have been accepted as part of a general campaign against the enemies of the faith and, although there were some complaints that the expeditions against heretics and schismatics diverted resources from the Holy Land, the extent of this opposition has been exaggerated. Only a few poets in the Languedoc even mentioned the Albigensian Crusade and the other critics of the expedition, Roger Wendover and the Northern French trouvères, were long-standing opponents of the papacy. The same applies to the critics of the crusades against the Staufen. They either came from areas already hostile to Rome, such as Ghibelline Italy, or they had personal reasons for attacking papal policy, for example an interest in the Spanish *Reconquista*, and they did not represent a large body of opinion. Admittedly these critics were usually more vociferous than the papacy's supporters. Nevertheless, the expeditions against Manfred and Conradin seem to have attracted recruits from a wide area, including Flanders, France, and the Guelf regions of Italy, and some crusaders fought in Europe and the Near East.

There was undoubtedly considerable disillusionment after the failure of Louis IX's Egyptian and North African cam-paigns. But the atmosphere of despondency does not seem to have been as severe as it had been after the reverse at Damascus in the mid twelfth century and it should be noted that there were no thirteenth-century equivalents of the annalist of Würzburg and Gerhoh of Reichersberg. In his memoir submitted to the Second Council of Lyons, Humbert of Romans referred to seven main types of critics of the crusade. But it must be remembered that the purpose of his work was to warn Gregory X of any possible source of criticism and he gave no indication of the extent of opposition. The significance of alternative ideologies such as the Joachite concept of apocalyptic conversion has also been exaggerated: such views were limited to their own small circle. Pacifist objections to the crusade have survived only because they were recorded by crusading apologists; and it should be stressed that the Cathar prohibition of homicide applied only to the *perfecti.*

Admittedly Gregory X's carefully laid plans for a crusade came to nothing, but this should not be attributed, as some historians have suggested, to unfavourable or even hostile public opinion and criticism of the crusading movement.[1] After the fall of Acre various proposals were put forward for the recovery of the Latin Kingdom; in the following years popes such as Nicholas IV, Benedict XI, and Clement V made repeated attempts to restore peace to Europe as a preliminary to sending an expedition to the East. The culmination of these efforts was the Council of Vienne in 1312. A number of recent studies have shown that in the fourteenth century princes and nobles remained eager to avenge the Muslim victories,[2] but their efforts were frustrated by dissension and internal problems in the West, as well as the difficulties of organizing and financing a major expedition to the Near East. At a more popular level, there was also continued enthusiasm for crusading and this was highlighted by the reaction to the reported Mongol capture of the Holy Land in 1300 and the 'crusade of the poor' in 1309.[3]

In brief, an analysis of criticism of crusading in the Central Middle Ages shows that, although from the beginning there was bitter resentment of abuses, fundamental criticism of the concept itself was rare; and in 1274 the expeditions in Europe and the Latin East still enjoyed considerable support from the faithful. There is no evidence to justify the claim that the thirteenth century saw a significant decline in popular enthusiasm.

[1] See Throop, 104, 147, 171, 213–14.

[2] See Cardini, 332–46; Tyerman, 57–75; Keen, 45–63; and Siberry, 'Criticism of Crusading in Fourteenth century England'.

[3] See Schein, 'The West and the Crusades', especially 14–16, 27, 263–70 and 'Gesta Dei per Mongolos 1300: The Genesis of a Non-event', *EHR* xciv (1979), 818–19.

Bibliography

Adam Marsh, *Epistolae*, ed. J. S. Brewer, *Monumenta Franciscana*, i, R S 4 (London, 1858)

Adam of Perseigne, 'Lettres d'Adam de Perseigne à ses correspondants de Maine, XIIe-XIIIe siècles', ed. J. Bouvet, *La Province du Maine*, 2nd ser. xxxii (1952), 1-20

Aimeric de Péguilhan, *Poems*, ed. W. P. Shepard and F. M. Chambers (Illinois, 1950)

Alan of Lille, *Contra haereticos*, PL ccx

— *Textes inédits*, ed. M. T. d'Alverny, Études de philosophie médiévale, LII (Paris, 1965)

Alberic of Troisfontaines, *Chronica*, MGH SS xxiii

Albert of Aix, *Historia Hierosolymitana*, RHC Occ. iv

Albert of Beham, 'Die Aventinischen Excerpte aus den Acten des Albert von Beham', ed. C. Höfler, in *Albert von Beham und Regesten Pabst Innocenz' IV*. (Stuttgart, 1847)

Alexander III, *Opera*, PL cc

Alexander IV, *Registres*, ed. C. Bourel de la Roncière *et al.* (Paris, 1902-31)

Alexander of Bremen, *Expositio in Apocalypsim*, ed. A. Wachtel, Die deutschen Geschichtsquellen des Mittelalters, 500-1500, II (Weimar, 1955)

Ambroise, *L'estoire de la guerre sainte*, ed. G. Paris (Paris, 1897)

Analecta hymnica medii aevi, xxi, xxxiii (Leipzig, 1895-9)

Andrew of Hungary, *Descriptio victoriae a Karolo Provinciae Comite Reportatae*, MGH SS xxvi

Angelo of Clareno, *Historia septem tribulationum ordinis minorum*, ed. F. Ehrle, *Archiv für Literatur und Kirchen-Geschichte des Mittelalters*, ii (Berlin, 1866), 249-337

Anna Comnena, *Alexiad*, ed. B. Leib (Paris, 1937-45)

Annales Brunwilarenses, MGH SS xvi

Annales Corbeienses, MGH SS iii

Annales de Burtoneia, ed. H. R. Luard, *Annales monastici*, RS 36 (London, 1864-9), i

Annales de Dunstaplia, *Annales monastici*, iii

Annales de Oseneia, ibid. iv

Annales de Theokesberia, ibid. i

Annales de Waverleia, ibid. ii

Annales ecclesiastici, ed. O. Raynaldus *et al.*, ii (Lucca, 1747)

Annales Egmundani, MGH SS xvi

Annales Erphordenses, ibid.

Annales Floreffienses, ibid.

Annales Herbipolenses, ibid.
Annales Ianuenses, MGH SS xviii
Annales Magdeburgenses, MGH SS xvi
Annales Mantuani, MGH SS xix
Annales Marbacenses, MGH SS xvii
Annales Palidenses, MGH SS xvi
Annales Parchenses, ibid.
Annales Parmenses maiores, MGH SS xix
Annales Reicherspergenses, MGH SS xvii
Annales Reineri, MGH SS xvi
Annales Rodenses, ibid.
Annales Romoaldi Archiepiscopi Salernitani, MGH SS xix
Annales Sanctae Iustinae Patavini, MGH SS xix
Annales Sancti Disibodi, MGH SS xvii
Annales Sancti Jacobi Leodiensis, MGH SS xvi
Annales Sancti Pauli Virdunensis, ibid.
Annales Stadenses, ibid.
Anonymous of Halberstadt, *De peregrinatione in Greciam et adventu reliquiarum de Grecia libellus*, ed. P. Riant, *Exuviae sacrae Constantinopolitanae* (Paris, 1877–1904), i
Anselm, *Opera*, ed. F. S. Schmitt (Edinburgh, 1946–61)
Anthologie des troubadours XIIme-XIIIme siècles, ed. A. Jeanroy, rev. J. Boelcke (Paris, 1974)
Appendiculum ad Sigebertum anonymi Blandiniensis, extr. RHGF xiv
Archives administratives de la ville de Reims, ed. P. Varin (Paris, 1839–48)
Archives législatives de la ville de Reims, ed. P. Varin (Paris, 1840–52)
Arnold of Lübeck, *Chronica Slavorum*, MGH SS xxi
Augustine, *De civitate Dei*, Corpus Christianorum, series Latina, xlvii–xlviii (Turnhout, 1955)
Austorc d'Aurillac, 'Le troubadour Austorc d'Aurillac et son sirventes sur la septième croisade', ed. A. Jeanroy, *Mélanges Chabaneau, Romanische Forschungen*, xxiii (1907), 81–7
Austorc de Segret, 'Le sirventes d'Austorc de Segret', ed. C. Fabre, *Annales du Midi*, xxii (1910), 467–81

Baldric of Dol, *Historia Jerosolymitana*, RHC Occ. iv
Bartolf of Nangis, *Gesta Francorum Iherusalem expugnantium*, RHC Occ. iii
Bartholomew of Neocastro, *Historia Sicula*, RIS xiii (3) (new edn., Bologna, 1921–2)
Benedict of Aniane, *Opera*, PL ciii
Benedict of Nursia, *Regula monachorum*, ed. E. C. Butler (Freiburg, 1912)
Bernard of Clairvaux, *Epistolae*, PL clxxxii
— *Opera*, ed. J. Leclercq, C. H. Talbot, and H. M. Rochais (Rome, 1957–77)
Bernat Desclot, *Crònica*, ed. M. Coll i Alentorn (Barcelona, 1949–51)

Bernold of St Blasien, *Chronicon*, MGH SS v
Bertran de Born, *Poésies complètes*, ed. A. Thomas (Toulouse, 1888)
Biographies des troubadours, ed. J. Boutière and A. H. Schulz (2nd rev. edn., Paris, 1964)
Bonaventure, *Vita Sancti Francisci*, ed. P. G. Golubovich, *Biblioteca Bio-Bibliografica della Terra Santa e dell'Oriente Francescano* (Florence, 1906-27), i
Boniface de Castellane, 'Bonifazio di Castellane', ed. A. Parducci, *Romania*, xlvi (1920), 478-511
Bruno of Olmütz, 'Bericht des Bischof Bruno von Olmütz an Papst Gregor X. über die kirchlichen und politischen Zustände Deutschlands bei der Thronbesteigung Rudolphs von Habsburg', ed. C. Höfler, in 'Analecten zur Geschichte Deutschlands und Italiens', *Abhandlungen der historischen Classe der Königlich Bayerischen Akademie der Wissenschaften*, 3rd ser., iv (1846), 1-28
Bullaire de l'Église de Maguelone, ed. J. Rouquette and A. Villemagne (Paris and Montpellier, 1911-14)
Burchard of Ursperg, *Chronicon*, MGH SS xxiii

Caesar of Heisterbach, *Dialogus miraculorum*, ed. J. Strange (Cologne, 1851)
— 'Die Fragmente der Libri VIII miraculorum des Caesarius von Heisterbach' ed. A. Meister, *Römische Quartalschrift*, Supp. xiii (1901)
Calendar of patent rolls, 1258-66 (London, 1910)
Calixtus II, *Bullaire*, ed. U. Robert (Paris, 1891)
Carmina Burana, ed. A. Hilka and O. Schumann (Heidelberg, 1930)
Cartulaire de l'abbaye de Saint-Père de Chartres, ed. M. Guérard, Collection des cartulaires de France, II (Paris, 1840)
Cartulaire de l'abbaye de Saint-Pierre de Troyes, ed. G. Lalore, Collection des principaux cartulaires du diocese de Troyes, V (Paris, 1880)
Casus monasterii Petrishusensis, MGH SS xx
Catalogue of Romances in the Department of Manuscripts, British Museum, ed. J. A. Herbert, iii (London, 1910)
Catalogue of Western Manuscripts in the Old Royal and King's collections, British Museum, ed. J. P. Gilson and G. F. Warner, i (London, 1921)
Chanson de la croisade albigeoise, La, ed. E. Martin-Chabot (Paris, 1931-60)
Chansons de croisade, ed. J. Bédier and P. Aubry (Paris, 1909)
Chansons satiriques et bacchiques du XIIe siècle, ed. A. Jeanroy and A. Langfors (Paris, 1921)
Choix des poésies originales des troubadours, ed. M. Raynouard (Paris, 1816-21)
Chronica Bremensis, ed. H. Meibom in *Scriptores Germanici Rerum Germanicarum* (Helmstedt, 1688), ii
Chronica regia Coloniensis et continuationes, ed. G. Waitz, MGH Scr. rer. Germ. (Hanover, 1880)
Chronicle of Melrose, ed. A. O. and M. O. Anderson (Facsimile edition, London, 1936)

Chronicon anonymi Laudunensis canonici, extr. RHGF xviii
Chronicon Clarevallense, PL clxxxv
Chronicon coenobii Sancti Medardi Suessionensis, extr. RHGF xii
Chronicon Sancti Jacobi Leodiensis, extr. RHGF xvii
Chronicon Lirensis monasterii, extr. RHGF xxiii
Chronicon Mauriniacense, extr. RHGF xiv
Chronicon monasterii Campensis, ed. G. Eckertz, *Fontes adhuc inediti rerum Rhenanarum* (Cologne, 1864–70), ii
Chronicon Nicholai Ambianensis, extr. RHGF xiv
Chronicon Normanniae, extr. RHGF xxiii
Chronicon Petroburgense, ed. T. Stapleton (London, 1849)
Chronicon Rastedense, ed. H. Meibom, in *Scriptores Germanici Rerum Germanicarum* (Helmstedt, 1688), ii
Chronicon Turonense extr. RHGF xii, xviii
Chronique latine inédite des Rois de Castille (1236), ed. G. Cirot, *Bulletin hispanique*, xiv (1912), 353–74
Clement IV, *Registres* ed. E. Jordan (Paris, 1893–1945)
Close Rolls of the Reign of Henry III, 1242–7 (London, 1916)
Codex Italiae Diplomaticus, ed. J. C. Lünig (Frankfurt and Leipzig, 1725–35)
Conciliorum oecumenicorum decreta, ed. G. Alberigo *et al.* 3rd edn. (Bologna, 1973)
Conon de Béthune, *Les Chansons*, ed. A. Wallenskold (Paris, 1921)
Continuatio Gemblacensis, MGH SS vi
Continuatio Praemonstratensis, ibid.
Continuatio Sanblasiana, MGH SS xx
Corpus documentorum Inquisitionis haereticae pravitatis Neerlandicae, ed. P. Fredericq (Ghent, 1889–1903)
Correspondance administrative d'Alfonse de Poitiers, ed. A. Molinier (Paris, 1894–1900)
Councils and Synods with Other Documents Relating to the English Church, i, ed. D. Whitelock, M. Brett and C. N. L. Brooke (Oxford, 1982); ii, ed. F. M. Powicke and C. R. Cheney (Oxford, 1964)
Cronica Sancti Petri Erfordensis, ed. O. Holder-Egger, *Monumenta Erphesfurtensia* (Hanover, 1899)

Decreta Claromontensia, in R. Somerville, *The Councils of Urban II*, i, *Annuarium Historiae Conciliorum*, Supp. i (Amsterdam, 1972)
De expugnatione Lyxbonensi, ed. C. W. David (New York, 1936)
'Dekretalensammlungen des Gilbertus und Alanus nach den Weingartener Handschriften, Die', ed. R. von Heckel, *Zeitschrift der Savigny-Stiftung für Rechtsgeschichte, Kanonistische Abteilung*, lxxiii (1940), 116–357
Derniers troubadours de la Provence, Les', ed. P. Meyer, *Bibliothèque de L'Ecole des chartes*, xxx (1869), 245–97.
'Deux poésies latines relatives à la IIIe croisade', ed. H. Hagenmeyer, *Archives de l'Orient Latin*, i (1881), 580–5
'Deux troubadours Narbonnais: Guilhem Fabre et Bertran Alanhan',

ed. J. Anglade, *Bulletin de la commission archéologique de Narbonne*, viii (1905), 397-428

Devastatio Constantinopolitana, MGH SS xvi

Diplomatarium Norvegicum, ed. C. A. Lange and C. R. Unger, i (Christiania, 1849)

Diplomatarium Suecanum, ed. J. G. Liljegren, i (Stockholm, 1829)

Doctrina de compendre dictats, ed. P. Meyer, 'Traités catalans de grammaire et de poétique', *Romania*, vi (1877), 341-59

Documents of the Baronial Plan of Reform and Rebellion, 1258-67, sel. R. H. Treharne, ed. I. J. Sanders (Oxford, 1973)

Documents pour servir à l'histoire de l'Inquisition dans le Languedoc, ed. C. Douais (Paris, 1900)

Ebrard of Béthune, *Liber Antihaeresis*, Maxima Bibliotheca Veterum *Patrum*, ed. M. de la Bigne, xxv (Lyons, 1677)

Ekkehard of Aura, *Chronicon universale*, MGH SS vi

— *Hierosolymita*, RHC Occ. v

Elias de Barjols, *Le Troubadour Elias de Barjols*, ed. S. Stronski (Toulouse, 1906)

Elias Cairel, *Der Trobador Elias Cairel*, ed. H. Jaeschke (Berlin, 1921)

— 'Un sirventes historique d'Elias Cairel', ed. V. De Bartholomaeis, *Annales du Midi*, xvi (1904), 468-95

Emonis Chronicon, MGH SS xxiii

'Emprunts de Saint Louis en Palestine et en Afrique', ed. G. Servois, *Bibliothèque de l'École des chartes*, xix (1858), 283-93

Enquêtes administratives d'Alfonse de Poitiers, ed. P. Fournier and P. Guébin (Paris, 1959)

Epistola Sancti Ludovici regis de captione et liberatione sua, ed. F. Duchesne, *Historiae Francorum Scriptores* (Paris, 1636-49), v

Epistolae Cantuarienses, ed. W. Stubbs, RS 38 (London, 1865)

Epitaphe de Jean d'Eppé, ed. V. le Clerc, *Histoire littéraire de la France*, xxiii (Paris, 1856)

L'estoire d'Eracles empereur et la conqueste de la terre d'Outremer, RHC Occ. ii

Études sur les actes de Louis VII, ed. A. Luchaire (Paris, 1885)

Eugenius III, *Opera*, PL clxxx

— 'Text der Kreuzzugsbulle Eugens III.', ed. P. Rassow, *Neues Archiv der Gesellschaft für ältere deutsche Geschichtskunde*, xlv (1924), 300-5

Exuviae sacrae Constantinopolitanae, ed. P. Riant (Paris, 1877-1904)

Fidenzio of Padua, 'Liber recuperationis Terre Sancte', ed. P. G. Golubovich, *Biblioteca Bio-Bibliografica della Terra Santa e dell'Oriente francescano* (Florence, 1906-27) ii. 1-60

Foedera, conventiones, litterae et cuiuscumque generis acta publica inter reges Angliae et alios quosvis imperatores, reges, pontifices, principes vel communitates, ed. T. Rymer *et al.* (Facsimile edition, Farnborough, 1967)

'Formulaires de lettres du XIIe et du XIIIe siècles', *Notices et extraits des manuscrits de la Bibliothèque nationale*, xxxv (1896), 793–830

Freidank, *Bescheidenheit*, ed. W. Grimm (Göttingen, 1834)

Fulcher of Chartres, *Historia Hierosolymitana*, ed. H. Hagenmeyer (Heidelberg, 1913)

Fulk de Marseille, *Le Troubadour Folquet de Marseille*, ed. S. Stronski (Cracow, 1910)

Fulk de Romans, *Die Gedichte des Folquet von Romans*, ed. R. Zenker (Halle, 1896)

Garçon et l'aveugle, Le, ed. M. Roques (Paris, 1911)

Gaucelm Faidit, *Les Poèmes de Gaucelm Faidit, Troubadour du XIIe siècle*, ed. J. Mouzat (Paris, 1965)

Gautier de Coincy, *De sainte Léocade*, ed. E. Vilamo-Pentti, *Annales Academiae Scientiarum Fennicae*, lxvii. 2 (1950)

Gavaudan , 'Poésies du troubadour Gavaudan', ed. A. Jeanroy, *Romania*, xxxix (1905), 497–540

Gedichte der Troubadours, ed. C. A. F. Mahn (Berlin, 1856–73)

Geoffrey of Coldingham, *Liber de statu ecclesiae Dunelmensis*, ed. J. Raine, Historiae Dunelmensis Scriptores Tres, Surtees Society, IX (London, 1839)

Geoffrey of Vendôme, *Opera*, PL clvii

Geoffrey of Vigeois, *Chronicon*, extr. RHGF xii

Geoffrey of Villehardouin, *La Conquête de Constantinople*, ed. E. Faral (Paris, 1938–9)

Gerald of Wales, *Opera*, ed. J. S. Brewer *et al.*, RS 21 (London, 1861–91)

Gerhoh of Reichersberg, *Commentarius in Psalmos*, MGH Libelli de lite, iii (Hanover, 1897)

—— 'De investigatione Antichristi', ibid.

Gervais of Prémontré, *Epistolae*, ed. C. L. Hugo, *Sacrae antiquitatis monumenta historica, dogmatica, diplomatica*, i (Estival, 1725)

Gervase of Canterbury, *Opera historica*, ed. W. Stubbs, RS 73 (London, 1879–80)

Gesta abbatum Sancti Bertini Sithiensium: continuatio, MGH SS xiii

Gesta crucigerorum Rhenanorum, ed. R. Röhricht, *Quinti belli sacri scriptores* (Geneva, 1879)

Gesta episcoporum Leodiensium, MGH SS xxv

Gesta Francorum, ed. R. M. T. Hill (London, 1962)

Gesta Innocentii, PL ccxiv

Gesta obsidionis Damiate, ed. R. Röhricht, *Quinti belli sacri scriptores* (Geneva, 1879)

Gesta veterum comitum Barcinonensium, ed. P. de Marca, in *Marca Hispanica* (Paris, 1688)

Gil of Zamora, 'Biografías de San Fernando y de Alfonso el Sabio', publ. F. Fita, *Boletín de la Real Academia de la Historia*, v (1884), 308–28

Gilbert Crispin, 'La lettre de Gilbert Crispin sur la vie monastique', ed. J. Leclercq, *Studia Anselmiana*, xxxi (1953), 118–23

Gilbert Foliot, *Letters and charters*, ed. A. Morey and C. N. L. Brooke (Cambridge, 1967)

Gilbert of Tournai, *Collectio de scandalis ecclesiae*, ed. P. A. Stroick, *Archivum Franciscanum Historicum*, xxiv (1931), 33–62

— *Eruditio regum et principum*, ed. A. de Poorter (Louvain, 1914)

— *Sermones ad omnes status de novo correcti et emendati* (Lyons, 1511)

Gilles le Muisit, *Chronique*, ed. H. Lemaître (Paris, 1906)

Giovanni Villani, *Cronica*, ed. F. Gherardi-Dragomanni (Florence, 1845)

Gislebert of Mons, *Chronicon Hanoniense*, MGH SS xxi

Grandes chroniques de France, ed. J. Viard (Paris, 1920–53)

Gratian, *Decretum*, ed. A. Friedberg, *Corpus iuris canonici* (Leipzig, 1879–81), i

Gregory VII, *Epistolae vagantes*, ed. H. E. J. Cowdrey (Oxford, 1972)

— *Registrum*, ed. E. Caspar (Berlin, 1920)

Gregory IX, *Registres*, ed. L. d'Auvray (Paris, 1896–1955)

Gregory X, *Registres*, ed. J. Guiraud (Paris, 1892–1906)

Guibert of Nogent, *Gesta Dei per Francos*, RHC Occ. iv

Guilhem Adémar, *Poésies du troubadour Guilhem Adémar*, ed. K. Almquist (Uppsala, 1951)

Guilhem Anelier, *Der Troubadour Guilhem Anelier von Toulouse, vier provenzalische Gedichte*, ed. M. Gisi (Solothurn, 1877)

Guilhem Figueira, ein provenzalischer Troubadour, ed. E. Levy (Berlin, 1880)

Guilhem de Montanhagol, *Le Troubadour Guilhem de Montanhagol*, ed. J. Coulet (Toulouse, 1898)

Guillaume le Clerc, *Le Besant de Dieu*, ed. P. Ruelle (Brussels, 1973)

Guiot de Provins, *Les Œuvres*, ed. J. Orr (Manchester, 1915)

Guiraut de Bornelh, *Sämtliche Lieder des Troubadours, Giraut de Bornelh*, ed. A. Kolsen (Halle, 1910–35)

Gunther of Pairis, *Historia Constantinopolitana*, ed. P. Riant, *Exuviae*, i

Hadrian IV, *Opera*, PL clxxxviii

Hélinant de Froidmont, *Les Vers de la mort*, ed. F. Wulff and E. Walberg (Paris, 1905)

Helmold of Bosau, *Chronica Slavorum*, ed. H. Stoob (Darmstadt, 1963)

Henry of Albano, *Opera*, PL cciv

Henry of Huntingdon, *Historia Anglorum*, ed. T. Arnold, RS 74 (London, 1874)

Henry of Livonia, *Chronicon Lyvoniae*, ed. G. H. Pertz, MGH Scr. rer. Germ. (Hanover, 1874)

Historia de expeditione Friderici imperatoris, ed. A. Chroust, MGH Scr. rer. Germ. n.s.v (Berlin, 1928)

Historia Diplomatica Friderici Secundi, ed. J. L. A. Huillard-Bréholles (Paris, 1852–61)

Historia peregrinorum, ed. A. Chroust, MGH Scr. rer. Germ. n.s.v (Berlin, 1928)

Historia Vizeliacensis monasterii, extr. RHGF xii
Historical Manuscripts Commission, Fifth Report, HMSO (London, 1876)
— *Report on Manuscripts in Various Collections*, i, HMSO (London, 1901)
Honorius III, *Regesta*, ed. P. A. Pressutti (Rome, 1888–95)
Hostiensis, *Summa aurea* (Basle, 1573)
Hugh of Flavigny, *Chronicon*, MGH SS viii
Hugh of Mataplana, 'Arondeta de ton chantar m'azir', ed. G. Bertoni, *Annales du Midi*, xxv (1913), 58–64
Humbert of Romans, *De praedicatione sancte crucis* (Nuremberg, 1490)
— *Opus tripartitum*, ed. E. Brown, *Fasciculus rerum expetendarum et fugiendarum*, ii (London, 1690)

Innocent III, *Opera*, PL ccxiv–ccxvii
— *Selected letters concerning England*, ed. C. R. Cheney and W. H. Semple (London, 1953)
Innocent IV, *Registres*, ed. E. Berger (Paris, 1884–1921)
Itinerarium peregrinorum, ed. H. E. Mayer (Stuttgart, 1962)
Itinerarium regis Ricardi, ed. W. Stubbs RS 38 (London, 1864)
Ivo of Chartres, *Opera*, PL clxi

James of Vitry, *Historia Hierosolimitana*, ed. J. Bongars, *Gesta Dei per Francos* (Hanau, 1611), i
— *Lettres*, ed. R. B. C. Huygens (Leiden, 1960)
— *Sermones vulgares*, ed. J. B. Pitra, *Analecta novissima* (Paris, 1885–8), ii
Jerome, *Epistolae*, ed. I. Hilberg, Corpus scriptorum ecclesiasticorum Latinorum, LIV (Leipzig, 1909)
Joachim of Fiore, 'De vita Sancti Benedicti et de officio divino secundum eius doctrinam', ed. C. Baraut, *Analecta Sacra Tarraconensia*, xxiv (1951), 1–90
— *Expositio in Apocalypsim* (Venice, 1527)
— *Liber Figurarum (Il Libro delle Figure)*, ed. L. Tondelli, M. Reeves, and B. Hirsch-Reich (Turin, 1953)
— *Liber introductorius in Apocalypsim*, prefacing *Expositio* (Venice, 1527)
John of Ford, *Life of Wulfric of Haselbury*, ed. M. Bell, Somerset Record Society Publications, XLVIII (Frome, 1933)
John of Garland, *De triumphis ecclesiae*, ed. T. Wright (London, 1856)
— *Morale scholarium*, ed. L. J. Paetow (Berkeley, Calif., 1927)
— *Parisiana Poetria de arte prosaica, metrica et rithmica*, ed. T. Lawler (New Haven, Conn., 1974)
John of Joinville, *Histoire de Saint Louis*, ed. N. de Wailly (Paris, 1868)
John of Salisbury, *Historia Pontificalis*, ed. M. Chibnall (London, 1956)
— *Letters*, ed. W. J. Millor and C. N. L. Brooke (Oxford, 1955–79)
John of Tulbia, 'De Domino Iohanne rege Ierusalem', ed. R. Röhricht, *Quinti belli sacri scriptores* (Geneva, 1879)

Kreuzzugsbriefe aus den Jahren 1088-1100, Die, ed. H. Hagenmeyer (Innsbruck, 1901)

Lamentum lacrymabile, PL clv
Langue et la littérature Française, La, ed. K. Bartsch and A. Horning (Paris, 1887)
Layettes du trésor des chartes, ed. J. B. Teulet, J. H. Delaborde, *et al.* (Paris, 1863-1909)
Letters from the Northern Registers, ed. J. Raine, RS 61 (London, 1873)
'Lettre inédite de Hugues de Saint Victor aux chevaliers du Temple', ed. C. Sclafert, *Revue d'ascétique et de mystique*, xxxiv (1958), 275-99
Liber Censuum de l'église romaine, Le, ed. P. Fabre and L. Duchesne (Paris, 1905-52)
Liber de compositione castri Ambaziae et ipsius dominorum gesta, ed. L. Halphen and R. Poupardin, *Chroniques des comtes d'Anjou* (Paris, 1913)
Liber de poenitentia et tentationibus religiosorum, PL ccxiii
Liber extra, ed. A. Friedberg, *Corpus iuris canonici* (Leipzig, 1879-81), ii
Luke of Tuy, *Chronicon mundi*, ed. A. Schott, *Hispaniae illustratae seu rerum urbiumque Hispaniae, Lusitaniae, Aethiopiae et Indiae scriptores varii* (Frankfurt am Main, 1603-8), iii

Magna vita Sancti Hugonis, ed. D. L. Douie and H. Farmer (London, 1961-2)
Magnus of Reichersberg, *Chronicon*, MGH SS xvii
Maius chronicon Lemovicense, RHGF xxi
Manifestatio haeresis Albigensium et Lugdunensium, ed. A. Dondaine, *Archivum Fratrum Praedicatorum*, xxix (1959), 270-5
Martino da Canale, *Cronaca veneta*, in *Archivio storico italiano*, viii (1845), 268-766
Materials for the History of Thomas Becket, ed. J. B. Sheppard and J. C. Robertson (London, 1875-85)
Matthew of Edessa, *Chronique*, extr. RHC Doc. arm. i
Matthew Paris, *Chronica maiora*, ed. H. R. Luard, RS 57 (London, 1872-80)
—— *Flores historiarum*, ed. H. R. Luard, RS 95 (London, 1890)
—— *Historia Anglorum*, ed. F. Madden, RS 44 (London, 1866-9)
Menko, *Chronicon*, MGH SS xxiii
MGH Constitutiones, ed. L. Weiland *et al.* (Hanover, 1893-1906)
MGH Diplomata regum et imperatorum Germaniae, ix (Cologne, Vienna and Graz, 1969)
MGH Epistolae saeculi XIII e regestis pontificum Romanorum, sel. G. H. Pertz, ed. C. Rodenberg (Berlin, 1883-94)
Minnesangs Frühling, ed. K. Lachmann, M. Haupt, F. Vogt, C. von Kraus, rev. H. Moser and H. Tervooren (Stuttgart, 1977)
Minnesinger: Deutsche Liederdichter des zwölften, dreizehnten und vierzehnten Jahrhunderts, ed. F. von der Hagen (Leipzig, 1838)

Moneta of Cremona, *Adversus Catharos et Waldenses*, ed. T. A. Ricchinius (Rome, 1743)

Monk of Montaudan, *Les Poésies du Moine de Montaudan*, ed. M. J. Routledge (Montpellier, 1977)

Neidhart, *Die Lieder*, ed. E. Wiessner (Tübingen, 1955)

Nivard, *Ysengrimus*, ed. E. Voigt (Halle, 1884)

Odo of Deuil, *De profectione Ludovici VII in Orientem*, ed. V. G. Berry (New York, 1948)

Odo Rigaud, *Regestrum visitationum archiepiscopi Rothomagensis*, ed. T. Bonnin (Rouen, 1852)

Olim ou registres des arrêts rendus par la cour du roi, Les, ed. A. Beugnot, i (Paris, 1839)

Oliver of Paderborn, *Die Schriften*, ed. H. Hoogeweg (Tübingen, 1894)

Orderic Vitalis, *Ecclesiastical History*, ed. M. Chibnall (Oxford, 1969–81)

Originum Cisterciensium tomus I, ed. P. L. Janauschek (Vienna, 1877)

Origo et historia brevis Nivernensium comitum, extr. RHGF xii

Otto of Freising, *Chronica*, ed. A. Hofmeister, MGH Scr. rer. Germ. (Hanover, 1912)

—— *Gesta Friderici imperatoris*, ibid.

Oxford Book of Medieval Latin Verse, ed. F. J. E. Raby (Oxford, 1959)

'Papsturkunden in Florenz', ed. W. Wiederhold, *Nachrichten von der Königlichen Gesellschaft der Wissenschaften zu Göttingen, philologisch-historische Klasse* (1901), 306–26

'Papsturkunden in Malta', ed. P. Kehr, ibid. (1899), 369–410

'Papsturkunden in Spanien, Vorarbeiten zur Hispania Pontificia: (i) Katalonien (ii) Urkunden und Regesten', ed. P. Kehr, *Abhandlungen der Gesellschaft zu Göttingen, Philologisch-historische Klasse*, xviii (1926) 237–585

'Papsturkunden in Spanien: Navarra und Aragon (i)', ed. Kehr, ibid. xxii (1928), 253–600

Parnasse occitanien ou Choix des poésies originales des troubadours tirées des manuscrits nationaux, Le, ed. M. de Rochegude (Toulouse, 1819)

Paschal II, *Opera*, PL clxiii

Paulet de Marseille, 'Le Troubadour Paulet de Marseille', ed. E. Levy, *Revue des langues romanes*, xxi (1882), 261–89

Peire Cardenal, *Poésies complètes du troubadour Peire Cardenal*, ed. R. Lavaud (Toulouse, 1957)

—— 'Un sirventes de Cardinal, encore inédit en partie (1271–2)', ed. C. Fabre, *A Miscellany of Studies in Romance Languages and Literatures Presented to L. E. Kastner* (Cambridge, 1932), 217–47

Peire Vidal, *Poésies*, ed. J. Anglade (Paris, 1913)

Peirol, Troubadour of Auvergne, ed. S. C. Aston (Cambridge, 1953)

Perdigon, *Les Chansons*, ed. H. J. Chaytor (Paris, 1926)

Peter of Blois, *Opera*, ed. J. A. Giles (Oxford, 1846–7)

—— 'Un écrit de Pierre de Blois réédité', R. B. C. Huygens, *Revue Bénédictine*, lxviii (1958), 87–113

Peter Lombard, *Summa Theologica*, PL cxcii

Peter Tudebode, *Historia de Hierosolymitano itinere*, ed. J. H. and L. L. Hill (Paris, 1977)

Peter of Vaux de Cernay, *Hystoria Albigensis*, ed. P. Guébin and E. Lyon (Paris, 1926-30)

Peter the Venerable, *Letters*, ed. G. Constable (Cambridge, Mass., 1962)

— *Liber contra sectam sive haeresim Saracenorum*, ed. J. Kritzeck, *Peter the Venerable and Islam* (Princeton, 1964)

— *Statuta*, ed. G. Constable, Corpus consuetudinum monasticorum, VI (Siegburg, 1975)

'Pisaner Konzil von 1135 in der Überlieferung des Pisaner Konzils von 1409, Das', ed. D. Girgensohn, *Festschrift für Hermann Heimpel* (Göttingen, 1971-2), ii. 1063-1100

Poesie provenzali storiche relative all'Italia, ed. V. De Bartholomaeis (Rome, 1931)

'Poésies inédites des troubadours du Périgord', ed. C. Chabaneau, *Revue des langues romanes*, 3rd ser., xxx (1885), 157-61

Pons de Capdouilh, *Leben und Werke des Trobadors Ponz de Capduoil*, ed. M. von Napolski (Halle, 1879)

Primera Crónica General de España que mandó componer Alfonso el Sabio, ed. R. Menéndez Pidal (Madrid, 1955)

Proverbia, sententiaeque Latinitatis medii aevi, ed. H. Walther, Carmina Medii Aevi Posterioris Latina, II (Göttingen, 1963-7)

Pseudo-Joachim, *Praemissiones*, prefacing *Super Esaiam* (Venice, 1517)

— *Super Esaiam Prophetam* (Venice, 1517)

— *Super Hieremiam Prophetam* (Venice, 1525)

Quinque compilationes antiquae, ed. A. Friedberg (Leipzig, 1882)

Raimbaut de Vaqueiras, *Poems*, ed. J. Linskill (The Hague, 1964)

Raimon de Miraval, *Les Poésies du troubadour Raimon de Miraval*, ed. L. T. Topsfield (Paris, 1971)

Raimon de Tors, 'Raimon de Tors, trovatore marsigliese del secolo XIII', ed. A. Parducci, *Studi romanzi*, vii (1911), 5-59

Rainier of Sacconi, *Summa de Catharis*, ed. A. Dondaine, in *Liber de duobus principiis* (Rome, 1939)

Ralph of Coggeshall, *Chronicon Anglicanum*, ed. J. Stevenson, RS 66 (London, 1875)

Ralph of Diceto, *Opera historica*, ed. W. Stubbs, RS 68 (London, 1876)

Ralph Niger, *Chronica universalis*, extr. MGH SS xxvii

— *De re militari et triplici peregrinationis Ierosolimitane*, ed. L. Schmugge (Berlin, 1977)

Ramon Muntaner, *Crònica* (Barcelona, 1927-51)

Ranulf Higden, *Polychronicon*, ed. C. Babington and J. R. Lumby, RS 41 (London, 1865-86)

Raymond of Aguilers, *Historia Francorum qui ceperunt Iherusalem*, ed. J. H. and L. L. Hill (Paris, 1969)

Raymond of Peñafort, *Summa de casibus penitentiae* (Verona, 1744)
'Récit de la fondation de Mortemer, Le', ed. J. Bouvet, *Collectanea Ordinis Cisterciensium Reformatorum*, xxii (1960), 149–69
Recueil des actes de Philippe Auguste, ed. H. F. Delaborde (Paris, 1916–43)
Recueil des chartes de l'abbaye de Saint-Benoît-sur-Loire, ed. M. Prou and A. Vidier (Paris, 1900–7)
Regesta Diplomatica Historiae Danicae, i (Copenhagen, 1847)
Regesta Imperii, 1198–1272, comp. J. F. Böhmer, rev. J. Ficker and E. Winkelmann, ii (Innsbruck, 1892–4)
Regesta Pontificum Romanorum, comp. P. Jaffé *et al.* (Leipzig, 1885–8)
— comp. A. Potthast (Berlin, 1874–5)
Règle du Temple, La, ed. H. de Curzon (Paris, 1886)
'Requête adressée au roi de France par un vétéran des armées de Saint Louis et de Charles d'Anjou', ed. E. Berger, *Études d'histoire du Moyen Âge dédiées à Gabriel Monod* (Paris, 1896), 343–50
Richard of Devizes, *Cronicon de tempore regis Ricardi primi*, ed. J. T. Appleby (London, 1963)
Richard of Poitiers, *Chronicon*, extr. RHGF xii
Richard of San Germano, *Chronica*, MGH SS xix
Rigord, *Gesta Philippi Augusti*, ed. H. F. Delaborde (Paris, 1882)
Robert of Auxerre, *Chronologia*, extr. RHGF xviii
Robert of Clari, *La Conquête de Constantinople*, ed. P. Lauer (Paris, 1974)
Robert Grosseteste, Bishop of Lincoln, *Epistolae*, ed. H. R. Luard RS 25 (London, 1861)
Robert of Rheims, *Historia Iherosolimitana*, RHC Occ. iii
Robert of Torigni, *Chronica*, ed. R. Howlett, RS 82 (London, 1892)
Roderick of Toledo, *De rebus Hispaniae*, ed. A. Schott, *Hispaniae illustratae seu rerum urbiumque Hispaniae, Lusitaniae, Aethiopiae et Indiae scriptores varii* (Frankfurt am Main, 1603–8), ii
Roger Bacon, *Opera hactenus inedita*, ed. J. S. Brewer, RS 15 (London, 1859)
— *Opus maius*, ed. J. H. Bridges (London, 1897–1900)
Roger of Howden, *Chronica*, ed. W. Stubbs, RS 51 (London, 1868–71)
— *Gesta regis Henrici secundi*, ed. W. Stubbs, RS 49 (London, 1867)
Roger Wendover, *Flores historiarum*, ed. H. G. Hewlett, RS 84 (London, 1886–9)
Rolandinus of Padua, *Chronicon*, MGH SS xix
Rostand of Cluny, *Tractatus de translatione capitis S. Clementi*, PL ccix
Royal and Other Historical Letters Illustrative of the Reign of Henry III, ed. W. W. Shirley, RS 27 (London, 1862–6)
Rutebeuf, *Onze Poèmes concernant la croisade*, ed. J. Bastin and E. Faral (Paris, 1946)

Saba Malaspina, *Historia rerum Siciliarum*, RIS viii
Sacrorum conciliorum nova et amplissima collectio, ed. G. D. Mansi (Florence and Venice, 1759–98)

Salimbene, *Chronica*, MGH SS xxxii

Speculum Laicorum, ed. J. T. Welter (Paris, 1914)

Statuta Capitulorum Generalium Ordinis Cisterciensis, 1116–1786, ed. J. Canivez (Louvain, 1933–5)

Stephen of Bourbon, *Anecdotes historiques, légendes et apologues*, ed. A. Lecoy de la Marche (Paris, 1877)

Stephen of Grandmont, *Opera*, PL cciv

Stephen of Tournai, *Lettres*, ed. J. Desilve (Paris, 1893)

'Strange Crusader's Song, A', ed. H. Pflaum, *Speculum*, x (1935), 337–9

Suger, *Epistolae*, RHGF xv

Summa 'Elegantius in iure divino' seu Coloniensis, ed. G. Fransen and S. Kuttner (New York, 1969)

Thesaurus novus anecdotorum, ed. E. Martène and U. Durand (Facsimile edition, Farnborough, 1968–9)

Thomas Aquinas, *Summa Theologica*, ed. P. Caramello (Turin, 1962)

Thomas of Celano, *Vita S. Francisci*, ed. P. G. Golubovich, *Biblioteca Bio-Bibliografica della Terra Santa e dell'Oriente francescano*, (Florence, 1906–27), i

Thomasin von Zirclaira, *Der wälsche Gast*, ed. H. Rückert, (Quedlinburg, 1852)

'Three Troubadour Poems with Historical Overtones', ed. F. M. Chambers, *Speculum*, liv (1979), 42–54

Triennis et Biennis Decima, RHGF xxi

'Troubadours de Béziers, Les', ed. G. Azais, *Bulletin de la société archéologique de Béziers*, 2nd ser., i (1858), 187–290

Trovatori d'Italia, I, ed. G. Bertoni (Modena, 1915)

Uc de Saint Circ, *Poésies*, ed. A. Jeanroy and J. J. Salverda de Grave (Toulouse, 1913)

'Un document sur les débuts des Templiers', ed. J. Leclercq, *Revue d'histoire ecclésiastique*, lii (1957), 81–91

'Un recueil cathare: le manuscrit A6:10 de la "collection vaudoise" de Dublin', ed. T. Venckeleer, *Revue belge de philologie et d'histoire*, xxxviii (1960), 815–34

'Un sirventes contre Charles d'Anjou, 1268', ed. A. Jeanroy, *Annales du Midi*, xv (1903), 145–67

'Un sirventes en faveur de Raimon VII (1216)', ed. A. Jeanroy, *Bausteine zur romanischen Philologie: Festgabe für A. Mussafia* (Halle, 1905), 629–40

Urban IV, *Registres*, ed. J. Guiraud (Paris, 1901)

Vetera monumenta historica Hungariam sacram illustrantia, ed. A. Theiner (Rome, 1859–60)

Vincent of Beauvais, *Speculum morale, Biblioteca mundi* (Douai, 1624)

Vincent of Prague, *Annales*, MGH SS xvii

'Vision of Gunthelm and Other Visions Attributed to Peter the

Venerable, The', ed. G. Constable, *Revue Bénédictine*, lxvi (1956), 92–115

'Vision of the Monk of Eynsham', ed. H. E. Salter, *Cartulary of the Abbey of Eynsham*, Oxford Historical Society Publications, LI (Oxford, 1908)

Vita altera PL clxxxix

Vita beati Gaufredi, ed. J. Bosvieux, *Mémoires de la société des sciences naturelles et archéologiques de la Creuze*, iii (1862), 75–120

Vita Ludovici summatim complectens, RHGF xii

Vita Sancti Bernardi et res gestae, PL clxxxv

Vita secunda Sancti Bernardi abbati, ibid.

'Vita Sancti Raymundi', in 'Raymundiana seu Documenta quae pertinent ad S. Raymundi de Pennaforti vitam et scripta', ed. F. Balme and C. Paban, in *Monumenta Ordinis Fratrum Praedicatorum Historica*, vi (Rome and Stuttgart, 1900)

Walter Bronescombe and Peter Quivil, Bishops of Exeter, *Register*, ed. C. Hingeston-Radulph (London, 1889)

Walter Gray, Archbishop of York, *Register*, ed. J. Raine, Surtees Society (Durham, 1872)

Walter Map, *De nugis curialium*, ed. M. R. James, rev. R. A. B. Mynors and C. N. L. Brooke (Oxford, 1983)

Walther von der Vogelweide, *Die Gedichte*, ed. K. Lachmann, rev. C. von Kraus and H. Kuhn (Berlin, 1965)

—— *Werke*, ed. J. Schaefer (Darmstadt, 1972)

Wibald of Corvey, *Epistolae*, ed. P. Jaffé, *Monumenta Corbeiensia, Bibliotheca rerum Germanicarum* (Berlin, 1864–73), i

William of Andres, *Chronica Andrensis*, MGH SS xxiv

William le Breton, *Gesta Philippi Augusti*, ed. H. F. Delaborde (Paris, 1882)

William of Nangis, *Gesta Sancti Ludovici*, RHGF xx

William of Newburgh, *Historia rerum Anglicarum*, ed. R. Howlett, RS 82 (London, 1884–5)

William IX of Poitou, *Les chansons de Guillaume IX, duc d'Aquitaine*, ed. A. Jeanroy (Paris, 1913)

William of Puylaurens, *Cronica*, ed. J. Duvernoy (Paris, 1976)

William of St Denis, *Dialogus*, ed. A. Wilmart, *Revue Mabillon*, xxxii (1942), 80–132

—— 'Vie de Suger', ed. A. Lecoy de la Marche, *Œuvres de Suger* (Paris, 1867)

William of St Panthus, *Vie de Saint Louis*, ed. H. F. Delaborde (Paris, 1899)

William of Tripoli, *De statu Saracenorum*, in H. Prutz, *Kulturgeschichte der Kreuzzüge* (Berlin, 1883), 573–98

William of Tyre, *Historia rerum in partibus transmarinis gestarum*, RHC Occ. i

SECONDARY WORKS

Alphandéry, P., 'Les citations bibliques chez les historiens de la première croisade', *Revue de l'histoire des religions*, xcix (1929) 139-58

Andraud, P., *La Vie et l'œuvre du troubadour Raimon de Miraval* (Paris, 1902)

Anglade, J. *Histoire sommaire de la littérature méridionale au moyen âge* (Paris, 1921)

Atiya A. S., *The Crusade in the Later Middle Ages* (London, 1938)

Bailey, T., *The Processions of Sarum and the Western Church* (Toronto, 1971)

Baldwin, M. W., 'The Papacy and the Levant during the Twelfth Century', *Bulletin of the Polish Institute of Arts and Sciences in America*, iii (1945), 277-88

Bartlett, R., *Gerald of Wales, 1146-1223* (Oxford, 1982)

Beck, J., *La Musique des troubadours* (Paris, 1910)

Benito Ruano, E., 'La Iglesia española ante la caída del Imperio Latino de Constantinopla', *Hispania sacra*, xi (1958), 5-20

Berger, P. L., *The Social Reality of Religion* (London, 1969)

Berry, V. G., 'Peter the Venerable and the Crusades', *Studia Anselmiana*, xl (1956), 141-62

—— 'The Second Crusade', in *History of the Crusades*, i. 463-513

Biller, P., 'Medieval Waldensian Abhorrence of Killing pre-c.1400', *Studies in Church History*, xx (1983), 129-46

Bishko, C. J., 'The Spanish and Portugese Reconquest', in *History of the Crusades*, iii. 396-457

Bisson, T. N., 'Negotiations for Taxes under Alfonse of Poitiers', *XIIe Congrès international des sciences historiques: Études présentées à la commission internationale pour l'histoire des assemblées d'états, Vienne, 1965*, (Paris and Louvain, 1966), xxi. 77-102

Blake, E. O., 'The Formation of the "Crusade Idea" ', *Journal of Ecclesiastical History*, xxi (1970), 11-32

Bloomfield, M. W., 'Joachim of Flora: A Critical Survey of his Canon, Teachings, Sources, Biography and Influence', *Traditio*, xiii (1957) 249-313

—— 'Recent scholarship on Joachim of Fiore and his influence', in A. Williams (ed.) *Prophecy and Millenarianism: Essays in honour of M. Reeves* (London, 1980), 21-53

—— and Reeves, M., 'The Penetration of Joachism into Northern Europe', *Speculum*, xxix (1954), 772-93

Bouvet, J., 'Biographie d'Adam de Perseigne', *Collectanea Ordinis Cisterciensium Reformatorum*, xx (1958), 16-26, 145-52

Bredero, A. H., 'Jérusalem dans l'Occident médiéval', ed. P. Gallais and Y. J. Riou, *Mélanges René Crozet* (Poitiers, 1966), i. 259-72

Brooke, C. N. L., *London, 800-1216: The Shaping of a City* (London, 1975)

Brooke, R. B., *Early Franciscan Government* (Cambridge, 1959)
Brown, E. A. R., 'The Cistercians in the Latin Empire of Constantinople and Greece, 1204–76', *Traditio*, xiv (1958), 63–121
Brown, P. R. L., *Augustine of Hippo* (London, 1969)
Brundage, J. A., 'Adhémar of Puy: The Bishop and his Critics', *Speculum*, xxxiv (1959), 201–13
— 'The Army of the First Crusade and the Crusade Vow: Some Reflections on a Recent Book', *Mediaeval Studies*, xxxiii (1971), 334–44
— 'The Crusader's Wife: A Canonistic Quandary', *Studia Gratiana*, xii (1967), 425–41
— 'An Errant Crusader: Stephen of Blois', *Traditio*, xvi (1960), 380–95
— 'Holy War and the Medieval Lawyers', in T. P. Murphy (ed.), *The Holy War*, (Columbus, Ohio, 1974), 99–141
— *Medieval Canon Law and the Crusader* (Madison, Wis., 1969)
— Review of F. Lotter, *Die Konzeption des Wendenkreuzzugs, Speculum* liv (1979), 172–3
— 'A Transformed Angel (X 3.31.18): The Problem of the Crusading Monk', *Studies in Medieval Cistercian History Presented to J. F. O'Sullivan*, Cistercian Studies Series, XIII (Shannon, 1971), 55–63
Bulst-Thiele, M. L., 'Sacrae Domus Militiae Templi Hierosolymitani Magistri', *Abhandlungen der Akademie der Wissenschaften in Göttingen, philologisch-historische Klasse*, lxxxvi (1974)
Bumke, J. *Mäzene in Mittelalter* (Munich, 1979)

Cardini, F., 'The Crusade and the "Presence of Jerusalem" in Medieval Florence', in *Outremer: Studies in the History of the Crusading Kingdom of Jerusalem Presented to Joshua Prawer*, ed. B. Z. Kedar, R. C. Smail, and H. E. Mayer (Jerusalem, 1982), 332–46.
Caspar, E., 'Die Kreuzzugsbullen Eugens III.', *Neues Archiv der Geschellschaft für ältere deutsche Geschichtskunde*, xlv (1924), 285–300
Cate, J. L., 'A Gay Crusader', *Byzantion*, xvi (1942–3), 503–26
Cazel, F. A., 'The Tax of 1185 in Aid of the Holy Land', *Speculum*, xxx (1950), 385–92
Cheney, C. R., *Hubert Walter* (London, 1967)
— *Innocent III and England* (Stuttgart, 1976)
— 'Master Philip the Notary and the Fortieth of 1199', *EHR* lxiii (1948), 342–50
Christiansen, E., *The Northern Crusades* (London, 1980)
Classen, P., *Gerhoch von Reichersberg* (Wiesbaden, 1960)
Colleville, M., *Les Chansons allemandes de croisade* (Paris, 1936)
Compain, L., *Étude sur Geoffroi de Vendôme* (Paris, 1891)
Congar, Y. M. J., 'Église et cité de Dieu chez quelques auteurs cisterciens à l'époque des croisades', *Mélanges offerts à Étienne Gilson* (Paris, 1959), 173–203
— 'Henri de Marcy, Abbé de Clairvaux, Cardinal-Évêque d'Albano et légat pontifical', *Studia Anselmiana*, xliii (1958), 1–91
Constable, G., 'A Lost Crusading Sermon by St. Bernard on the Failure

of the Second Crusade', in *Studies in Medieval Cistercian History presented to J. F. O'Sullivan*, Cistercian Studies Series, XIII (Shannon, 1971), 49–55

— 'Monachisme et pèlerinage au Moyen Âge', *Religious Life and Thought (Eleventh and Twelfth Centuries)* (London, 1979), 3–27

— 'Opposition to Pilgrimage in the Middle Ages', ibid. 125–46

— 'The Second Crusade as Seen by Contemporaries', *Traditio*, ix (1953), 213–81

Corner, D., 'The *Gesta Henrici Secundi* and *Chronica* of Roger, Parson of Howden', *Bulletin of the Institute of Historical Research*, lvi (1983), 126–45

Cowdrey, H. E. J., 'Pope Urban II's Preaching of the First Crusade', *History*, lv (1970), 177–89

— Review of F. Lotter, *Die Konzeption des Wendenkreuzzugs*, *EHR* xciv (1979), 166–7

Daniel, E. R., 'Apocalyptic Conversion: The Joachite Alternative to the Crusades', *Traditio*, xxvi (1969), 127–54

Deane, H. A., *The Political and Social Ideas of St. Augustine* (New York, 1963)

De Bartholomaeis, V., 'Osservazioni sulle poesie provenzali relative a Federico II', *Memorie della R. Accademia delle scienze dell'Istituto di Bologna, Classe di scienze morali*, 1st ser. vi (1911–12), 97–125

Diez, F., *Leben und Werke der Troubadours* (2nd edn., Leipzig, 1882)

Donovan, J. P., *Pelagius and the Fifth Crusade* (Philadelphia, 1950)

Dossat, Y., 'Les Vaudois méridionaux d'après les documents de l'Inquisition', *Cahiers de Fanjeaux*, ii (1967), 207–22

Easton, S. C., *Roger Bacon and his Search for a Universal Science* (Oxford, 1952)

Eynde, D. van den, *L'Œuvre littéraire de Géroch de Reichersberg* (Rome, 1957)

Fabre, C., 'Le Troubadour Pons de Chapteuil, quelques remarques sur sa vie et sur l'esprit de ses poèmes', *Mémoires et procès-verbaux de la Société agricole et scientifique de la Haute-Loire*, xiv (1905–6), 25–51

Favier, J., 'Les finances de Saint Louis', in *Septième centenaire de la mort de Saint Louis: Actes des colloques de Royaumont et de Paris, Mai 1970*, ed. M. Roche and L. Carolus-Barré (Paris, 1976), 133–41

Flahiff, G. B., 'Deus non vult: A Critic of the Third Crusade', *Mediaeval Studies*, ix (1947), 162–88

— 'Ralph Niger: An Introduction to his Life and Works', *Mediaeval Studies*, ii (1940), 104–26

Fossier, R., 'L'essor économique de Clairvaux', in *Bernard de Clairvaux* (Paris, 1953), 95–114

Fournier, P. and Le Bras, G., *Histoire des collections canoniques en Occident depuis les fausses décrétales jusqu'au Décret de Gratien* (Paris, 1931–2)

France, J., 'An Unknown Account of the Capture of Jerusalem', *EHR* lxxxvii (1972), 771–84

Fransen, G., 'La date du Décret de Gratien', *Revue d'histoire ecclésiastique*, li (1956), 521–31

Galbraith, V. H., *Roger Wendover and Matthew Paris* (David Murray Lecture, University of Glasgow, 1944)

Gaztambide, J. G., *Historia de la bula de la cruzada en España* (Vitoria, 1958)

Gillingham, J. B., 'Roger of Howden on Crusade', in D. O. Morgan (ed.), *Medieval Historical Writing in the Christian and Islamic Worlds* (London, 1982), 60–76

Glaser, H., 'Wilhelm von Saint Denis: Ein Humanist aus der Umgebung des Abtes Suger und die Krise seiner Abtei von 1151 bis 1153', *Historisches Jahrbuch*, lxxxv (1965), 257–323

Gransden, A., *Historical Writing in England c.550 to c.1307* (London, 1974)

Green, D. H., *The Millstätter Exodus* (Cambridge, 1966)

Haines, K., 'Attitudes and Impediments to Pacifism in Medieval Europe', *Journal of Medieval History*, vii (1981), 369–89

Hallam, E. M., *Capetian France, 987–1328* (London, 1980)

Hamilton, B., 'Reynald of Châtillon: The Elephant of Christ', *Studies in Church History*, xv (1978), 97–109

Hehl, E. D., *Kirche und Krieg im 12. Jahrhundert* (Stuttgart, 1980)

Hill, J. H. and L. L., 'Contemporary accounts and Later Reputation of Adhémar, Bishop of Puy', *Medievalia et Humanistica*, ix (1955), 30–9

Histoire générale de Languedoc, ed. C. Devic and J. Vaissete, rev. A. Molinier *et al.* (Toulouse, 1879–1904)

History of the Crusades, ed.-in-c. K. M. Setton (Madison, Wis., 1969–)

Hoepffner, E., 'La biographie de Perdigon', *Romania*, liii (1927), 343–64

Holdsworth, C. J., 'Ideas and Reality: Some Attempts to Control and Defuse War in the Twelfth Century', *Studies in Church History*, xx (1983), 59–79

Hoogeweg, H., 'Die Kreuzpredigt des Jahres 1224 in Deutschland mit besonderer Rücksicht auf die Erzdiöcese Köln', *Deutsche Zeitschrift für Geschichtswissenschaft*, iv (1890), 54–74

Housley, N. J., *The Italian Crusades: The Papal-Angevin Alliance and the Crusades against Christian Lay Powers, 1254–1343* (Oxford, 1982)

—— 'Politics and Heresy in Italy: Anti-Heretical Crusades, Orders and Confraternities, 1200–1500', *Journal of Ecclesiastical History*, xxxii (1982), 193–208

Jamison, E., 'The Sicilian Norman Kingdom in the Mind of Anglo-Norman Contemporaries', *Proceedings of the British Academy*, xxiv (1938), 237–85

Jeanroy, A., *Bibliographie sommaire des chansonniers français du moyen âge* (Paris, 1918)
— *Bibliographie sommaire des chansonniers provençaux* (Paris, 1916)
— 'Les "biographies" des troubadours et les "razos"; leur valeur historique', *Archivum Romanicum*, i (1917), 289–306
— *La poésie lyrique des troubadours* (Paris, 1934)
— 'Le soulèvement de 1242 dans la poésie des troubadours', *Annales du Midi*, xvi (1904), 311–30
— 'Les Troubadours dans les cours de l'Italie du Nord aux XIIe et XIIIe siècles', *Revue historique*, clxiv (1930), 1–26
Jenkins, C., *The Monastic Chronicler and the Early School of St. Albans* (London, 1922)
Johnson, E., 'The German Crusades in the Baltic', in *History of the Crusades*, iii. 545–86
Jordan, E., *Les Origines de la domination angevine en Italie* (Paris, 1909)
Jordan, W. C., *Louis IX and the Challenge of the Crusade* (Princeton, 1979)

Karp, T., 'Troubadours and trouvères', in *The New Grove Dictionary of Music and Musicians*, xix (London, 1980)
Kay, R., 'The Albigensian Twentieth of 1221–3: An Earlier Chapter in the History of Papal Taxation', *Journal of Medieval History*, vi (1980), 307–16
— 'An Eyewitness Account of the 1225 Council of Bourges', *Studia Gratiana*, xii (1967), 63–80
Kedar, B. Z., 'The General Tax of 1183 in the Crusading Kingdom of Jerusalem: Innovation or Adaptation', *EHR* lxxxix (1974), 339–45
— 'A Passenger List of a Crusader Ship: Towards the History of the Popular Element on the Seventh Crusade', *Studi medievali*, 3rd ser. xiii (1972), 267–80
Keen, M., 'Chaucer's Knight, the English Aristocracy and the Crusade', in V. J. Scattergood and J. W. Sherborne (eds.) *English Court Culture in the Later Middle Ages*, (London, 1983), 45–63
Kennan, E., 'Innocent III and the First Political Crusade: A Comment on the Limitations of Papal Power', *Traditio*, xxvii (1971), 231–49
— 'Innocent III, Gregory IX and Political Crusades: A Study in the Disintegration of Papal Power', in *Reform and Authority in the Medieval and Reformation Church*, ed. G. F. Lytle (Washington, DC, 1981), 15–35
Kippenberg, B., 'Minnesang', in *The New Grove Dictionary of Music and Musicians*, xii (London, 1980)
Kritzeck, J., *Peter the Venerable and Islam* (Princeton, 1964)

Labande, E. R., 'Saint Louis pèlerin', *Revue d'histoire de l'église de France*, lvii (1971), 5–18
Langlois, C. V., *La Vie en France au Moyen Âge d'après quelques moralistes du temps* (Paris, 1908)

Lea, H., *A History of the Inquisition in the Middle Ages* (New York, 1906)

Leclercq, J., 'Gratien, Pierre de Troyes et la seconde croisade', *Studia Gratiana*, ii (1954), 583–93

— *The Love of Learning and the Desire for God* (2nd rev. edn., New York, 1974)

— *Pierre le Vénérable* (Abbaye S. Wandrille, 1946)

Lecoy de la Marche, A., 'La prédication de la croisade au treizième siècle', *Revue des questions historiques*, xlviii (1890), 5–29

Lefebvre, C., 'Hostiensis', in R. Naz (ed.) *Dictionnaire de droit canonique*, v (Paris, 1953)

Leff, G., *Heresy in the Later Middle Ages*, (Manchester, 1967)

Lewent, K., *Das altprovenzalische Kreuzlied* (Berlin, 1905)

Linehan, P. A., 'Documento español sobre la Quinta Cruzada', *Hispania sacra*, xx (1967), 177–82

— 'The *Gravamina* of the Castilian church in 1262–3', *EHR* lxxxv (1970), 730–54

— 'Religion, Nationalism and National Identity in Medieval Spain', *Studies in Church History*, xviii (1982), 161–92

— *The Spanish Church and the Papacy in the Thirteenth Century* (Cambridge, 1971)

Lomax, D. W., *The Reconquest of Spain* (London, 1978)

Lommatzsch, E., *Gautier de Coincy als Satiriker* (Halle, 1913)

Longnon, J., 'Les troubadours à la cour de Boniface de Montferrat en Italie et en Orient', *Revue de synthèse*, n.s. xxiii (1948), 45–60

— 'Les vues de Charles d'Anjou pour la deuxième croisade de Saint Louis: Tunis ou Constantinople', *Septième centenaire de la mort de Saint Louis: Actes des colloques de Royaumont et de Paris, Mai 1970*, ed. M. Roche and L. Carolus-Barré (Paris, 1976), 183–97

Lotter, F., *Die Konzeption des Wendenkreuzzugs* (Sigmaringen, 1977)

Lunt, W. E., *Financial Relations of the Papacy with England to 1327* (Cambridge, Mass., 1939)

— *The Valuation of Norwich* (Oxford, 1926)

McGinn, B., 'St. Bernard and Eschatology', *Studies presented to J. Leclercq*, Cistercian Studies Series, XXIII (Washington DC, 1973), 161–85

— 'Iter Sancti Sepulchri: The Piety of the First Crusaders', in B. K. Lackner and K. R. Philp (eds.), *Essays on Medieval Civilization* (Arlington, Tex., 1978), 33–72

Mackay, A. *Spain in the Middle Ages: From Frontier to Empire, 1000–1500* (London, 1977)

Maurer, F., *Die politischen Lieder Walthers von der Vogelweide* (Tübingen, 1954)

Mayer, H. E., *The Crusades*, tr. J. Gillingham (London, 1972)

— 'Henry II of England and the Holy Land', *EHR* xcvii (1982), 721–40

— Review of J. S. C. Riley-Smith, *What were the Crusades?*, *Speculum*, liii (1979), 841–2

— 'Zur Beurteilung Adhémars von Le Puy', *Deutsches Archiv für Erforschung des Mittelalters*, xvi (1960), 547–53

Mayr-Harting, H., 'Functions of a Twelfth Century Recluse', *History*, lx (1975), 337–53

Mazzarino, S., *The End of the Ancient World*, trs. G. Holmes (London, 1966)

Merkel, C., 'L'opinione dei contemporanei sull'impresa italiana di Carla I d'Angio', *Atti della R. Accademia dei Lincei*, 4th ser., *Classe di Scienze morali, storiche e filologiche*, iv (1888), 275–435

Mitchell, S. K., *Studies in Taxation under John and Henry III* (New Haven, Conn., 1914)

Moormán, J. R. H., *A History of the Franciscan Order* (Oxford, 1968)

Morey, A., and C. N. L. Brooke, *Gilbert Foliot and his Letters* (Cambridge, 1965)

Morris, C., 'Equestris ordo: Chivalry as a Vocation in the Twelfth century', *Studies in Church History*, xv (1978), 87–97

— *Medieval Media: Mass Communication in the Making of Europe* (inaugural lecture, University of Southampton, 1972)

— 'Propaganda for War: the Dissemination of the Crusading Ideal in the Twelfth Century', *Studies in Church History*, xx (1983), 79–101

Mortier, R. P., *Histoire des maîtres généraux de l'ordre des frères prêcheurs* (Paris, 1903–9)

Nelli, R., *Le Phénomène cathare* (Paris, 1964)

Nothdurft, K. D., 'Studien zum Einfluß Senecas auf die Philosophie und Theologie des zwölften Jahrhunderts', *Studien und Texte zur Geistesgeschichte des Mittelalters*, vii (Leiden and Cologne, 1963), 47–201

Paetow, L. J., 'The Crusading Ardor of John of Garland', *Essays Presented to Dana C. Munro* (New York, 1928), 207–22

Painter, S., 'The Crusade of Theobald of Champagne and Richard of Cornwall', *History of the Crusades*, ii. 463–87

Patschovsky, A., *Der Passauer Anonymus: Ein Sammelwerk über Ketzer, Juden, Antichrist aus der Mitte des 13. Jahrhunderts*, MGH Schriften, XXII (Stuttgart, 1968)

Pauli, R., 'Die Chroniken des Radulphus Niger', *Nachrichten von der Gesellschaft der Wissenschaften zu Göttingen* (1880), 569–89

Pelikan, J., *The Growth of Medieval Theology, 600–1300* (Chicago, 1978)

Pfeiffer, P. L., 'Die Cistercienser und der zweite Kreuzzug: Die Cistercienser und der unglückliche Ausgang des II. Kreuzzuges', *Cistercienser-Chronik*, xlviii (1935), 145–50

Pissard, H., *La Guerre sainte au pays chrétien* (Paris, 1912)

Plehn, H., 'Der politische Charakter von Matheus Parisiensis', *Staats- und socialwissenschaftliche Forschungen*, iii. 14 (1897)

Porges, W., 'The Clergy, The Poor and the Non-combatants on the First Crusade', *Speculum*, xxi (1946), 1–23

Powicke, F. M., 'The Compilation of the *Chronica maiora* of Matthew Paris', *Proceedings of the British Academy*, xxx (1944), 147–61
— *Stephen Langton* (Oxford, 1928)
Prawer, J., *Histoire du royaume latin de Jerusalem* (Paris, 1969–70)
Preger, W., 'Beiträge zur Geschichte der Waldesier im Mittelalter', *Abhandlungen der Bayerischen Akademie der Wissenschaften: philosophisch-historische Klasse*, xiii (1877), 179–250
Purcell, M., 'Changing Views of the Crusade in the Thirteenth Century', *Journal of Religious History*, ii (1972), 3–20
— *Papal Crusading Policy, 1244–91* (Leiden, 1975)

Queller, D. E., *The Fourth Crusade* (Leicester, 1978)
— T. K. Compton, and D. A. Campbell, 'The Fourth crusade: The Neglected Majority', *Speculum*, xlix (1974), 441–65

Reeves, M., 'The Abbot Joachim's Disciples and the Cistercian Order', *Sophia*, xix (1951), 355–71
— 'History and Prophecy in Medieval Thought', *Medievalia et Humanistica*, n.s. v (1974), 51–75.
— *The Influence of Prophecy in the Later Middle Ages: A Study in Joachimism* (Oxford, 1969)
— *Joachim of Fiore and the Prophetic future* (London, 1976)
— and Hirsch-Reich, B., *The Figurae of Joachim of Fiore* (Oxford, 1972)
— 'The Seven Seals in the Writings of Joachim of Fiore', *Recherches de théologie ancienne et médiévale*, xxi (1954), 211–48
Riant, P., *Expéditions et pèlerinages des Scandinaves en Terre sainte* (Paris, 1865)
Richard, J., *The Latin Kingdom of Jerusalem* (Amsterdam, 1979)
— 'La papauté et la direction de la première croisade', *Journal des Savants* (1960), 49–59
— *La Papauté et les missions d'Orient au moyen âge, XIIIe–XVe siècles* (Rome, 1977)
— *Saint Louis: roi d'une France féodale, soutien de la Terre sainte* (Paris, 1983)
Riley-Smith, J. S. C., 'An Approach to Crusading Ethics', *Reading Medieval Studies*, vi (1980), 3–20
— 'Peace Never Established: the Case of the Kingdom of Jerusalem', *TRHS*, xxviii (1978), 87–103
— *What were the Crusades?* (London, 1977)
— and Riley-Smith, L., *The Crusades: Idea and Reality, 1095–1274* (London, 1981)
Rocher, D., *Thomasin von Zerklaere—Der wälsche Gast 1215–16* (Paris, 1972)
Röhricht, R., *Die Deutschen im Heiligen Lande* (Innsbruck, 1894)
Roquebert, M., *L'Epopée cathare* (Toulouse, 1970–7)
Rougemont, D. de, *Passion and Society* (London, 1940)
Rousset, P., 'Etienne de Blois, croisé, fuyard et martyr', *Genava*, n.s. xi (1963), 183–95

—— *Histoire d'une idéologie: La Croisade* (Lausanne, 1983)

—— 'L'idée de croisade chez les chroniqueurs d'Occident', *Storia del medioevo, Relazioni del X congresso internazionale di scienze storiche*, iii, Biblioteca storica Sansoni, n.s. XXIV (Florence, 1955), 547–63

—— *Les Origines et les caractères de la première croisade* (Neuchâtel, 1945)

Rowe, J. G., 'Paschal II, Bohemond of Antioch and the Byzantine Empire', *Bulletin of the John Rylands Library*, xlix (1966–7), 165–202

Runciman, S., 'The Decline of the Crusading Idea', *Storia del medioevo, Relazioni del X Congresso internazionale di scienze storiche*, iii. Biblioteca storica Sansoni, n.s. XXIV (Florence, 1955), 637–52

—— *The Sicilian Vespers* (Cambridge, 1958)

Russell, F. H., *The Just War in the Middle Ages* (Cambridge, 1975)

Sainte-Marie, H. de, 'Les lettres de saint Anselme de Cantorbéry et la Règle Bénédictine', *Mélanges Bénédictins publiés à l'occasion du XIVe centenaire de la mort de saint Benoît* (Abbaye S. Wandrille, 1947), 259–321

Schein, S., 'Gesta Dei per Mongolos 1300: The Genesis of a Non-event', *EHR* xciv (1979), 805–20

Schmandt, R. H., 'The Fourth Crusade and the Just War Theory', *Catholic Historical Review*, lxi (1975), 191–221

Schmugge, L., 'Zistercienser, Kreuzzug und Heidenkrieg', *Die Zistercienser: Ordensleben zwischen Ideal und Wirklichkeit* (Cologne, 1980), 57–68

Schwinges, R. C., *Kreuzzugsideologie und Toleranz* (Stuttgart, 1977)

Siberry, J. E., 'Criticism of Crusading in Fourteenth-century England', in *'Crusade and Settlement' Papers: Proceedings of the First Society for the Study of the Crusades and Latin East Conference, Cardiff, 1983*, ed. P. W. Edbury (forthcoming)

—— 'Missionaries and Crusaders, 1095–1274: Opponents or Allies?', *Studies in Church History*, xx (1983), 103–10

Smail, R. C., 'Latin Syria and the West, 1149–87', *TRHS* xix (1969), 1–21

Smalley, B., 'Sallust in the Middle Ages', in R. R. Bolgar (ed.), *Classical Influences on European Culture, 500–1500* (Cambridge, 1971), 165–75

Smith, A. L., *Church and State in the Middle Ages* (Oxford, 1913)

Somerville, R., 'The Council of Clermont and the First Crusade', *Studia Gratiana*, xx (1976), 323–38

Southern, R. W., *St. Anselm and his Biographer* (Cambridge, 1963)

—— 'Peter of Blois: A Twelfth-century Humanist?', *Medieval Humanism and Other Studies* (Oxford, 1970), 105–35

Spence, R., 'Gregory IX's Attempted Expeditions to the Latin Empire of Constantinople: the Crusade for the Union of the Latin and Greek Churches', *Journal of Medieval History*, v (1979), 163–76

Spiegel, G. M., ' "Defence of the Realm": Evolution of a Capetian Propaganda Slogan', *Journal of Medieval History*, iii (1977), 115-34

Stenton, D. M., 'Roger of Howden and Benedict', *EHR* lxvii (1953), 574-82

Stephenson, C., 'The Aids of the French Towns in the Twelfth and Thirteenth Centuries', in B. Lyon, (ed.) *Medieval Institutions* (New York, 1954), 1-41

Stickel, E., *Der Fall von Akkon* (Frankfurt, 1975)

Strayer, J. R., 'The Crusades of Louis IX', in *History of the Crusades*, ii. 487-522

Stroick, P. A., 'Verfasser und Quellen der *Collectio de scandalis ecclesiae*', *Archivum Franciscanum Historicum*, xxiii (1930), 3-41, 273-99, 433-66

Swietek, F. R., 'Gunther of Pairis and the *Historia Constantinopolitana*', *Speculum*, liii (1979), 49-79

Sypher, F. J. and E., *Ysengrimus by Magister Nivardus* (New York, 1980)

Tangl, G., *Studien zum Register Innocenz' III* (Weimar, 1929)

Throop, P. A., *Criticism of the Crusade: A Study of Public Opinion and Crusade Propaganda* (Amsterdam, 1940)

—— 'Criticism of papal crusade policy in Old French and Provençal', *Speculum*, xiii (1938), 379-413

Topsfield, L. T., *Troubadours and Love* (Cambridge, 1975)

Toubert, P., 'Les Déviations de la Croisade au milieu du XIIIe siècle: Alexandre IV contre Manfred', *Le Moyen Âge*, lxix (1963), 391-9

Treharne, R. F., *The Baronial Plan of Reform, 1258-65* (Manchester, 1932)

Tyerman, C. J., 'Marino Sanudo Torsello and the Lost Crusade: Lobbying in the Fourteenth Century', *TRHS* xxxii (1982), 57-75

Vacandard, E., *Vie de saint Bernard* (Paris, 1895)

Van Cleve, T. C., *The Emperor Frederick II of Hohenstaufen* (Oxford, 1972)

—— 'The Fifth Crusade', *History of the Crusades*, ii. 377-429

Varga, L., 'Peire Cardenal était-il hérétique', *Revue de l'histoire des religions*, cxvii (1938), 205-31

Vaughan, R., *Matthew Paris* (Cambridge, 1958)

Vicaire, M. H., 'Les clercs de la croisade', *Cahiers de Fanjeaux*, iv (1969), 260-81

Villey, M., *La Croisade: essai sur la formation d'une théorie juridique* (Paris, 1942)

Waddell, H., *The Wandering Scholars* (London, 1927)

Wakefield, W. L. and Evans, A. P., *Heresies of the High Middle Ages* (New York, 1969)

Warren, W. L., *Henry II* (London, 1973)

Wentzlaff-Eggebert, F. W., *Kreuzzugsdichtung des Mittelalters* (Berlin, 1960)

Werf, H. van der, *The Chansons of the Troubadours and Trouvères* (Utrecht, 1972)

West, D. E., 'The Education of Fra Salimbene of Parma: The Joachite Influence', in A. Williams (ed.), *Prophecy and Millenarianism: Essays in Honour of M. Reeves* (London, 1980), 191-217

Willems, E., 'Cîteaux et la seconde croisade', *Revue d'histoire ecclésiastique*, xlix (1954), 116-52

Willems, L., *Étude sur l'Ysengrimus* (Ghent, 1895)

Williams, J. R., 'William of the White Hands and Men of Letters', *Anniversary Essays in Medieval History by Students of C. H. Haskins* (Boston, 1929), 365-89

Williamson, D. M., 'The Legate Otto in Scotland and Ireland, 1237-41', *Scottish Historical Review*, xxviii (1949), 12-30

— 'Some Aspects of the Legation of Cardinal Otto in England, 1237-41', *EHR* lxiv (1949), 145-74

Winter, F., *Die Cistercienser des nord-östlichen Deutschlands* (Gotha, 1868-71)

Wolff, R. W., 'The Latin Empire of Constantinople, 1204-61', *History of the Crusades*, ii. 187-235

Wolfram, G., 'Kreuzpredigt und Kreuzlied', *Zeitschrift für deutsches Alterthum und deutsche Litteratur*, xxx (1886), 89-132

Wood, M. M., *The Spirit of Protest in Old French Literature* (New York, 1917)

Yewdale, R. B., *Bohemond I, Prince of Antioch* (Princeton, 1924)

UNPUBLISHED THESES

Daniel, E. R., 'Joachim of Flora and the Joachite Tradition of Apocalyptic Conversion in the Later Middle Ages', (Ph.D. Virginia, 1966)

Gere, R. H., 'The Troubadours, Heresy and the Albigensian Crusade', (Ph.D., Columbia, 1955)

Grossman, R. P., 'The Financing of the Crusades', (Ph.D. Chicago, 1965)

Nickson, M. A. E., 'A Critical Edition of the Treatise on Heresy Ascribed to Pseudo Reinerius with an Historical Introduction', (Ph.D., London, 1962)

Schein, S., 'The West and the Crusades: Attitudes and Attempts, 1291-1312', (Ph.D., Cambridge, 1980)

Index